The Weight Loss Cure "They" Don't Want You To Know About

Also by Kevin Trudeau

Natural Cures "They" Don't Want You To Know About

More Natural Cures Revealed: The Previously Censored Brand Products That Cure Disease

Mega Memory

The Weight Loss Cure "They" Don't Want You To Know About

KEVIN TRUDEAU

Alliance Publishing Group, Inc.

This edition published by Alliance Publishing Group, Inc.
For information, address:
Alliance Publishing Group, Inc.
P.O. Box 207
Elk Grove Village, IL 60009

ISBN 13: 978-0-9787851-0-9
ISBN 10: 0-9787851-0-X

Library of Congress Control Number: 2006940486

Manufactured in the United States of America
22 21 20 19 18 17 16 15 14 13 12

Contents

Acknowledgments

I would like to acknowledge Dr. A.T.W. Simeons for his discoveries in the area of weight loss and his manuscript *Pounds and Inches: A New Approach to Obesity*, from which most of this book has been derived. Special thanks go to the hundreds of doctors that allowed me the hours required for interviews and reviewing the gargantuan amounts of documents that substantiate the protocols outlined in this book. The authors and producers of the books, documentaries, and films listed in the Appendix deserve praise for their fearlessness in exposing the truth about the corruption within the food, drug, and weight loss industries. My sincere gratitude goes to "Dr. Fritz" for personally introducing me to the Simeons "weight loss cure protocol," and allowing me to be cured of my lifelong affliction. Praise is also due to Pam Farley for her dedication and countless hours of typing my dictated words, allowing this book to become a reality.

Disclaimer

The author of this book is not a medical doctor. He has no formal medical training. As a reporter and journalist, he is presenting in this book his observations and personal experience of the various weight loss methods developed and practiced by doctors from around the world. Before beginning any weight loss program you should consult a licensed health care provider and be monitored throughout the entire weight loss process. This book is not intended to provide medical advice, diagnose illness, or in any way attempt to practice medicine. It is not intended to replace personal medical care from a licensed health care practitioner. Doing anything recommended or suggested in this book must be done at your own risk. This book is based on, and inspired by, a true story. Much of this book comes directly from the manuscript entitled *Pounds and Inches: A New Approach to Obesity*, authored by A.T.W. Simeons, M.D. This book is also derived from the author's memory and best recollection of events. Dates, names, locations, and actual events may have been changed, embellished, exaggerated, or fictionalized for dramatic effect. The author is forced to include this disclaimer due to the litigious nature of today's world, and the expected attacks, criticisms, and attempts to suppress and discredit this work.

Introduction

Read this book cover-to-cover. You are being exposed to one of the greatest kept secrets, and greatest discoveries in the cause and cure for the affliction of obesity. The corruption in the established medical community resulting in unscrupulous pharmaceutical conglomerates to take advantage of the vulnerabilities of the overweight by selling them outrageously expensive and dangerous surgical procedures and drugs is more than scandalous and appalling, it should be regarded as criminal. The true root causes of obesity are now known, yet this information is not only being hidden from you, but is being debunked and discredited by those who have financial interests in keeping this knowledge suppressed.

The methods of curing the condition of obesity without expensive drugs and surgery in a totally safe manner are also being debunked and discredited. These inexpensive, effective, and safe methods of losing weight and keeping the weight off forever are being hidden from the public. Those who have financial interests in keeping people obese are the main culprits. The shock and outrage is the number of well-known government agencies, associations, and publicly traded corporations that all have a direct financial self interest in keeping obesity rates going up.

This book opens up Pandora's box in relation to the weight loss industry, food industry, and drug industry, and how they are all working together to keep America and the world getting fatter, fatter, and fatter.

More importantly, this book not only outlines the problem, but gives you the workable solution!

Lose Thirty Pounds In Thirty Days...Guaranteed

First they ignore you, then they laugh at you, then they fight you, then you win.
—Mahatma Gandhi

You are about to learn about the greatest medical discovery relating to obesity and weight loss of all time. The cause of obesity and weight gain has finally been discovered. The cure has also been discovered. It has been used and tested for over thirty years by over 100,000 people with virtually 100% success. The most amazing fact is that the true cause and cure for obesity and weight gain has been systematically and purposefully debunked, discredited, and hidden from the public. Now, for the first time since the cause and cure of obesity and weight gain was discovered over thirty years ago, this information is finally being revealed to the world!

This is not my discovery. I am simply reporting on the facts relating to this medical discovery. The cause and cure for obesity was discovered by a top British medical doctor over thirty years ago. He opened a clinic in a hospital in Rome, treating the rich and famous for over twenty years. His clients included hundreds of members from various royal families throughout Europe, major Hollywood celebrities, and some of the wealthiest people in the world. He was paid enormous sums of money to keep the cure a secret. The results were spectacular.

Before I go on telling you about the history of this discovery, I want to explain in simple terms what results you can expect. When you do "the weight loss cure protocol," as it is now called,

1

you should lose about one pound per day. This means in thirty days you should lose approximately thirty pounds. Exactly how much weight you lose will depend upon how much total weight you need to lose. If you only need to lose thirty pounds total, then you are more likely to lose twenty pounds in thirty days. If you need to lose 100 pounds, then you could expect to lose more than thirty pounds in the first thirty days. I have reviewed thousands of files of people that have done this protocol over the last thirty years. Almost everyone loses about one pound per day while on the protocol. This is important. The weight loss cure is not a diet, not an exercise program, not a psychological behavior modification program, or some other system that is supposed to help you lose weight. The weight loss cure actually addresses and corrects the physiological cause of obesity, weight gain, and inability to lose weight.

When you read this book cover-to-cover you will learn the true cause of obesity, weight gain, and the body's inability to lose weight. You will learn why food companies are making us fat on purpose. Most importantly, you will learn the simple protocol that you can easily do that will cure the basic underlying cause that makes us fat. There is absolutely not even one weight loss diet, program, system, pill, or anything else that addresses the true cause as to why we are fat. Even the government admits that nothing works for permanent weight and fat loss.

I know from personal experience that nothing works because I have virtually tried them all. I have struggled with weight my whole life. When I was growing up there were only one or two kids in each class that were considered fat. We were called "husky" or "big boned" or "healthy looking." I was that kid. Compare this with kids today. Statistics show that if we were to use the same standards of what was considered "fat" back in the 1940s, it would show that over 60% of children between the grades one through twelve are overweight. Compare this with the 1940s, where less than 1% of the children were considered overweight. I was one of the overweight kids. Throughout my life I tried everything to lose weight and keep it off. I went to "fat farms" for weeks at a time; I hired personal trainers and exercised as much as five hours a day. I tried every pill sold, every new diet, every miracle device, subliminal tapes, hypnosis, laser therapy, and more. I bought the prepackaged food. I even hired a private chef to prepare specific meals that would help me lose weight and keep it off. I tried every diet you've heard of: the blood-type diet, the low carb diet, Atkins, South Beach, low calorie, vegetarian, food combining, high protein, raw, the grapefruit diet, the chocolate diet, NutriSystem, Slim Fast, Jenny Craig, Weight Watchers, and probably a hundred more different kinds of diets. I tried every specific kind of exercise program, every herb, and homeopathic or nutritional product sold that promised to reduce my appetite, burn fat, and solve my weight issue forever. I drank so many different miracle protein shakes that it virtually drove me mad. I would lose some weight, but always gained it right back. Nothing really ever worked.

Many of you are in a similar situation. You've tried everything, yet nothing really ever works. When I say works, what does that mean? Yes, if you do any diet and exercise program you may, in fact, lose some weight. The problem is during the diet, exercise, or weight loss program you are usually hungry, grumpy, fatigued, have food cravings, need to use super human willpower, and feel deprived and miserable. The weight you lose is never the fat in the problem areas. You actually lose water, structural fat, and muscle. The biggest problem is that these weight loss programs lower your metabolism, and increase your appetite. They actually make it so the body gains weight quicker, stores more fat in the problem areas, and makes it even harder in the future to lose weight and fat. This is why when you stop the diet, exercise, or weight loss program you very quickly gain all the weight back, plus more! The scariest thing is the weight you gain back is the fat that is stored in the problem areas that is virtually impossible to lose. Diet, exercise, and weight loss programs actually make you fatter in the long-term.

The fact is, fat people and thin people have different ways in which their bodies operate.

Here are the common problems that people who are overweight have to deal with. Individuals who are dealing with weight issues, generally speaking, have the following characteristics, which are quite different from people who are not dealing with weight issues. These are some of the common denominators that virtually all fat people have:

1. **Their body metabolism is low.** What this means is when a fat person eats food their body does not burn the food as fuel at a very high rate. People who are naturally thin burn food and calories quickly. Up until now there has never been a treatment that truly addressed this particular problem. This is one of the reasons why when a person goes on a weight-loss program and actually loses some weight, they gain all the weight back very quickly. If you don't correct low metabolism then you are destined to be fat your whole life.

2. **High hunger.** Thin people can never understand this. A fat person is physically hungry more often and at a higher intensity than the naturally thin person. Thin people always say that fat people don't have enough self-control to stop eating. This is not true. The thin person cannot comprehend the physiological, intense, and almost constant hunger that the fat person has to deal with. It has nothing to do with self-control. This is a real, gnawing, tortuous, intense physical hunger. This is one of the reasons why naturally thin people and exercise gurus have no right to author a book on how to lose weight. They have never really had to deal with the real issues that overweight people deal with.

3. **Eating when you're not hungry.** Fat people also have a problem with "emotional eating" or cravings. Certain food cravings fall into the above hunger category as they are physiological in nature. Other food cravings or emotional eating occur when you are physically not hungry, but you are "hungry" to fill an emotional need. This is actually physical in nature. I have read over 300 diet books and only two give any real solutions that address this problem.

There are two other issues relating to obesity. The first is genetics. As amazing as it sounds, genetics do not play a major role as a cause for obesity. Genetics do determine general body shape, but are not the main cause for a low metabolism, intense and constant physical hunger, or emotional eating.

The other issue is that specific foods, or kinds of foods, actually make you gain weight very quickly. Nutritionists and doctors always talk about calories, fat, protein, carbohydrates, and sodium. Some are now more advanced and talk about simple carbohydrates, complex carbohydrates, and the glycemic index levels of foods. (Foods high on the glycemic index fall into the category of highly refined or super highly refined, causing massive spikes in insulin secretion, leading to increased food cravings and hunger, and making the body increase fat deposits.) Some talk about saturated or unsaturated fats. All of these components have some level of importance. However, nutritionists and doctors virtually never mention the most important and significant components of food which lead to weight gain and obesity. The most significant components of food that play the largest role in weight gain and obesity are food additives, chemicals, and food processing techniques! It's not the food itself; it's not really the calories, the amount of fat, the amount of carbohydrates, sodium, glycemic index level, or protein. It's *how* food is processed and the man-made chemicals and additives in the food that actually cause weight gain and obesity. These include bovine growth hormone and antibiotics injected into meat, poultry, and dairy products, flavor enhancers, such as monosodium glutamate, artificial sweeteners such as NutraSweet (aspartame) and Splenda (sucrolos). This also includes man-made sugars such as high fructose corn syrup, corn syrup, dextrose, sucrose, fructose, highly refined white sugar, processed molasses, processed honey, malto dextrin, etc., plus the over 15,000 chemicals that are routinely added to virtually every product you buy, including conventionally grown fruits and vegetables. Man-made trans fats such as hydrogenated or partially hydrogenated oils cause weight gain and obesity. Additionally, food processing techniques such as pasteurization, which is now done on virtually every product in a bottle or carton, homogenization, and irradiation (which is done to over 50% of all food products sold in America) all cause weight gain.

As part of "the weight loss cure protocol" all of these issues are addressed and corrected easily and permanently.

As I tried various methods to lose weight I experienced several problems that most of you are familiar with. While on every "weight loss program" the first problem was that the weight didn't come off very quickly. This was always frustrating and de-motivating. With "the weight loss cure protocol" this problem is solved. I lost six pounds the very first day. I lost twenty-nine pounds in the first twenty-one days. I lost a total of forty pounds in six weeks. When you are losing weight every day this keeps your motivation to continue with the program very high. The next problem with every other weight loss system I tried is that I was always hungry and miserable. With the "weight loss cure protocol" mild hunger only lasts for a couple of days. Then, almost miraculously, hunger is virtually nonexistent. This made staying on the protocol very easy and pleasant. With other weight loss programs I was tired, grumpy, and had food cravings. With "the weight loss cure protocol" I had tons of energy, was happy and excited, with no food cravings at all. With other weight loss programs you don't actually lose the fat in the "trouble areas." No matter how much weight you lose you still have fat around the hips, thighs, buttocks, and waist. Your stomach never gets flat. With "the weight loss cure protocol" you are actually burning and releasing the fat in these troubled areas. Your body is completely reshaped. You lose massive amounts of inches. Your stomach gets flat! Your waist gets much smaller. It's the only method known that burns and releases these secure fat reserves, dramatically changing the shape of your body. The before and after photos of people who have done this protocol look as though they have had liposuction! With most other weight loss methods time-consuming exercise is required. Although exercise is always encouraged, with this protocol no exercise is required. While I did this cure I purposely did no exercise at all to make sure these spectacular and almost miraculous results could be achieved without exercise. In reviewing the records of thousands of people that have done "the weight loss cure protocol" over the last thirty years, I can report that no exercise is *required* and the spectacular results are consistently achieved even without any exercise!

This weight loss approach is quite different than anything else in the treatment of obesity. There are no hunger and food cravings. You have increased energy. You lose weight from the very first day. You lose approximately one pound per day. You lose fat in the trouble areas. You lose massive amounts of inches.

Your body is completely reshaped as if you got liposuction. Your success in reducing inches and fat, combined with no hunger, no cravings, no feelings of deprivation, and no depression keep you motivated to stay on the protocol. There has never been a weight loss treatment that is so easy and works so well. One of the most exciting things that people experience is a fast and dramatic flattening of the stomach. Weighing yourself in the morning, and looking at yourself in the mirror, is one of the most exciting and motivating experiences patients do while on this protocol.

Every person who has lost weight in the past knows that the process of losing weight is hard, miserable, frustrating, depressing, and full of deprivation. Even with massive exercise, fat in the trouble areas is virtually impossible to lose. This protocol solves all these issues.

The biggest challenge with all other weight loss programs however, is keeping the weight off permanently. No other weight loss system corrects and cures the basic problems overweight people deal with or the true cause of obesity. When you stop a weight loss program, statistics show that almost everyone gains the weight back very quickly. We all know that we actually gain the weight back faster than we lost it! This is because no weight loss program cures and corrects the low metabolism, the intense and constant hunger, or the emotional eating and food cravings. This "weight loss cure protocol" does in fact "cure" and correct these problems. When you finish the protocol your metabolism is reset to the normal level. Your physical hunger is reset to the normal level. The emotional eating issues and food cravings are gone forever. This means when you finish this protocol you will be able to be a normal person in relation to your eating and weight. Your hunger will be completely normalized. You will be able to eat any food you want. Your body will burn the food you eat so that it does not turn to fat. Your hunger and appetite mechanisms will be regulated so that you have an intense feeling of fullness with no physiological food cravings. You will have no desire to eat when you are not hungry. For some of you, this will be a new and life-changing experience. Imagine going to a buffet and eating a normal amount of food and feeling totally full and satisfied. Imagine not having to deal with willpower or deprivation.

Imagine not being hungry throughout the day. Imagine no longer being a slave to food or your weight. This cure may be the answer to your prayers.

As I mentioned, I have struggled with my weight my whole life. I've constantly dealt with hunger. I had to use willpower to reduce the amount of food I ate. I was constantly thinking about food, desiring food, and wanting food. When I ate foods I enjoyed in the amounts I wanted to, I would gain weight quickly. Because my metabolism was abnormally low, as it is with most fat people, I would gain weight even if I ate normal quantities of food. For the last twenty years I have researched almost every known weight loss treatment. Like Oprah, my weight was constantly going up and down like a yo-yo. I would work really hard with diet and exercise and get my weight to 195 pounds, then in just a short period of time I would go back up to 240 pounds. At my peak I weighed close to 300 pounds. The lowest I ever got was 185 pounds. The whole process was hard and made me miserable. It was always easy to gain weight and very difficult to lose it. In my first book, *Natural Cures "They" Don't Want You To Know About*, I list thirty-two dos and don'ts that help you lose weight and keep the weight off. Since doing those things my weight situation dramatically improved. Still, I was not cured. I still dealt with low metabolism and high hunger. This meant keeping the weight off was unpleasant and difficult. I also dealt with an inability to flatten my stomach and lose the fat in the problem areas. My search for a solution to the obesity problem has been going on for over twenty years.

I read over 300 books on weight loss. The problem with the majority of these books is they are written by people who have never personally had a weight problem. These authors never had to deal with the issues that fat people deal with. They were never seriously overweight or obese. They never dealt with constant and intense physical hunger. They never experienced massive and overwhelming and compulsive food cravings or emotional eating when they weren't hungry. They never looked in the mirror and saw grotesque fat deposits over their body that no matter how much diet and exercise they did, they still couldn't lose it. These so-called diet and weight loss experts could never tell me how to lose weight easily, reshape the body, and lose the trouble area fat and keep the weight off for good. They only shared theories that did not address the true causes of obesity.

The other group of authors who write these weight loss and diet books are people who are still fat themselves! It annoyed me when I read these books. If the information in the books actually worked, then why was the author still fat? Why was the author unable to reshape their body and lose the fat in the trouble areas? Obviously, these authors didn't know what they were talking about. Their ideas and weight loss systems obviously didn't solve and correct the true causes of obesity. It is interesting to note that I personally met and interviewed many of these weight loss and diet gurus, fitness and exercise gurus, and executives who run the weight loss pre-packed food companies, diet pill companies, and weight loss aides companies. I can tell you this, these people have either never had a weight problem so they don't know what they're talking about, are still fat, which means they don't know what they're talking about, or are simply in the weight loss business to make money. After twenty years, the search for the most effective and permanent weight loss method seemed to be an impossible task. I was about to give up.

I began thinking that maybe it would be better to give up the weight loss miracle search. I was tired of going to restaurants, wanting and craving food, yet constantly depriving myself of the pleasure of eating. I was getting fed up with constantly being hungry. I was tired of constantly trying to motivate myself with such phrases as, "Nothing tastes as good as being thin feels." The fact is I, like most fat people, got great pleasure in eating. The thought of resigning myself to the fact that I would be a jolly fat guy for the rest of my life began to have much appeal. The only true weight loss miracle, if there was one, would have to be something that was incredibly easy to do, or I was no longer interested in even trying it. It had to work fast; it had to get rid of the fat deposits in the trouble areas; it had to reshape my body and flatten my stomach. Most importantly, when I finished losing all the fat, inches, and weight I wanted, I needed to be able to eat anything I wanted, any time I wanted, as much as I wanted, and never gain the weight back. I had to live without deprivation, without using willpower, without crazy exercise, without hunger, and without craving and wanting food all the time. I actually thought, although this was a tall order, that the end result was an achievable goal. I had seen people who have never had a weight problem. They eat everything they want, as much as they want, without exercise, yet always remain thin. The question was, is there a way to get *my* body to operate like *theirs*?

My idea for this ultimate weight loss miracle was exciting. However, I felt finding such a cure would be like hitting the lottery. But you know people do hit the lottery! I didn't know it, I didn't expect it, but I was about to find the greatest weight loss discovery of all time.

◇ ◇ ◇

In the Bavarian region of Germany an anti-aging clinic exists for the rich and famous. Kings, queens, members of royal families from around the world, celebrities, and billionaires routinely come to this small, semi-secret anti-aging clinic. The medical doctor who runs the clinic administers anti-aging therapies such as chelation, blood oxygen, and most importantly, live cell therapy. In my first book, *Natural Cures "They" Don't Want You To Know About,* I tell the story about how I was born with a deformed heart and was treated and cured with live cell therapy. I explained how this all-natural, non-patentable, inexpensive therapy has been made illegal in America by the FDA because it would adversely affect the profits of the pharmaceutical companies. Live cell therapy is one of the most effective health enhancing and anti-aging treatments in the world. The rich and famous who secretively received this therapy experience almost superhuman health and vitality. Some people get the treatment once in their life. Others get several treatments in their lifetime. Most, however, receive the therapy every year or two. Having had the treatment over twenty years ago, I decided it was time for me to start a regular administering of live cell therapy. The treatment is painless, takes five minutes, has no side effects, is inexpensive, and would allow me a nice vacation in Bavaria. I was looking forward to experiencing Oktoberfest, hiking the Alps, and doing some sightseeing among the castles and lovely villages throughout the region. When I arrived at the clinic the doctor gave me a private tour of the patient archive room. I first had to sign a confidentiality nondisclosure statement promising not to reveal the names of any of the past or current patients. I looked through thousands of photographs of past and current patients who regularly come for the live cell therapy. What I saw blew my mind. It was virtually a who's who of world leaders, billionaires, celebrities and royalty. This had to be one of the best kept secrets in medical anti-aging therapy. The doctor and I chatted about my medical condition and what I had hoped the treatment would achieve. A complete battery of blood tests and hormone tests were done in addition to dozens of other medical tests to assess my condition. Many patients come with serious medical conditions such as heart disease, MS, arthritis, diabetes, or cancer. The doctor is very clear that he does not treat these conditions; he only administers the anti-aging and health enhancing live cell therapy, and other anti-aging treatments. These therapies promote health in the body by stimulating and revitalizing internal organs and glands. Only the body heals disease. I had no preexisting known medical condition. I simply wanted a "tune-up." I had no symptoms that needed to be dealt with. The doctor asked if there was anything specific that I wanted to achieve physically. I joked that I wished I could lose some weight and keep it off forever! The doctor paused and very seriously and matter-of-factly stated that there was a cure for obesity that I could receive while at the clinic. I was about to brush him off figuring that it was just another diet and exercise program. I was, however, intrigued when he used the word "cure." I asked how it worked. He went on to say that a British medical doctor, in the late 1950s, discovered that all overweight people have a low metabolism, constant and intense hunger, and massive food cravings causing them to eat when they are not hungry. This M.D. also discovered that fat is stored in three areas of the body. First, structural fat around the joints and organs; second, normal fat reserves throughout the entire body; and third, secure or abnormal fat reserves, which are known as the "problem areas." In women, these problem areas generally include the hips, thighs, buttocks, waist, stomach, and behind the upper arms; in men, the upper chest, back, neck, waist, and stomach. These secure or abnormal fat reserves (the problem areas) are never released no matter how much diet and exercise you do. The body retains these fat reserves as a survival mechanism and will only release them after ninety days of starvation as a last resort so that the person does not die. They are also released during pregnancy so that if a pregnant woman has no food, the unborn fetus still receives the nutrition needed to be a fully nourished healthy baby. The doctor went on to say that the protocol developed by this British M.D. virtually cures the cause of obesity. During the treatment, which lasts between three and six weeks, a person will lose about a pound a day. You will have no hunger and your energy levels will be high. You will have no food cravings and you will not feel deprived. You will not need willpower. Although exercise is encouraged, you do not need to exercise. Most importantly, the weight you will be losing will be almost all fat. You will lose very little, if any, muscle. The fat you lose will be from the problem areas or the secure fat reserves. This means your body will be reshaped. It will look as if you have had liposuction. You will not lose the structural fat that you need for good health. When you are finished with the protocol your hypothalamus gland will be reset. Your internal body weight set point will be lowered. Your metabolism will rise and be reset at a much higher level. Your physiological hunger will be reduced dramatically back to a normal level. You will no longer experience food cravings or need to eat for emotional reasons. You will be cured and you will not gain the weight back.

This sounded too good to be true. If this was real, this was an answer to my prayers. I was highly skeptical. The doctor then escorted me to the confidential patient files. Being a best selling author in the health field, a journalist, and having signed the confidentiality nondisclosure agreement, the doctor allowed me to review the patient files. Incredibly detailed and accurate records were kept on the people that had been treated with this weight loss protocol. The statistics were astonishing. Almost everyone lost a pound a day from the very first day they started the protocol. The before and after photos were startling. Every patient saw a dramatic flattening of their stomach. Wherever the patient held on to fat shrunk the most; the waist, hips, thighs, buttocks were all completely reshaped. Remember, this was without exercise of any kind. With women, even though some lost sixty to eighty pounds, the breasts did not reduce, but rather became firmer. Men lost the spare tire around the waist and the fat around their upper chest vanished. The faces of these patients did not look drawn, rather the skin glowed, was taught and tight, and wrinkles diminished dramatically. Everyone looked ten to fifteen years younger. The weight loss numbers were astounding:

- 7 pounds in 7 days
- 10 pounds in 7 days
- 12 pounds in 7 days
- 18 pounds in 7 days
- 12 pounds in 14 days
- 16 pounds in 14 days
- 21 pounds in 14 days
- 18 pounds in 14 days
- 20 pounds in 21 days
- 25 pounds in 21 days
- 35 pounds in 21 days
- 45 pounds in 21 days
- 20 pounds in 30 days
- 28 pounds in 30 days
- 35 pounds in 30 days
- 45 pounds in 30 days
- 60 pounds in 30 days

These are actual results from actual patient records.

The weight loss numbers were beyond anything I had hoped for. Every person's results were slightly different based on a multitude of factors, including age, gender, and how much they needed to lose. The heavier a person was the faster they lost. One statistic that stood out was everyone who was sixty pounds or more overweight lost at least a pound a day during the six-week treatment. Most importantly though was the fact that the weight they were losing was not muscle or structural fat—these people were losing almost 100% fat directly from the problem areas, completely reshaping and re-sculpting their bodies. The results were fast and effective. There has never been a weight loss protocol that burns off these secure problem area fat deposits and reshapes and re-sculpts the body so effectively. Nothing even comes close. The fact is the majority of weight loss protocols never even touch these problem area fat reserves.

The comments from the patients in these records repeatedly stated that they were not hungry at all, had tons of energy, and were overwhelmingly excited about the results. Since many of the patients come back annually to the clinic, the long-term effects were of great interest to me. These thousands of records proved that people could lose fat faster than any other known weight loss system and do so virtually effortlessly. The big question was would the weight and fat stay off? In follow-up observations the statistics showed 85% of the patients kept the weight off (within 10%) after one, two, and five years. The most exciting statistic was no one gained *all* the weight back. The other important point was in the very small percentage that did gain *some* weight back; the record showed that these people gained the weight over a very long period of time while at the same time gorging themselves on food on a daily basis. In other words, they gained the weight back very slowly. It was actually hard for them to gain the weight back. I compared this with every other weight loss method. Remember, with other weight loss methods the weight comes off very slowly. It is hard to lose the weight. You gain the weight back quickly and easily. It is very frustrating! *This* protocol was exactly the opposite. You lose the weight and fat *quickly* and *effortlessly*, and it is very difficult and slow for you to gain the weight back. Remember, over 85% kept the weight off. No other weight loss method comes close with these successful results. Needless to say, I was utterly impressed. More than that, I was excited and motivated to start the protocol. I felt like I had found Aladdin's lamp and the genie was granting my weight loss miracle wish.

◇ ◇ ◇

I woke up early the day I was to start "the weight loss cure protocol." I believed I was about to start a brand new chapter in my life. Up until now I had been consumed with the constant battles with my weight—hunger, food cravings, constant dieting, losing weight and gaining weight, spending thousands of dollars on pills, powders, potions, teas, and every weight loss program sold. I was sick and tired of having clothes that were either too tight or too big. Could it be that I would never have to be on a diet ever again? Could it be that I could eat whatever I wanted anytime I wanted and as much as I wanted without having to worry about gaining weight? The thoughts of what my life was going to be like as a thin person with a normal hunger and appetite, without any crazy food cravings, and never having to deal with willpower, deprivation, or feeling hungry was so exciting I could barely stand it. I knew I was not alone; I knew that obese, fat, and overweight people were now the vast majority of Americans. The overweight problem is starting to permeate the globe. Back in the 1940s less than 1% of the American population was considered obese. Less than 10% were considered overweight. Using the same standards as was used in the 1940s, today over 80% of Americans are overweight! Over 50% are obese. On *CNN* it was reported that the average woman in America is 5'4" tall and weighs 165 pounds. This means that the average woman in America is medically classified as obese. America is by far the fattest and unhealthiest country on planet Earth. Every year more and more people are on diets, eating diet food, choosing low calorie, low fat, low carb products, and consuming record amounts of diet pills, powders, and potions. Record numbers of people are purchasing exercise equipment and working out in gyms. The diet and weight loss industry is estimated at over a $150 billion a year business. Yet, each year people are getting fatter and fatter and fatter. Nothing is working. So many questions filled my mind. If this weight loss cure, discovered and developed by a prominent British medical doctor, was so effective, why has it remained a secret for over thirty years? If there are tens of thousands of long-term success stories why doesn't everyone know about it? First it had to work for me before I investigated further and told the world about this medical weight loss miracle cure.

Here are my personal results. Before I started the protocol I weighed 231 pounds, with a forty-two inch waist. Five weeks later, I weighed 195 pounds, with a thirty-four inch waist. I did no exercise at all during the protocol. I was slightly hungry for the first two days, but then I had virtually little or no hunger at all. The two things that all my friends noticed mostly were that I looked ten years younger and my skin was incredibly clear. The other most exciting thing to me was everyone noticed how flat my stomach was. This is very exciting for anyone who has a weight problem. The protocol was everything that I hoped it would be—no hunger, no food cravings, no grumpiness, no feeling of deprivation, no fatigue, a dramatic loss in not only weight but fat; most importantly a dramatic reshaping of the body with the burning of the secure problem area fat deposits. Although this is not a diet, I am happy to report that this will be the last "diet" you will ever need. The success rate of this protocol in keeping the weight off forever is unmatched, nothing comes close. The speed and amount of weight and fat you lose is unmatched, nothing even comes close. The ease and effortlessness in which you lose the weight and keep it off is unmatched, nothing even comes close.

Before you learn the exact protocol it is important to know the real untold reasons why you are fat, why you have a low metabolism, why you have intense and constant hunger, why you have uncontrollable food cravings and eat when you're not hungry, and why it is so hard to lose weight yet so easy to gain it. It is also important that you know why this weight loss cure has been debunked, discredited, and hidden from the public for so many years. You must also know the truth about the tens of thousands of people, including major celebrities, royalty, and other members of the rich and famous who have secretively been treated with this protocol and the spectacular, miraculous results they have achieved. I am not a medical doctor. I am a researcher, investigator, and journalist blowing the whistle and reporting on one of the best kept secrets in the area of weight loss.

Let's learn *why* you are fat and *who* is making you fat. You'll be surprised to learn it's not your fault that you're fat!

CHAPTER TWO

It's Not Your Fault You Are Fat

If people let the government decide what foods they eat and what medicines they take, their bodies will soon be in a sorry state as are the souls who live under tyranny.

—Thomas Jefferson

People are overweight, fat, and obese all over the world. America, however, has the highest percentage of overweight people, fat people, and obese people in the world. In America specifically, more people are on diets, eating diet food, and taking diet pills and products than ever before. More weight loss books are purchased than ever. More "lite," low carb, low fat, no sugar, low calorie, and diet food is purchased and consumed than ever. More people are exercising than ever before. Yet, each year the percentage of people in America that are overweight, fat, and obese continues to rise. This trend is rapidly spreading around the world, but no country comes close to America in terms of the percentage of people that are overweight, fat, and obese. As I mentioned in the last chapter, in the 1940s less than 10% of the population of America was considered fat. Using the same standards as in the 1940s, today over 80% of the population is considered fat. The problem continues to get worse. Every diet system has failed. Even government statistics show that there has never been a diet plan, program, or product that has worked.

The most common myth is that to lose weight and keep it off you must eat less and exercise more. This is even the U.S. Government's "law" in relation to selling weight loss products. Fat people are told they have no willpower or self-control. This is untrue in most circumstances. I am here to tell you it's not your fault you're fat. When you understand the reasons why you are fat and why every diet and exercise program has failed, you will be free to experience "the weight loss cure protocol" and cure yourself of the bondage of being a slave to food, hunger, cravings, deprivation, and obesity once and for all.

The key that no one addresses is that fat people and naturally thin people have bodies that operate quite differently. A fat person's metabolism is abnormally low. A thin person's metabolism is normal or slightly high. This means if a naturally thin person and a fat person ate the exact same amount of food over a one-week period, the thin person would not gain any weight and the fat person would gain weight. When your metabolism is abnormally low your body cannot burn the food as fuel. When food is not burned for fuel the excess must be converted to fat, thus increasing your weight and making you fatter. This is the first condition which must be corrected if you want to experience rapid weight loss and, more importantly, be able to eat whatever you want in the future without gaining any weight. "The weight loss cure protocol" is the only method known that cures this problem.

In addition to having a low metabolism, fat people generally eat larger quantities of food than naturally thin people. This has nothing to do with self-control or willpower. Thin people cannot understand the very real fact that fat people have an abnormally high, intense, and constant real, gnawing, physical hunger. Fat people are hungry with more intensity than thin people. When fat people eat food they do not get a feeling of fullness. When fat people eat food their hunger stays high much longer, causing them to eat more food. Thin people have their hunger mechanism shut off very quickly and their hunger stays low or nonexistent for many, many hours after they eat even a small quantity of food. Fat people, on the other hand, get hungry very quickly even after consuming a large meal. This is one of the reasons why fat people are so miserable while dieting. Nothing addresses the intense and prolonged *real* hunger. If this physical abnormality is not corrected you are destined to live your life in misery and with feelings of deprivation. This intense and prolonged hunger is a physical abnormality which is corrected and brought back to normal with "the weight loss cure protocol."

The other reason fat people consume large quantities of food is they have uncontrollable intense food cravings to eat, even when they are not physically hungry. This is sometimes called emotional eating, but is actually a physical abnormal condition. Thin people do not understand just how overwhelming and uncontrollable these food cravings and urges can be. There is not a weight loss program ever developed that permanently corrects this condition. This is another reason why weight loss programs fail. If this condition remains intact, the person trying to lose weight or keep the weight off is constantly struggling with these food cravings and urges; therefore living in more misery and deprivation. Thin people cannot understand that these uncontrollable intense food cravings and urges are no different than a drug addict's cravings for more drugs. "The weight loss cure protocol" corrects this physical abnormality once and for all.

Fat people also eat the wrong *types* of foods. This is a sub-symptom of hunger and food cravings. When hunger and food cravings are corrected, this symptom is automatically corrected. Upon completion of "the weight loss cure protocol" you will no longer have high intense hunger or uncontrollable food cravings for the types of food that make weight gain happen rapidly. This does not mean you will be restricted to certain kinds of food. On the contrary, when you finish "the weight loss cure protocol" you will be able to eat any food you want in any amount you want any time you want. What will occur, however, is that because the physical abnormalities have been corrected, your body will no longer crave or have intense hunger for certain types of food. This is a freeing experience leading to a life where you are no longer a slave to food or your uncontrollable cravings.

Genetics play a relatively minor role in obesity. It is true that we all have different genetic makeups. This means some people have blue eyes, and others have brown eyes. Genetics determine why some people are tall and others are short. Genetics do, in fact, determine basic body shape and structure. This means some people are genetically programmed to be thin and others to be heavier. This is important. Not everyone has the genetic body type and bone structure to be a tall, skinny runway model. Some people are built naturally wider and thicker. This does not mean, however, that you are destined to be overweight, fat, or obese. It simply means that everyone's body will look different. Remember, there are tens of thousands of people that have been treated with "the weight loss cure protocol" over a thirty year time period. The results are virtually 100 % successful. Even if you have a major genetic abnormality resulting in low metabolism or intense high hunger, "the weight loss cure protocol" will correct this.

If you've read my first two books, *Natural Cures "They" Don't Want You To Know About* and *More Natural Cures Revealed*, you know that treating symptoms is never the answer. When a symptom is found we must ask, what is the cause of that symptom? When we find the cause or causes of a symptom we must then ask what is the cause or causes of that! We must continue finding the cause until we get to the *root cause* of the symptom. When we address and correct the *root cause*, all the *symptoms* vanish. The first question then is what is the *cause* of a low metabolism? Remember, almost every fat person has a low metabolism. In order to lose weight rapidly and keep it off forever your metabolism has to be brought back to normal, or even slightly elevated. With a high metabolism you can eat any kind of food you like, in any quantity you want, and your body will burn it off and not convert it to fat. This means you never have to diet ever again, and you will never gain weight. This will be achieved when you do "the weight loss cure protocol."

So the *main* reasons for obesity are low metabolism, constant and intense hunger, food cravings, and eating when you're not hungry. There is one more main reason for obesity, which is abnormally storing fat in secure problem area fat reserves throughout the body. We'll talk more about that later. First, let's start by addressing low metabolism.

So *why* is your metabolism abnormally low? What is the *cause,* or *causes*? The number one cause of a low metabolism is the hypothalamus gland operating abnormally. The question then is what causes the hypothalamus gland to operate abnormally, creating low metabolism and a condition where the person cannot burn as fuel all the food they consume even if they are consuming small quantities. This means that a person eating even small amounts of food cannot lose weight and actually gains weight. There are a multitude of reasons why the hypothalamus does not work properly. These include genetics, a clogged liver, Candida yeast overgrowth, a clogged colon, artificial sweeteners, trans fats, food additives, growth hormones and antibiotics in food, monosodium glutamate, lack of sun, lack of sleep, nutritional deficiencies, heavy metal toxicity, parasites, yo-yo dieting, eating eradiated food, eating pasteurized food, eating genetically modified food, lack of walking, non-prescription and prescription drugs, chlorine and fluoride from the water you drink and bathe in, high fructose corn syrup and other man-made sweeteners, propylene glycol and other chemicals introduced into the body through the skin in the form of lotions and creams, carbonated drinks, electromagnetic frequency exposure from cell phones and other wireless devices, and traumatic stressful incidences in our life. There are many other causes.

Let's briefly discuss several of these causes as many of them are themselves caused by other factors. This way you can see the interrelation of these causes and how many actually cause other problems to develop, which in turn can cause additional problems to develop, all leading to the creation of an abnormally operating hypothalamus, resulting in high hunger and low metabolism.

1. **Genetics.** It is true that everyone is born with different metabolic rates. Some people are naturally born with super high metabolisms. Other people are born with abnormally low metabolisms. This is a physical condition. Your metabolism, if caused by genetics, will be corrected once and for all through "the weight loss cure protocol."

2. **A clogged liver.** Virtually every fat person tested has a sluggish, clogged liver. This is caused by non-prescription and prescription drug use, trans fats, including hydrogenated oils, artificial sweeteners, Candida yeast overgrowth, and many other factors. A clogged liver always results in low metabolism and high storing of body fat.

3. **Candida yeast overgrowth.** In your intestine you have good and bad bacteria. If you've ever taken an antibiotic in your

life, the antibiotic destroyed the good bacteria. This allows bad bacteria, including Candida yeast, to abnormally over-grow. The Candida clogs the colon, making digestion and metabolism slow. It also creates gas and bloating, as well as food cravings for bread, pasta, cheese, and sugar. Over time, the Candida turns into a fungus and spreads throughout the entire body. Unless you correct this problem you will always have food cravings, gas, bloating, low metabolism, slow digestion, and you will never have a flat stomach.

4. **A clogged colon.** If you are not having three bowel move-ments a day you have a clogged colon. The colon gets clogged by non-prescription and prescription drugs, lack of water, lack of fiber, lack of walking and exercise, lack of digestive enzymes in the food we eat, and many other fac-tors. In autopsies, medical doctors have found as much as thirty pounds of undigested fecal matter in people's colons. Unless you clean your colon, digestion will remain slow, metabolism will remain slow, food cravings will remain high, hunger will remain high due to lack of nutrients being absorbed properly, and you will never get a flat stomach.

5. **Lack of enzymes.** Today's food supply is void of living enzymes. Any food in a jar or a can has been pasteurized, meaning it has been heated to over 180 degrees for thirty minutes, killing all the enzymes in the food. Microwaving food kills the enzymes. Even commercially grown fruits and vegetables are devoid of enzymes due to the gassing used in the ripening process and dowsing the fruits and vegetables in heavily chlorinated water, and irradiation. Without enough enzymes you can never correct low metabolism and will always have gas, bloating, constipation, and slow digestion.

6. **Underactive thyroid.** Thyroid production can be low due to non-prescription and prescription drugs, nutritional defi-ciencies, and fluoride in the water you drink and bathe in. If you have an underactive thyroid, this must be corrected or you will be stuck with a low metabolic rate. "The weight loss cure protocol" corrects this.

7. **Inefficient pancreas**. The pancreas secretes insulin. People with a weight problem have a pancreas that is not operating properly and have insulin tolerance problems. This is caused by a multitude of factors, including non-prescription and prescription drugs, Candida overgrowth, nutritional deficiencies, a clogged liver and colon, artificial sweeteners, high fructose corn syrup, and other considerations. If you do not correct insulin intolerance you will continue to have abnormally high amounts of fat in your body and continue to store more fat abnormally high.

8. **Hormonal imbalances**. Hormones partially regulate metabolism. Hormonal imbalances are caused in part by stress; chemical additives in food; chlorine and fluoride in water you drink, shower, and bathe in; cosmetics, lotions, and creams you put on your skin; Candida overgrowth; a sluggish liver and colon; and many more factors.

9. **Artificial sweeteners**. All man-made artificial sweeteners slow metabolism. This includes aspartame and sucralose. These go by the trade names NutraSweet and Splenda.

10. **Monosodium Glutamate (MSG)**. This is called an excitotoxin. It is a man-made chemical that should never be consumed. MSG is now sometimes listed on food labels as "spices," "flavors" or, in many cases, does not have to be listed at all.

11. **Lack of water**. Most people are dehydrated and don't know it. Lack of pure water hydrating the cells leads to a low metabolic rate.

12. **Carbonated drinks**. These block calcium absorption, leading to nutritional deficiencies which lower metabolism. This includes diet drinks.

13. **Lack of sleep**. This means less than seven hours per night. Research show this leads to obesity.

14. **Cold water drinks**. Drinking ice cold liquids slows metabolism.

15. **Lack of sun**. The sun stimulates metabolism plus alleviates depression and stress.

16. **Nutritional deficiencies**. Without proper nutrition your metabolism cannot be normal. The most common deficiencies include calcium, zinc, magnesium, Vitamin C, Vitamin E, and other amino acids and cofactors, including CLA and chromium.

17. **Heavy metal toxicity**. Most people are loaded with heavy metals, including mercury from amalgam fillings. These heavy metals clog the liver, colon, and affect circulation.

18. **Poor circulation**. Without proper circulation metabolism will stay low. People's circulation is poor due to clogged arteries, which is caused by trans-fats, homogenized dairy products, and chlorine in the water. Other causes include vitamin and mineral deficiencies, heavy metal toxicity, Candida overgrowth, and misaligned feet and ankles. Lack of walking and exercise are also a factor.

19. **Lack of oxygen**. Most people have lower than normal levels of oxygen in their blood and cells. This is caused by poor breathing habits, nutritional deficiencies, lack of exercise, a clogged liver and colon. It is also caused by non-prescription and prescription medications.

20. **Allergies**. Environmental and food allergies are caused by Candida overgrowth, a clogged liver and colon, poor circulation, parasites, heavy metal toxicity, and many other factors.

21. **Parasites**. Almost 100% of overweight people have parasites. A clogged liver and colon, Candida, heavy metal toxicity, and nutritional deficiencies are the main causes.

22. **Yo-yo dieting**. Every time you go on a diet and lose weight and gain it all back you are in fact lowering your body's internal thermostat and internal body weight set point. Every time you diet to lose weight your metabolism goes lower.

23. **Lack of sweating**. The skin is the largest organ in the body. It must breathe and eliminate toxins on a regular basis. Sweating is a natural body process. Lack of sweating leads to a clogged lymphatic system and sluggish metabolism.

24. **Low muscle mass.** If your body does not have normal amounts of muscle your metabolism will always be low. Increasing muscle mass always leads to a high metabolism.

25. **Air conditioning.** Research shows that air conditioning lowers metabolism.

26. **Breakfast.** Eating no breakfast keeps metabolism low.

27. **EMS.** Electromagnetic frequencies are generated from all wireless devices, including wireless phones, cell phones, laptop computers, and even TV and computer screens. They have an adverse affect on every cell in the body, lowering metabolic rate.

28. **Eating before bed.** Filling your stomach before bed, with highly refined or super highly refined easily digestible food, promotes low metabolism.

29. **Genetically modified food.** In America most fruit, vegetables, and dairy products have been genetically modified, creating food that is in fact man-made. The body does not know how to react to these abnormal food products, causing metabolism to be lowered.

30. **Food additives.** If food is not 100% organic, the food is loaded with herbicides, pesticides, chemical fertilizers, antibiotics, and over 15,000 man-made chemicals. This is unique to America. American produced food absolutely, positively, 100% will make you fat.

31. **Lack of walking.** In America the average person walks less than one-tenth of a mile per day. In other countries people walk five miles or more a day. The body is designed to walk. Lack of physical movement results in a constant lowering of the metabolic rate.

The above list is just to give you an idea of some, not all, of the factors that we deal with every day, keeping our metabolism low. The list may seem overwhelming. The bad news is this list is just the tip of the iceberg. The really bad news is if you are fat right now, due to the above factors, and many more factors, your metabolism is so abnormally low that you are virtually a prisoner to your weight problem and lack of energy. The good news is that your metabolic condition can be corrected easily and effortlessly and in a very short period of time using "the weight loss cure protocol." The even better news is once you get your metabolism back up to normal you can keep it there for the rest of your life and not fall back into the trap that has kept you fat.

Low metabolism keeps you tired, fatigued and lethargic. Low metabolism means that even if you go on a low calorie, low fat, low carb diet combined with exercise, you still will have a hard time losing weight. Low metabolism means even if you just look at food you seem to gain weight! When you correct your metabolic rate and bring it back to normal you will experience a dramatic increase in energy, depression and moodiness will vanish, your motivation in life will increase, sexual desires increase, your skin, hair, and nails will look younger and healthier, all body functions become healthier, and your immune system is strengthened. You become less susceptible to colds, flues, illness, and disease. Evidence suggests lifespan increases. You will feel like a brand new person.

I mentioned that fat people seem to be hungry all the time. The intensity of hunger causes the person to consume large quantities of food. The frequency of the hunger causes the person to eat more often. This intense constant hunger needs to be normalized or the person will live in misery and deprivation. What causes this intense and constant hunger? The causes include:

1. **Abnormal hypothalamus gland.** The hypothalamus is the body's master gland. It is the master gland that regulates metabolism. It is also the master gland that regulates physiological hunger. This gland does not operate in a normal state in fat people. It must be reset and normalized in order to eliminate intense and constant physical hunger. The reasons that the hypothalamus is operating abnormally include genetics, a clogged liver, Candida overgrowth, a clogged colon, lack of digestive enzymes, nutritional deficiencies, stress, high fructose corn syrup, artificial sweeteners, microwaved food, MSG, lotions and cosmetics put on the skin, non-prescription and prescription drugs, fluoride and chlorine in the water you drink, bathe, and shower in,

dehydration and lack of water, carbonated drinks, ice cold drinks, trans-fats, lack of sun, food additives, genetically modified food, heavy metal toxicity, lack of oxygen, environmental and food allergies, parasites, yo-yo dieting, air conditioning, lack of sleep, EMS, lack of fiber, and several other factors.

As you can see, the hypothalamus in an abnormal state is the main cause for both low metabolism and intense constant hunger. There are two other interesting factors that cause the hypothalamus to be in this abnormal state, making metabolism very low and hunger very real, intense, and constant.

The first factor that can cause the hypothalamus to lower metabolism and create intense hunger is the lack of all the various "tastes" in food we eat on a daily basis. The basic tastes that should be present in most meals throughout the day include saltiness, sourness, sweetness, bitterness, and savoriness. "Subtastes" include temperature, texture, smells, astringency, fat, tingly numbness, spiciness, lack of spiciness, or coolness. When the body does not get stimulated with all of these "tastes" as well as scents, the hypothalamus is tricked into believing the body lacks food, thus lowers metabolism and increases hunger. In an ideal world all of your meals would have all of these tastes and scents, thus keeping metabolism high and hunger low.

The other factor, and most interesting and significant cause of intense and constant hunger, is that food manufacturers are specifically and purposely creating food, using manufacturing processes, using food additives, and using chemicals that specifically are designed to affect the hypothalamus and increase hunger when you eat the food. Food manufacturers are making food with the sole purpose of creating a physical chemical addiction to the food. I have personally been in the chemists' labs where the directives are to create food that increase hunger, lower metabolism, get a person physically addicted to the food (like a drug), and make people fatter. Food companies are publicly traded corporations. These publicly traded international conglomerates have only one objective...to increase profits! The only way they can increase profits is to produce food at the lowest possible cost and to get more people to buy and eat more food. This is why publicly traded food companies are producing genetically modified food using chemical poison fertilizers, herbicides, pesticides, and other dangerous growing methods. This is why food is ripened with poisonous gas, injected with chemical preservatives and flavoring agents, eradiated, pasteurized, bathed in poisonous chlorine baths, injected with antibiotics, growth hormones, and other deadly drugs. Food is produced in an unnatural, abnormal way. Fruits and vegetables are not grown, they are manufactured! They are made to grow abnormally fast, look the same, and last ten to twenty times longer than nature intended. Every bit of commercially produced fruits, vegetables, meat, dairy, poultry and fish is purposefully laced with thousands of man-made chemical agents, hormones, and drugs. Every commercially made grain or food product in a bag, box, jar, or can has been altered from the way nature intended. They are all, with the exception of 100% organic, loaded with some of the over 15,000 man-made chemicals that the U.S. Government allows to be put in the food. Most of these chemicals don't even have to be listed on the labels!

The main reason why it's not your fault you're fat is that the American food supply is being produced purposely to make you fat! This is why when thin people from other countries come to America and eat what they think is the same food that they were eating in their own country, they unexpectedly gain weight rapidly. Generally speaking, the bread in America will make you fat. The bread in other countries will not. The milk, butter, and cheese in America will make you fat. The milk, butter, and cheese in other countries will not. The meat, poultry, and farm-raised fish in America will make you fat. The meat, poultry, and wild fish in other countries will not. The pasta, rice, and potatoes made in America will make you fat. The rice, pasta, and potatoes grown in other countries will not. Even the fruits and vegetables conventionally grown in America can make you fat. The fruits and vegetables grown in many other countries will not. You see, it is not the calories, the fat, the protein, the simple or complex carbohydrates, the sodium, or the glycemic index rate of food that is the main culprit that is making you fat. It is the man-made chemicals, additives, and food processing techniques that are the main issues. It's the man-made trans fats, the man-made high fructose corn syrup, the man-made artificial sweeteners, the genetically modified food, the pasteurization of food, the irritating and microwaving of food, the growth hormones and drugs in the meat and dairy products, the chemicals in the lotions and creams we put on our skin, and the chlorine and fluoride in the water we drink and bathe in that are the real reasons we get fat.

In my first book, *Natural Cures "They" Don't Want You To Know About,* I talk at length about how food is produced in America. I would encourage you to read my first two books, *Natural Cures "They" Don't Want You To Know About* and *More Natural Cures Revealed*. They will give you an insider's view of how the food industry in America is specifically making you fat.

There is another important cause of why the hypothalamus is operating abnormally, keeping our metabolism low and hunger high. When a person consumes small amounts of food for a 24-hour period, followed by consuming a massive quantity of calories and foods high on the glycemic index, the hypothalamus gets shocked and begins to create the conditions for abnormally storing fat, lowering metabolism, and increasing appetite. Think of the average person who goes to bed, wakes up eating little or no breakfast, skips lunch, and then in the evening has a huge meal. This is the ideal, perfect storm scenario to shock the hypothalamus into operating abnormally, thus creating obesity.

It may appear that there is no way out of this trap. It may seem like it is impossible to reset the hypothalamus and normalize the hunger. The good news is "the weight loss cure protocol" will quickly and easily reset your hypothalamus, thus eliminating the intense and constant hunger that you have. The even better news is when you are finished with the protocol you will be able to eat any kind of food you want. You will be able to eat cheeseburgers, French fries, ice cream, cookies, cakes, bread, pasta, cheese, butter, cream, steak, pizza, Mexican food, mashed potatoes and gravy, virtually any kind of food you want. Remember, when your hypothalamus is reset, your metabolism will be high and you will no longer have intense and constant hunger. You will automatically and effortlessly be eating normal quantities of food without ever feeling hungry or deprived. Your body will naturally burn the food as fuel, giving you abundant energy and guaranteeing that you do not gain the weight back.

Let's address the uncontrollable, compulsive urges to eat when you're not hungry, and food cravings. Sometimes this is called emotional eating. It is actually triggered by the hypothalamus. What causes these massive uncontrollable food cravings, making you eat even when you're not physically hungry? The basic causes are: mental and emotional stress, Candida overgrowth, a clogged liver, a clogged colon, lack of digestive enzymes, nutritional deficiencies, hormonal imbalances, artificial sweeteners, non-prescription and prescription drugs, high fructose corn syrup, food additives, microwaved food, MSG, lotions, creams and cosmetics on the skin, environmental and food allergies, parasites, lack of fiber, and several other factors.

You will again notice that the causes of food cravings are the same causes of low metabolism and intense and constant hunger. I would like to address the two most significant causes of these food cravings.

The first is Candida yeast overgrowth. Your intestine is loaded with good and bad bacteria. If you have ever taken an antibiotic, the antibiotic killed the good bacteria in your gut. This allowed the bad bacteria, including Candida yeast, to overgrow abnormally. When Candida overgrows in the intestine it burrows itself into the intestinal wall. It also turns into a fungus spreading throughout the entire body. The yeast and the fungus feed on simple carbohydrates such as sugar, yeast, bread, pasta, cake, ice cream, etc. Candida is the main cause of carbohydrate food cravings. It is also a major cause of constipation, gas, bloating, and a protruding stomach and waist. It causes depression, lack of concentration, a feeling of spaceyness and fatigue. When the Candida burrows itself into the intestinal wall it creates pockets where food is trapped. When food is trapped in the intestine it begins to turn toxic. Interestingly enough, these toxic food particles create actual cravings for that food while at the same time producing allergic reactions to that food. It's a catch-22. The condition actually makes you crave foods that make you feel bad.

The Candida condition also creates a second cause of food cravings which is parasites. These parasites feed on the body, creating nutritional deficiencies. The person then develops massive and uncontrollable cravings for certain kinds of food. The body, however, cannot assimilate the nutrients effectively due to the clogged liver and colon; therefore, the food cravings come back frequently and persist.

There is an emotional, mental aspect to food cravings as well. These are linked to stressful emotional experiences we've had in our life. They are also linked to the massive brainwashing and programming that we have had from all of the food advertisements. Without going into great detail, I know from personal inside experience that food companies use the most sophisticated mind programming technology when producing advertisements for certain foods. The television ads and print ads for food are designed to create emotional triggers that actually make us crave food when these triggers are set off. This is almost like having a post-hypnotic suggestion implanted in our mind. When the trigger is set off you experience an uncontrollable overwhelming craving and urge to eat certain kinds of food. This urge is so powerful it causes you to crave and want specific food even when you are not hungry. This is, again, why I say it's really not your fault that you're fat.

The good news is that as part of "the weight loss cure protocol" you will be able to eliminate these food cravings at both levels. You will no longer be a slave to the food companies.

As you can see, I am exposing and blowing the whistle on dirty secrets that the food companies do not want you to know about. This is one of the reasons why I am personally attacked, debunked, and discredited in such a massive way through the news media. Food companies spend billions of dollars in advertising in virtually every magazine, newspaper, television network, and radio network. These media outlets are controlled by the advertisers. I, therefore, am the enemy of the food industry. I want people to be cured of their obesity, food cravings, low metabolism, and intense hunger. If you are cured you will automatically and effortlessly be eating and buying less food. The food industry, on the other hand, wants everyone's metabolism low, hunger and food cravings high, making sure more and more people continue to buy and eat more food every year. The food industry wants you fat and physically and emotionally addicted to their food!

It's Profitable Keeping You Fat

In my first book, *Natural Cures "They" Don't Want You To Know About*, I explain how it always all about the money. I highly recommend you read that book as well as my last book, *More Natural Cures Revealed: Previously Censored Brand Name Products That Cure Disease*. These books go into great detail of how the corporate system works relating to the drug industry and the food industry. As a former insider and current whistle-blower, I expose how the money flows and why it is profitable for these industries to keep people fat and sick. Following the money trail answers all questions. The drug industry knows that people who are overweight, fat, and obese have more medical symptoms and buy and take more non-prescription and prescription drugs. There is a financial motivation to keep people overweight. Overweight people are sicker and great customers for the drug companies. Remember that the same group of about 300 families that control the world-wide pharmaceutical industry also control most of the publicly traded food producers and manufacturers. Members of the food industry and the drug industry regularly have secret meetings to determine how they can each increase the other's profits. In Oslo, Norway I was personally at one of these secret meetings. Remember, drug companies and food companies are publicly traded corporations whose only objective is to increase profits and shareholder value. Their only goal is to sell more of their products. Drug companies have publicly stated that they want more and more people buying and using more and more of their drugs. The do not want to prevent or cure disease. Doing so would put them out of business. Their only objective is to convince people through the use of their deceptive advertising that they need to be taking more and more drugs on a regular basis. Food companies simply want to sell more and more food. Their publicly stated objectives are to get more and more people consuming larger and larger amounts of food. These industries work together. Drugs, both non-prescription and prescription, have side effects that include lowering metabolism and increasing hunger. This makes people fatter, making them buy more food, increasing the profits of the food companies. This also makes people sicker, therefore, buying and using more drugs. It is a preplanned vicious cycle.

Food companies specifically make food by using genetic engineering techniques, food processing techniques, and adding chemicals into the food that create disease in the body. Just like the tobacco industry knew that smoking cigarettes cause cancer and other diseases, yet lied about it for fifty years, so too do the current food producers and manufactures know that their genetically modified chemically laced food products cause cancer, heart disease, arthritis, MS, lupus, depression, and a host of other illnesses. One board member from the Mayo Clinic, whose identity must be kept secret, shared with me the data showing that virtually all cancerous tumors are loaded with pesticides and herbicides used in the production of most commercial food! The food companies are making food purposefully to create new illnesses. The food companies, for example, designed and engineered food that would create the epidemic of such diseases as acid reflux disease, depression, insomnia, restless leg syndrome, constipation, high blood pressure, and high cholesterol. The drug companies knew this in advance. This is why when a new disease becomes common there is already a drug ready to be marketed! The food companies also are specifically putting chemicals in the food, in many cases not listing them on the label that are designed specifically to increase appetite, get you physically, chemically addicted to the food like a drug, and make you fat. This way the food companies are assured that each person will be consuming more and more food every year. This increases their profits.

Both the drug industry and food industry are using sophisticated brainwashing techniques in their deceptive advertising, virtually programming our minds with mental triggers that give us overwhelming compulsive cravings and urges for a specific food and drugs. I know this factually because I was directly involved on a covert basis in this activity for almost twenty years. This is why 80% of Americans are overweight. This is also why the obesity problem is now spreading around the world.

A sub-industry that has a financial incentive to keep you fat is the diet industry. The weight loss or diet industry consists of companies that sell exercise equipment, weigh loss pills, powders and potions, prepackaged food, low fat, low carb, and low calorie food, and every other weight loss treatment marketed and sold. The vast majority of the companies involved in the weight loss industry are owned directly or indirectly by the same people that own and control the food industry and drug companies. These weight loss companies have data in their internal documents showing that their products and programs do not work. The most significant secret data reveals that these companies know that the number of overweight people will continue to increase year after year, thus increasing their profits. These weight loss and diet companies are taking advantage of desperate vulnerable people who are struggling with their weight. The most amazing insider secret I want to blow the whistle on is the fact that the same unscrupulous people will sell ten different worthless diet aids over time to the same person. These marketers know that the first diet product will not work. When a customer buys the product, the companies know in a month or two the person will still be fat, and therefore will be a prime customer for their next worthless diet aid. This cycle repeats itself over and over again. The products are marketed under different names and companies so that you don't know it's the same people selling you the various products. This is nothing more than a money making scam.

These marketing scams can be quite comprehensive. These corporations use books, doctors, media outlets, TV and radio talk show hosts, combined with selling supplements, and prepackaged food, all under the "brand" they are trying to promote. Two prime examples include the Atkins diet and Dr. Phil's shape up program.

Atkins started with a book that was based on Dr. Stillman's research from the late 1960s. Major corporations saw the power in the Atkins' brand and an opportunity to make hundreds of millions in profits. They then produced a line of Atkins branded products which sold like hotcakes. The problem was the people running the Atkins organization did not believe in the Atkins program. They were not on the Atkins program. They did not use the Atkins products. They created products, and then lied about the ingredients on the label. They knew that the products would not help people lose weight. They were not interested in whether people lost weight; they were only interested in whether they themselves would make money. I knew Dr. Atkins personally. I believe he was a sincere, genuine man with a deep belief in his program. The money people that took over his organization, I believe, were only in it for the money. I know this because I was in business with them. I knew the people involved, I talked with them on a regular basis, and I have firsthand knowledge of their true money hungry motivation. I remember having lunch with the Atkins executives at Graziano's restaurant in Niles, Illinois. All the Atkins executives were fat! They laughed about all the "suckers" who were buying Atkins products. The whole conversation revolved around how much money we all could make. There was no concern about the people and their desperate need to lose weight permanently. It was all money, money, money!

Dr. Phil is another example. I do not know Dr. Phil. I have never met him. He may be totally genuine and sincere with his desire to help people lose weight. What I do know is that he wrote a book on weight loss that promoted a line of weight loss supplements and meal replacements using his name. It is no secret that this was a coordinated market effort to create huge profits. We do know that a class action suit was filed by customers who bought the products and felt the only thing they lost was their money. With no admission or finding of wrongdoing the organizations settled with the unhappy customers for $10 million. Dr. Phil is one of the weight loss gurus and authors that is still fat! With all due respect to Dr. Phil, how could he write a book about losing weight when he is still fat himself? If he and others like him had programs that worked, they should be skinny.

When a new diet book comes out there is a preplanned sophisticated comprehensive marketing program preestablished to include selling branded diet aids, prepackaged food, or other weight loss programs. I can tell you this is never designed to cure obesity. These books, diet aids, and prepackaged food products are designed only to increase profits for the people selling them.

It is sad that overweight people are being taken advantage of—all in the name of profit. Everyone knows that none of these programs work. Even if a person loses some weight, the major problems and true causes of obesity are never addressed. People are miserable during the weight loss process. People are hungry and feel deprived. The problem area fat never goes away. People are tired, depressed, and grumpy. When they finish these weight loss programs they remain a slave to hunger, fatigue, portion control, counting calories, fat, or carbs, or being unable to enjoy the foods they like. The worst part of all is almost everyone gains all the weight back and puts more weight on. The real travesty is every one of these programs actually makes the condition worse because they leave the person with a lower metabolism than before and an even higher hunger than they had at the beginning of their weight loss regime.

I am revealing this "weight loss cure protocol" because it worked for virtually 100% of the tens of thousands of patients that used it over the last thirty plus years. I am revealing this discovery because it worked for me! I believe that if you follow this protocol your weight loss issues will be cured and you can live the rest of your life as a normal, thin, happy person!

Why Other Weight Loss Programs Don't Work and Actually Make You Fat

There are a lot of myths and theories about weight loss. We hear things such as: eat fewer calories, exercise more, eat low fat, low carb, low glycemic food, food combining, etc. There are hundreds of special hard to follow diets such as the blood type diet, the high protein diet, the raw food diet, the low fat diet, the low carb diet, the low sodium diet, the high fiber diet, the low calorie diet, the vegetarian diet, the macrobiotic diet, the grapefruit diet, the South Beach diet, the Atkins diet, the Slim Fast diet, the Opti-fast diet, etc. There is even a chocolate diet, the skip a day diet, the Mediterranean diet, and the list goes on. There are weight loss programs which include Jenny Craig, NutriSystem, Sugar Busters, Weight Watchers, and others. These diet programs do not work and actually make you fatter in the long run. None of them address the true causes as to why you are overweight. Not one of them resets the hypothalamus. None of them raise and reset your metabolism. None of them correct the intense and constant hunger. None of them correct the uncontrollable food cravings and urges to eat when you are not hungry. Most importantly, no matter how much weight you may lose doing these programs, none of them get your body to release the secure abnormal trouble area fat deposits. None of these programs reshape your body.

The whole concept that you have to count calories, eat certain foods and eliminate others, count fat or carbohydrate grams is completely unnatural and unnecessary. If you travel around the world and look at people that are naturally thin, none of them are on a diet! None of them do crazy exercise programs! They eat real food, and lots of it.

In France people eat bread, cheese, butter, chocolate, and drink wine. Everyone is thin. In Italy people eat pizza, pasta, Gelato ice cream, bread, and tons of fat. Everyone is thin. In Germany people drink beer, eat cake, sausages, bread, butter, and potatoes. Everyone is thin. In Asia people eat rice, noodles, fish, and drink sake. Everyone is thin. All the diet theories are myths, lies, and deceptions. Throughout the world people eat tons of carbs, tons of fat, tons of salt, drink beer, wine, and other alcohol, eat ice cream and other deserts, have bread with real butter, yet everyone remains thin. No one is drinking diet sodas. No one eats low fat food. No one uses artificial sweeteners. They eat real food—real, full fat milk, cheese, and butter. They eat chicken and other poultry with the skin on! No one drinks light beer—they drink full carb and full calorie beer. Why are people thin in these other countries, eating large quantities of real food on a regular basis? Simple. The food is produced differently than in America. In America, for example, the beef is injected with bovine growth hormone and loaded with antibiotics and other drugs. The beef is fed genetically modified, chemically produced grain and ground up dead animals. The beef produced in America is different from the beef produced in other countries. It's not that beef makes you fat; it's the chemicals and growth hormones and drugs put in the American beef that makes you fat. The bread in America is loaded with high fructose corn syrup, dextrose, sucrose, or other man-made sweeteners that lower metabolism, increase appetite and make you fat. They are also loaded with chemical preservatives and stabilizers which make you fat. In other countries bread is made with flour, water, salt and yeast. It's not that bread makes you fat; it is American bread that makes you fat. Again, the American food supply is being produced and designed specifically and purposefully to make you fat.

The prepackaged food diets are probably the worst. They are loaded with monosodium glutamate, high fructose corn syrup, and thousands of man-made chemicals. When you go on any of these diets you may lose some weight initially, but you will not lose the secure trouble area fat deposits. You will not reshape your body. The chemicals in this food will continue to lower your metabolism and increase your hunger, which is why when people stop these programs they immediately gain all the weight back, plus more. This is why it's so hard to lose weight. This is why losing weight takes a long time. This is also why gaining weight is so easy and takes such a short period of time. In the movie documentary *Super Size Me*, Morgan Spurlock ate only at McDonalds for one month. He gained twenty-eight pounds in one month. He gained the weight fast and effortlessly. This is because McDonald's food is specifically and purposely made to make you gain weight. McDonald's, for example, even puts sugar on their French fries! They even publicly announced that they are now adding MORE SUGAR into their buns! He also got physically, chemically addicted to the McDonald's food. In between meals he was depressed and had an overwhelming craving for McDonald's food. He exhibited all the common symptoms of a drug addict. When he ate his next McDonald's meal his depression, symptoms, and cravings went away. He said he felt like a heroin addict getting a fix. McDonald's does this purposefully. It wants its customers to be physically, chemically addicted to its food just like a drug dealer wants his victims addicted to drugs. It's the way they guarantee you'll be coming back for more. McDonald's even calls people who eat three or more meals a week at their restaurants "heavy users"!

The scariest part of the documentary was the fact that after seven months of diet and exercise Morgan still had not lost the twenty-eight pounds! This is why diets don't work. Diets and diet food only make the problem worse and make it harder than ever to lose weight in the future.

Diet supplements also do not work. There are many supplements sold that claim to increase metabolism and reduce hunger. These include hoodia and effedra. There are hundreds of pills containing combinations of vitamins, minerals, amino acids, herbs, algaes, plant extracts, and other various supplements. Some of these do in fact temporarily increase metabolism and lower appetite. None of them, however, have long-term effect. The major problem with these supplements is that when you stop taking the supplement your metabolism goes down even lower than before. Your appetite also can come back twice what it was when you started. Therefore, these supplements make your condition worse. They make it harder for you to keep the weight off and make it even easier for you to gain weight in the future. None of these supplements release the problem area fat reserves or reshape the body.

Those who think exercise is the answer are mistaken. Exercise in any form is recommended and has benefits. Exercise will slightly raise metabolism and slightly lower hunger. Exercise will not, however, release the problem area fat reserves and reshape your body. If you've ever gone to the gym and seen some of the aerobics instructors who exercise three to four hours a day yet still have all the problem area fat around the hips, thighs, and buttocks you know this is true. If exercise was required in order for a person to be thin, why is it that there are tens of millions of people around the world who eat everything they want, never exercise, yet remain lean and thin? Exercise is good and beneficial, but it is not the answer and will not cure the cause of obesity.

Fasting was once called a treatment for obesity. It is not. In researching fasting clinics around the world and reviewing the records of the participants it is conclusive that the majority of the people gain all the weight back very quickly after fasting. Fasting is for cleansing the body from toxins. It is highly encouraged and beneficial. I fast on a regular basis to clean toxins out of the body. There are many kinds of fasts. Fasting should only be done under the supervision of a licensed health care practitioner. Cleaning the body of toxins will help everything in your body work more efficiently and better. The health benefits of fasting are quite extensive. It is not, however, a cure or treatment for obesity.

Laxatives, diuretics, skipping meals, amphetamines, thyroid drugs, liquid diets, fiber drinks, human growth hormone, testosterone injections, acupuncture, laser treatments, homeopathic remedies, and weight loss teas all do not cure the underlying cause of obesity. These treatments, like all others, do not permanently correct and normalize metabolism or hunger. None of them release the problem area fat deposits. They generally make the problem worse in the long run.

A question that comes up often is why do some people have more problem area fat deposits than others? The hypothalamus gland determines where the body stores fat. There are three basic areas where fat is stored in the body. First is structural fat. This is good fat which surrounds the joints and internal organs. You do not want to lose this fat. Second are the normal fat reserves spread throughout your body. Third are the secure problem area fat reserves. The problem area fat reserves are designed as a survival mechanism. Once fat is stored there, no matter how much diet and exercise you do, this fat will not be released. This is the problem with diet and exercise alone. When you do any diet and exercise program you will lose water, structural fat, normal fat reserves, and muscle mass. The problem area fat will never be released. This is why people who have done constant yo-yo dieting tend to have sore and painful joints, and a sore and painful heel. This means that your body has burned off the good needed structural fat. This is why reduced calorie dieting is not only ineffective, but causes more physical problems. The reason why some people store more fat in these secure abnormal problem area fat deposits is because the hypothalamus gland is not operating properly. "The weight loss cure protocol" releases these abnormal secure problem area fat deposits and, more significantly, resets your hypothalamus so that in the future if you do consume more than your body burns the excess will not be stored abnormally in these secure problem area fat reserves. This is another reason why this protocol has been called a cure by the medical doctors who have used it with their patients.

It is important to note that "the weight loss cure protocol" normalizes body function. This treatment resets the body to a normal state. The body needs and requires that it have *some* secure fat reserves for survival. These secure fat reserves are never released with the exception of two instances. First, as a survival mechanism for the human species, these fat reserves are in fact released during pregnancy. This is why in third world countries mothers who consume only a few hundred calories a day during pregnancy still deliver healthy full weight babies. The other time that the body releases these fat reserves is at the point of starvation. This is how prisoners in concentration camps were able to survive. The problem is, when the hypothalamus gets in an abnormal state it abnormally puts fat in these secure abnormal fat reserves at a much higher rate than normal. "The weight loss cure protocol" corrects this problem.

The bottom line is that the major reasons why you are overweight, fat, or obese is your metabolism is abnormally low, your hunger is abnormally intense and constant, you have uncontrollable food cravings causing you to eat when you are not hungry, and when you have excess food that has not been burned off, your hypothalamus stores an abnormally high amount of the excess in the secure problem area fat reserves which will never be released no matter how much you diet and exercise. "The weight loss cure protocol" will once and for all correct this condition.

Who discovered this cure? How was it discovered? Why has it been suppressed and kept a secret for so long? The amazing story will surprise you!

CHAPTER THREE

The Weight Loss Cure Discovered

A new scientific truth does not triumph by convincing its opponents and making them see the light, but rather because its opponents eventually die, and a new generation grows up that is familiar with it.
—*Max Planck, German Physicist*

In the 1950s obesity was a rare occurrence. In Europe less than a quarter of 1% of the population was considered obese; less than 3% were fat; less than 6% were considered slightly overweight. Europe had just been devastated by the Second World War. Food was scarce. People ate food that was grown and harvested, usually within a mile of where they lived. Everything was relatively fresh. Fruits, vegetables, and grains were not genetically modified. There were no artificial chemical fertilizers. Herbicides, pesticides, and insecticides were never used. Cows roamed freely and ate grass and hay. They were not injected with growth hormone, antibiotics, or other drugs. Meat and poultry was killed and butchered in local neighborhoods and purchased fresh. Bread was made daily with flour, water, salt, and yeast. Pasteurization and irradiating of food, killing all the enzymes and nutritional value, was not practiced. Microwaving of food was an unheard of technology. Artificial sweeteners like saccharin, aspartame, and sucrolos were nonexistent. High fructose corn syrup, dextrose and the over 15,000 chemical additives commonly used today were an unheard of concept. Monosodium glutamate and other flavor enhancing excitotoxins were not even imagined. People ate real

43

food. Diet sodas, low fat, low calorie, low carb items were not even considered. People ate real, full fat, full carb, full calorie food.

Due to the devastation of the war, people routinely walked over five miles daily as part of their normal routine. Moving their body as the body was intended was part of normal life. Bending, lifting, pushing, pulling, carrying, reaching were not activities done in exercise classes, but rather acts performed in the normal course of living day-to-day. People did not sit for hours in front of televisions or computers, as computers were nonexistent and televisions were scarce. People drank tea and coffee with real sugar and full fat cream. High calorie and high carb beer and wine were the drinks of choice. Being slightly overweight, fat, or obese was a rarity indeed.

It was at this time that a prominent physician, Dr. A.T.W. Simeons, M.D., became interested in the medical condition of obesity. Born in London, Dr. Simeons graduated in medicine summa cum laude at the University of Heidelberg. His post-graduate studies were done in Germany and Switzerland. He was appointed to a large surgical hospital near Dresden. Early in his career he became engrossed in the study of tropical diseases and joined the School of Tropical Medicine in Hamburg. He spent two years in Africa. In 1931, he went to India, where he stayed for eighteen years. He was awarded the Red Cross Order of Merit by the Queen of England for discovering the use of an injectable remedy for malaria, and a new method of staining malaria parasites, now known as the "Simeons stain." During the Second World War he held several important posts under the government of India, conducting extensive research on bubonic plague and leprosy control. In 1949 he moved to Rome, treating patients at the Salvator Mundi International Hospital. During his career he authored several medical books and contributed to many scientific publications.

Dr. Simeons, M.D., was regarded as one of the top research doctors in Europe. Traveling the world, Dr. Simeons became fascinated with the unique and rare condition known as obesity. Up until this time in history the majority of people that were slightly overweight, fat, or obese were the rich. The reasons were well known. The rich had plenty of food to eat and did not have to perform any physical labor. Taking in more calories than the body burns through normal metabolism and physical activity creates an excess which must be stored in the body. This creates excess weight. By simply lowering caloric intake and increasing physical activity the body very quickly and easily burned off the excess fat and weight. People today are not so lucky. What Simeons observed was the unique and rare situation where poor impoverished people became obese even though their calorie consumption was quite low and their physical exertion level was quite high. This made no logical sense. Thus began his fascination with the cause and treatment of obesity. Dr. Simeons very quickly became one of the most knowledgeable experts on every known theory relating to the cause of obesity. He also became one of the world's foremost experts on every treatment used around the world to handle the obesity condition. During this time, it was mostly only the rich and famous that had issues with obesity. In today's terms the profit potential or market for weight loss treatments was incredibly small. If anyone was slightly overweight they simply reduced their food intake and increased their physical activity for a week or two and the condition was easily and almost effortlessly corrected. In Simeons's day, obesity was not the epidemic that it is today. The drug and food companies had not yet figured out a way to actually make us fat, make us intensely and constantly hungry, or get us physically addicted to food. The drug and food companies had not yet figured out a way to mess up our metabolisms and fat storing mechanisms, virtually making it impossible for people to lose weight and fat.

Simeons worked with thousands of individual overweight, fat, and obese patients and studied the results with incredible due diligence. Every new theory, every new method, every new lead was considered. He personally tested and critically evaluated everything used around the world for obesity. The results were always disappointing and lacked uniformity. The nature of the obesity disorder was a mystery to every doctor and expert around the world. Remember, at this time obesity was relatively rare. Today, using the same standards as then, over 50% of Americans classify as being obese, and 80% are overweight or fat. The standard theory, which is still what governments and health organizations around the world claim, is that people are fat simply because they eat too much and do not exercise as much as they should. Simeons believed this was neither the whole truth nor the last word in the matter. Simeons believed that over-eating is a result of a deeper disorder and not the true cause. For years Simeons tested and studied patient after patient. He completed multiple clinical trials and published these in scientific journals. During his research Simeons received hundreds of inquiries from research institutes and doctors around the world. It seemed that Simeons was the only doctor trying to find the true cause of this condition instead of trying to find a way to profit from the marketing or sale of some "treatment" for the condition. After sixteen years of trial and error, Simeons discovered a theory as to the true cause of obesity. Once believing he knew the cause, he then could come up with a way to cure the condition permanently.

His basic findings were that obesity, in all forms, is an abnormal functioning of various parts of the body. It is a medical condition. People suffering from this particular disorder get fat regardless of whether they eat excessively, normally, or less than normal! A person suffering from this disorder will still get fat, stay fat, and never lose the problem area fat no matter how much they diet and exercise. Most importantly, Simeons discovered that when a person is free of this disorder, he will never get fat even if he frequently overeats and does not exercise. When the condition is severe, fat accumulates very rapidly. When the condition is moderate, a person gradually increases fat and weight. When the condition is mild, the weight can remain steady for long periods of time with very slow accumulation of fat, yet fat still accumulates abnormally. Whether the person has a severe, moderate, or mild condition, any loss of weight using any diet and exercise treatments is only achieved with much discomfort, is only temporary, and is rapidly regained as soon as the reducing regime is relaxed or stopped.

In order for Simeons to achieve true success he determined his treatment must be equally effective in both men and women, in all age groups, and for severe, moderate, and mild forms of obesity. This way, Simeons would know that his treatment in fact corrected the underlying cause of the disorder. To further prove that the treatment, in fact, cured the disorder, all patients must have the ability to eat normally any food he pleases in any amounts without regaining abnormal fat or weight after the treatment. These requirements were met during the research. Simeons then could legitimately speak of "curing" obesity rather than just reducing weight. Never before or since has a true cure for obesity been a legitimate claim.

Three Kinds of Fat

There are three kinds of fat in the human body. The first is structural fat. It surrounds the organs and joints. It is important at protecting the organs, arteries, and keeping the skin smooth and taught. It also provides cushioning under the bones of the feet and joints.

The second type of fat is the normal fat reserves used as fuel when the body is dealing with nutritional or calorie insufficiencies. This fat is spread all over the body. Structural and normal fat reserves are in fact normal and needed for good health. Interestingly enough, when people do any type of diet and exercise weight reducing regimes, it is *this* fat plus muscle that is lost. This is why people who lose weight with every other diet and exercise program have a sore heel, sore feet, sore joints, develop arthritis, and have sagging, old looking skin. They are losing important structural fat, some normal fat, and important muscle mass.

The third type of fat is abnormal, secure reserves of fat. This third fat is a reserve of fuel, but unlike the normal, readily accessible fat reserves spread throughout the body, this fat is located in what is called the "problem areas." In women this is most often the hips, thighs, and buttocks. In men it is most often the waist and upper chest. This fat is stored as a survival mechanism and is only released in the most severe nutritional emergency when the body is close to near starvation. It is also released during pregnancy to ensure the survival of the unborn fetus. In obese patients the body abnormally stores most of its fat reserves in these areas. This creates a grotesque disfiguration of the body shape and guarantees that the person will virtually find it impossible to lose weight and fat in the future.

When an obese person tries to lose weight using any diet and exercise program he loses normal fat reserves, structural fat, and muscle. The patient feels weak and hungry. They look tired and their face and skin become drawn and haggard. To their frustration, the hips, thighs, buttocks, belly, and upper arms show little improvement. The problem areas and grotesque body shape that the patient wants so desperately to correct stays virtually the same. The important structural fat covering their bones gets less and less. Their skin wrinkles and they look old and miserable. This is why dieting and exercise programs can be one of the most depressing and frustrating experiences a person can have.

Because this is a medical physical condition, obese patients feel horrible when trying to reduce. They actually feel physically better when they are staying at their current weight or gaining weight.

Remember, because this is an abnormal physical condition, the basic theories of simply reducing calories and increasing physical activity to lose weight are not true. Many obese patients actually gain weight when reducing calories and increasing physical activity, going against the conventional wisdom held by the majority of the medical community. Every doctor who has studied obese patients under strictly controlled conditions knows this is true even though it is beyond accepted medical knowledge and understanding.

As part of Simeons's research the thyroid gland, the pituitary gland, the pancreas, the adrenals, the gallbladder, and over 100 other physiological functions were tested. No direct, consistent correlation between obesity and these various body functions were found. The only common denominators in all obese patients were a constant and abnormally intense physical hunger, abnormally low body metabolism, abnormally high food cravings and desires to eat when not hungry, and the body's abnormally storing excess fat in the secure problem area fat reserves. Therefore, the theory that obesity is caused by overeating and not enough exercise and can be cured only by under-eating and exercising more is categorically false and leads to misery in the patient and utter failure.

Simeons's greatest discovery was that these conditions were caused by an abnormal functioning of the hypothalamus gland. The hypothalamus gland remains a mystery in the medical profession. Little knowledge as to its functioning is known. Doctors and medical experts simply do not know what the hypothalamus actually does and how it does it. The question that Simeons wrestled with was if the hypothalamus is functioning abnormally in obese people, what caused this abnormality? The next question was how could this abnormality be corrected? The third question was could this abnormality be corrected permanently so as not to return, thus curing the condition of obesity forever?

During the time of Simeons's research, DNA testing and other medical diagnostic technologies were not available. In many respects Simeons had theorized. Today's advancements in medical diagnostic techniques are proving that his theories were correct. His first theory was that the hypothalamus abnormality was caused by a genetic abnormality. If a person was born with a hypothalamus that did not function properly, their obesity simply wasn't their fault. The second theory as to why a person's hypothalamus would be operating abnormally leading to obesity was that at some point in the person's life their hypothalamus was massively and abruptly overtaxed. Simeons believed that this could be caused by a massive and sudden dramatic, stressful, or emotional event, or series of events, that occurred in a person's life. This would produce an incredible release of hormones, shocking the hypothalamus and, in effect, resetting abnormally high its fat-storing regulators and hunger-producing regulators.

Simeons also concluded that when a person consumed massive amounts of calories in a short period of time this would also cause the hypothalamus to function abnormally. He found the situation worsened when a person ate little or nothing for twenty-four hours right before this large consumption of food, and if the food lacked sufficient amounts of fiber, and was super highly refined.

As I previously mentioned, it is interesting to note that a common denominator of obese people today is that they do this exact regime almost on a daily basis. For example, a fat person today eats dinner at 7:00 p.m. They go to bed, and wake up and skip breakfast. They work all day and skip lunch. They go home in the evening and consume a massive meal twenty-four hours since their last intake of food. This causes a severe negative reaction to the hypothalamus. In Simeons's day, trans fats, high fructose corn syrup, monosodium glutamate, growth hormones, and other chemical man-made additives were not present in the food supply. Today's research is conclusive that these substances make the problem 100 times worse.

Eating a meal in a fast food restaurant is a guaranteed way to mess up your hypothalamus and push it into an abnormal state, lowering metabolism, increasing hunger, and guaranteeing large amounts of fat will be stored in the problem areas making it virtually impossible to lose. A standard meal in a fast food restaurant consists of over 2,500 calories! Combine that with the massive amounts of man-made trans fats, high fructose corn syrup, artificial sweeteners, MSG, etc. and you have the absolute perfect method to create an abnormally operating hypothalamus guaranteeing you'll become obese. The fast food industry has done this purposefully. This is not a conspiracy, this is pure economics. It is in the financial best interest of the fast food industry to make you fat, and get you physically, chemically addicted to the food like a drug. Fat people buy and eat more food.

Simeons also discovered that constant dieting also creates this abnormal hypothalamus condition. After the Second World War, Simeons observed 6,000 grossly underfed Polish refugees. These Poles were housed in a British refugee camp in India. They were fed normal British army rations; they were not overeating, and engaged in more physical activity than 90% of Americans do today. Surprisingly, within about three months 85% of these Poles were suffering from obesity! This is why dieting doesn't work. Dieting does not address the cause of obesity; dieting makes the condition worse.

Simeons also observed that another cause of the creating of an abnormally operating hypothalamus was the massive consumption of highly refined food with little fiber. Highly refined food, such as white flour and white sugar, causes slow digestion and a dramatic spike in insulin secretion by the pancreas, thus overtaxing the hypothalamus causing is abnormal function resulting in low metabolism, intense and constant hunger, and the storing of fat in the secure fat reserves.

It is interesting to note that in Simeons's day Candida overgrowth was virtually nonexistent. Today, however, over 80% of the American population has a Candida overgrowth. This Candida overgrowth leads to a slowing of the digestion, which leads to overtaxing of the hypothalamus, leading to its abnormal functioning, which creates obesity. In Simeons's day highly refined food was not common. Today, fast food restaurants, and regional and national chain restaurants, serve food that is over 90% classified as highly refined. Much of this food is more than highly refined; it is classified as super highly refined. These include trans fats, which is anything hydrogenated or partially hydrogenated, and high fructose corn syrup. This is another reason why 80% of Americans can be classified as being overweight, and 50% being classified as obese. The food we are being sold is causing the hypothalamus to operate abnormally, creating the condition of obesity.

Believing he had discovered the cause of obesity was an abnormally functioning hypothalamus gland, Simeons's task now became finding a way to correct this abnormal functioning. Most discoveries are made during a "eureka moment." Simeons had such a moment. Being excited with the fact that he truly believed he had found the root cause of obesity, he was also skeptical that he could discover a way to cure the condition. The question that persisted in his mind was if these secure problem fat reserves were in fact normal in small amounts, what would trigger the body to release this fat in those who had abnormally high amounts of this abnormal secure fat deposits? The eureka moment came.

Simeons recalled that while traveling in India, he observed pregnant women giving birth to full-size, full-weight healthy babies. This was not unique in itself. What was interesting was the fact that India was a third world country devastated by the war. Food was scarce. People walked for miles and engaged in high amounts of physical activity. The pregnant women were eating a few hundred calories a day. They were walking for miles and doing strenuous physical chores. Two interesting observations were made. The babies delivered were full size and weight and perfectly healthy. The second was the women, after delivering their children, were skinny. Simeons theorized that these secure fat reserves were a survival mechanism, and during pregnancy were released in order to ensure the health of the unborn baby. It was known that when a woman became pregnant a hormone-like substance was created in the body. Where this substance was created, why it was created, and how it was created was a mystery to the medical profession. The substance is called "human chorionic gonadotrophin," or hCG.

Simeons also recalled that a rare medical condition was becoming rather common in India at this time. Young boys were not developing their sexual organs normally. They were called "fat boys." They had underdeveloped genitals. They also possessed abnormally large breasts, hips, buttocks, and thighs, and abnormal fat around their bellies. The medical treatment of this condition was a small amount of hCG. The observations were that these patients would immediately lose their ravenous appetite. Surprisingly, they neither gained nor lost any weight. What was strange was that their body shapes changed dramatically. The hips, thighs, buttocks, belly, and breast fat all seemed to melt away. Simeons believed that this reshaping of the body meant that fat deposits that were held in these secure abnormal reserves were being burned as fuel. The boys' energy increased, appetite and food consumption decreased, and their dispositions were elevated. They seemed to be happier.

Simeons wondered if hCG could play a role in getting the hypothalamus out of its abnormal operating state back to normalcy, therefore normalizing metabolism, hunger, and the storing of fat in the secure area fat reserves. He wondered if hCG combined with a complete protocol could release the secure fat deposits in obese patients, thus reshaping their bodies, making them slimmer and more aesthetically beautiful than they could ever imagine. He wondered if this could be a way to keep the structural fat and muscle while simultaneously have the body release and burn off these abnormal grotesque bad fat deposits.

Thousands of test patients and years later, Simeons had perfected his "weight loss cure protocol." The results were astonishing. Almost 100% of patients were losing approximately one pound per day while on the protocol. They were not losing structural fat or muscle. They were losing the abnormal secure fat deposits. People's bodies were being completely reshaped. There was no hunger or feeling of deprivation during the treatment; no exercise was required. In follow-up studies almost 80% of the people did not gain the weight back. The surprising observations included the dramatic improvement in various medical conditions. Patients with diabetes dramatically improved or were totally cured of their diabetes. Rheumatism, arthritis, high cholesterol, high blood pressure, gout, and peptic ulcers all improved or were completely cured. Simeons was ecstatic with the results. More importantly, his patients felt like his miracle weight loss cure had given them a new life.

Simeons opened his clinic as part of the Salvator Mundi International Hospital in Rome, Italy to treat obese patients. Doctors from all over the world flocked to Italy as the word spread about this breakthrough medical discovery that was curing obesity. Medical journalists, researchers, scientists, and physicians wanted to see firsthand how Simeons was administering his weight loss protocol to patients.

Although obesity was not common at the time, those patients dealing with the affliction were in many cases desperate to find a cure. In his book *Pounds and Inches: A New Approach to Obesity,* Dr. Simeons recalls one such patient. "I remember the case of a lady who was escorted into my consulting room while I was engaged on the telephone. My back was to her when she sat in the chair in front of my desk. When I turned to greet her I saw a woman who seemed to have the symptoms of anorexia. Her dry skin hung loosely over the bones of her face. Her neck was scrawny and collar bones and ribs stuck out from deep hollows. I was confused as why she would seek an appointment with me knowing that I specialize in curing obesity. I asked what I could do for her. She replied that she needed to lose weight. I tried to hide my surprise, but she must have noted the astonished expression on my face. She smiled and said, 'I know you think I'm mad, but look at this.' With that she rose and came around to the side of my desk. Jutting out from a tiny waist were grotesquely enormous hips, thighs and buttocks. I became excited knowing this would be a true test case. She received the protocol and a virtual medical miracle occurred. The abnormal fat on her hips, thighs and buttocks were transferred evenly to the rest of her body that had been severely depleted of important and healthy structural fat from years of severe dieting. At the end of the treatment this very small woman had lost an astonishing eight inches around her thighs. Her face looked fresh and full of life. The ribs were no longer visible. Her skin was tight and wrinkle free. She looked like a new person. Because the protocol releases abnormal fat reserves and promotes healthy fat distribution for the structural fat, she experienced one of the most dramatic body reshaping and sculpting I had ever seen. Not surprising to me was that her weight stayed the same."

This is a unique case. The woman did not need to lose weight, she needed to lose the abnormal fat reserves while at the same time regain the healthy structural fat so she would look proportionately correct and regain her health.

A bizarre twist that would lead to Simeons's "weight loss cure protocol" becoming one of the most closely guarded medical secrets of all time was about to occur. Remember, in the 1950s and 1960s being overweight, fat, or obese was relatively rare. The majority of people dealing with this condition were upper class and very well-to-do. The vast majority was very slightly overweight or considered very slightly fat. By today's standards these same people would be called average, normal, athletic, or even thin. A very small percent were considered obese at this time. It's interesting to note that these very same obese people of the 1950s and 1960s today would only be called stocky, or chunky. The fact is today's fat people are actually morbidly, grossly obese. It's hard for people in America to really grasp this fact. While I was living in Australia I had a friend who was always called the fattest guy in Sydney. Wherever we went he stood out like a sore thumb because he was so fat. He was fatter than everyone else by a very wide margin. On one occasion we decided to take a trip together to Las Vegas. He loved to eat and wanted to visit one of the famous Las Vegas food buffets. As we stood in the buffet line with dozens of other people my friend smiled and said to me, "I'm not the fat guy here!" He was right. Comparing him to the others in the buffet line, my friend would not have been considered fat. Think about it.

Simeons, therefore, had a clientele that included well-to-do, high society, wealthy individuals from around the world. Although much of Simeons's research was published in prestigious medical journals, news of his cure spread mostly by word of mouth. At this time, it was an embarrassment for most people to say they were receiving treatment for obesity. The news about his cure and spectacular results spread slowly. Not surprising to Simeons, the amount of professional jealousy within the medical community also stifled the spreading of the truth about this medical breakthrough that cured obesity.

Professional jealousy is hard for the average person to understand. We assume when a breakthrough medical discovery is made, the medical community, the news media, and governments around the world would embrace and rejoice in such a discovery that is for the betterment of mankind. Throughout history this has proven to never be the case. Imagine a room filled with 100 people trying to solve a puzzle. The first person that correctly solves the puzzle will be given worldwide accolades, praise, and achieve high status and wealth. All the people in the room want to win the contest. They all want the glory that goes along with being the discoverer of the answer. When one person finally solves the puzzle and wins the prize, are the others ecstatic and happy that they failed? Are they happy that they will remain in obscurity while the lucky victor gets all the glory? No. They wonder if he cheated; they claim the solution to the puzzle is not correct at all. Human nature dictates that they loath and despise him. This happens in all areas of research. It is more prevalent than any average person can imagine. In 1850, a German philosopher noted, "All truth passes through three stages. First, it is ridiculed; second, it is violently opposed; third, it is accepted as self-evident."

The fact is medical breakthroughs are always ridiculed and violently opposed. History proves that it takes decades before new discoveries become generally accepted in medical circles. They are always criticized, debunked, and discredited.

This is made clear in the movie *Sister Kenny* (1946). This movie discusses the treatment of polio. At the turn of the century polio created the same fear that the word cancer does today. The established profitable medical treatment was to put affected limbs in irons to prevent distortion. Unfortunately, this resulted in paralysis for life. Sister Kenny was not a medical doctor. She was merely a nurse working with patients who were afflicted with polio. Sister Kenny worked with thousands of patients proving that muscles could be reeducated and the patients could walk again. She proved that the irons actually inhibited the recovery of patients and were an ineffective treatment. The arrogance and professional jealousy within the medical community prevented her "cure" to be accepted in medical circles. Medical experts believed only "qualified doctors" could develop treatment methods. The movie chronicles how the medical establishment not only debunked and discredited her effective treatment methods, but actually stopped her from continuing to cure children of their polio affliction. Only after twenty years did the established medical hierarchy accept Sister Kenny's proven and workable treatment for patients afflicted with polio. In the minds of the medical elite Sister Kenny, or anyone outside the medical hierarchy, couldn't possibly discover or develop a useable treatment that was better than what the established medical scientific community had failed to produce. This movie looks like fiction. When you watch it you cannot believe the stonewalling, jealousy, and profit motives involved in health care and medical treatments. Watch the movie. It proves fact is stranger than fiction. The movie is a completely accurate historical portrayal of how breakthrough medical discoveries produced outside of the established scientific medical community, with the potential of disrupting the status quo and pharmaceutical profits, are always stonewalled, debunked, and discredited.

Simeons's "weight loss cure protocol" discovery received similar treatment. Although no one could deny the clinical evidence of its virtual 100% success rate, critics and opponents of his treatments became widespread. None of these critics ever used the protocol on patients. They did not interview patients who had received the treatment. They did not even read the abstracts, double-blind studies, or any of the extensive detailed clinical research produced. Simeons was not dismayed. He continued to treat patients and achieve almost 100% success.

Since most of Simeons's patients came from the wealthy elite from around the world, news of Simeons's success in treating obesity reached a member of one of the leading royal families in Europe. Due to a promise of confidentiality, I will not release the name of this family. The princess of this royal household was ridiculed for her obese condition. Under the most secret circumstances, the princess was treated by Dr. Simeons using his "weight loss cure protocol" for a period of six weeks. The results were nothing less than miraculous. The princess lost almost sixty pounds. More importantly, the reshaping and re-sculpting of her body allowed her for the first time to be photographed in a swimsuit. This photograph made the front page of major newspapers around the world. Speculation as to how she was transformed from an obese, grossly disfigured woman to this new sexy starlet became the talk of high society circles around the globe.

The secret of Simeons's treatment was revealed covertly through royal households, Hollywood celebrities, and the rich and famous. Virtually overnight Simeons was bombarded with requests from these well-known public figures to treat them, yet keep their participation, as well as the treatment itself, a closely guarded secret. The enormous amounts of money offered Simeons convinced him to do just that. For the next ten years Simeons's clinic and treatment went underground. He treated thousands of the super rich, celebrities, and royalty. He continued to refine his treatment. The results continue to be virtually 100% successful.

Even under the veil of secrecy rumors began to circulate about this mysterious doctor secretly working out of a hospital in Rome, with a miracle cure for obesity. Thousands of doctors would travel to Rome trying to find if there was a real obesity cure or if the rumors were merely myth and legend. Simeons rarely, but on occasion shared his secret with only the most prominent of doctors under the promise to keep the treatment secret and not reveal it in the public domain. These doctors in turn treated wealthy patients in their own clinics around the world in a nonpublic and rather secretive way. All were amazed at the spectacular consistent results they achieved with their patients. One thing is for sure, you can't keep a secret secret.

Doctors being so excited about the results would share Simeons's cure with other doctors.

◇ ◇ ◇

At an anti-aging seminar in Amsterdam, Holland, a young up-and-coming pioneer in anti-aging live cell therapy, Dr. Fritz (per his request, this is not his real name), inadvertently overheard a most prominent Dutch physician explaining to a colleague a weight loss cure that he was using with his patients with miraculous results. Dr. Fritz inquired from the Dutch physician wanting more information. The Dutch doctor refused to give Fritz any details claiming confidentiality promises. Over the next few months Dr. Fritz, practicing in Germany, made repeated attempts to get more information from the Dutch doctor. His requests went unanswered. Fritz was undaunted. He persisted with phone calls, telegrams, and letters. For over two years Fritz attempted to communicate with this doctor and get any information anywhere in the world about a so-called weight loss or obesity cure. Fritz knew that this Dutch doctor was one of the most prominent, well respected physicians in the world. He knew that if this doctor was doing something that was having miraculous results with obese patients it had to be legitimate. Finally, after two years of searching and coming up empty, Fritz traveled to Holland and made an unannounced visit to the Dutch doctor. Fritz was politely told the doctor was unavailable for a private visit. Fritz was relentless. He stayed in Holland two weeks. Each day he would visit the doctor's clinic and home asking for an appointment; each time he was denied. Fritz traveled back to Germany without answers. For the next year Fritz forgot about an obesity cure. He focused on his anti-aging live cell therapy. He appeared on Oprah, made speeches to the rich and famous in New York, Hollywood, Chicago, and Palm Beach. He developed a super wealthy clientele including kings of several countries, some of the most famous Hollywood celebrities, and billionaires from some of the most well-known families in the world.

It was over a year since Fritz traveled to Amsterdam and made his futile attempts at talking to the famous, prominent Dutch physician. Unexpectedly, Fritz received a surprise phone call from the very doctor that he had been trying to communicate with. The Dutch physician apologized for his inaccessibility. He explained that the obesity cure was real, but because of a promise of strict confidentiality he could not reveal the exact protocol. Now, however, the doctor was retiring and was impressed with Fritz's curiosity, open mindedness, and tenacity. Fritz himself had become quite well known in well to do circles. The Dutch doctor was impressed with Fritz's work and his prominent clientele. If Fritz would travel to Amsterdam, the doctor would share "the weight loss cure protocol."

In Amsterdam Fritz learned of Dr. Simeons's research. He was told the history of how "the weight loss cure protocol" was discovered. Fritz reviewed the patient records and was astonished at the seemingly miraculous weight loss results. The before and after pictures of the patients were startling. The fact that the patients kept the weight, fat, and inches off after the treatment was equally impressive. Results like this never existed. Fritz promised to keep the protocol secret and make it available only to his private patients. Simeons was still operating his clinic in Rome at the hospital at this time. Fritz decided a trip to Rome to watch the treatment administered by the discoverer himself would be invaluable. Little did Fritz know, time was of the essence.

◇ ◇ ◇

Dr. Simeons received yet another hug combined with tears of joy from a grateful patient. Over the years, patient after patient would come in desperate, despondent, and depressed about their inability to become thin. Each time, a few short weeks later, these same patients would be ecstatic, joyful, and exuberant over their dramatic weight loss, reshaping of their bodies and new lives as a thin person. Simeons had been struggling for years with the fact that there were millions of people around the world that were suffering needlessly with their weight issues when the cure was available. In the 1950s and 1960s very few people had major weight problems. Each year the percentage of people who were dealing with this condition was dramatically increasing. Simeons knew that publicizing his work could be disastrous. He knew that like all medical discoveries, it would be highly criticized, debunked, and discredited. Professional jealously within the medical community was more intense than ever before. There were many groups, organizations, and industries that absolutely did not want a weight loss cure to be accepted. The drug companies wanted to patent drugs for weight loss. Food companies wanted fat people, not thin people, so that they could sell more food. The diet food industry was beginning to blossom and those companies didn't want anything that could adversely affect their products' market share. Releasing the cure publicly would result in personal ridicule and could be personally financially devastating.

Simeons decided to go half way. He thought that he would write a small manuscript, publish it himself, and make it available only to doctors. The manuscript would detail "the weight loss cure protocol." This way people around the world who were suffering with an overweight condition could finally end their misery; at the same time, being a small self-published manuscript not available to the general public, would allow the cure to fly under the radar, preventing widespread and massive criticism and ridicule.

Simeons did not know, however, how corporate espionage works. Today we know that virtually all major corporations engage tens of thousands of investigators that do secret, covert, undercover work against competitors or anyone doing anything that could be potentially adverse their profits. We know today, as reported in the news, that the chairwoman of Hewlett Packard was indicted criminally for having her company engage in illegal investigations of staff members and members of the media. These investigations include going through people's trash, hacking into their computers, planting listening devices in homes, offices, and cars, wire tapping telephone calls, and reviewing private e-mails. Corporate executives today admit that this is common practice and is done by virtually all corporations.

Simeons was not aware that such eavesdropping was taking place. The fact was that Simeons's weight loss cure was something the drug companies, food industry, and even governments did not want revealed. Remember that Simeons first discovered the causes which make the hypothalamus act abnormally, thus making people fat. The food industry at this time had discovered the same thing. They, however, were using this knowledge to specifically *create* food that would create obesity. There was great fear that Simeons's research would expose the food companies' plan to create an obese world.

Simeons wrote his manuscript; he self-published the work, printing only a few hundred copies. That was enough to seal his fate.

◇ ◇ ◇

The year is 1970. Fritz called Simeons to set up a meeting. He was introduced to Simeons by the Dutch doctor, which guaranteed Fritz an audience with Simeons. Simeons was in the process of quietly releasing his self-published manuscript to doctors around the world. Fritz and Simeons agreed to a visit in three weeks. Fritz could stay as long as he wanted to review files, interview patients, and observe the administering of the protocol. Fritz's idea was to return to his clinic in Germany and offer this obesity cure to his private patients. He had not planned promoting or publicizing the fact that he was treating obesity. His clinic would go on as usual and Fritz would have the gratification of seeing his patients cured of their obesity dilemma and be able to live normal, happy, healthy lives.

Three weeks later Fritz arrived in Rome. Arriving at the clinic to meet Dr. Simeons, Fritz was greeted by the head nurse. The clinic seemed abuzz with activity and confusion. Apprehension seemed to fill the air. When Fritz asked the head nurse to see Dr. Simeons, the nurse nervously said, "You need to call the doctor's wife, here is the number, and there is the phone." Fritz walked to the reception desk and dialed the number. Upon introducing himself the woman on the other end of the phone said sharply, "You need to come to the house immediately," and gave Fritz the address. Grabbing a taxi, Fritz headed for the address given. He knew something was wrong. Twenty minutes later, he arrived at the doctor's home and knocked on the door. There was a long pause, and then the door swung open. A terrified woman stood before Fritz—"He's dead."

◇ ◇ ◇

Fritz talked to the doctor's widow and discovered Simeons had died just a week before. It was said he died in his sleep from natural causes. It was sudden and unexpected. Simeons's widow was gracious, but obviously distraught. There was no immediate family and Simeons's widow seemed to be having a hard time dealing with all the details and pressures one would expect having a spouse, and the only breadwinner, die so unexpectedly. Fritz politely asked if he could be of assistance. Simeons's widow said yes. Fritz wound up staying in Rome over a month helping Simeons's widow and the clinic deal with the issues that arise when such a tragedy occurs. During this time Fritz interviewed the clinic's staff, gaining insights to the weight loss cure. He reviewed patient records, research notes, internal clinical studies, and the detailed data relating to Simeons's work. He interviewed patients, some of whom were treated ten years earlier. The more Fritz reviewed the facts about "the weight loss cure protocol" the more impressed and astonished he became with the results.

Simeons printed only a few hundred copies of his manuscript detailing "the weight loss cure protocol." Most of these were sent out to doctors the week before his death. There were less than thirty copies that remained in the possession of Simeons's widow. Fritz intuitively knew that securing the manuscripts was vitally important. Simeons's widow felt an obligation to Fritz for his help. Fritz went back to Germany with the last 30 remaining copies of Simeons's manuscript!

◇ ◇ ◇

Back in Germany Fritz began using "the weight loss cure protocol" and achieving the same spectacular results. Thousands of the most famous Hollywood celebrities, kings, queens, princes, princesses, and some of the wealthiest people in the world have come to Fritz's clinic and received treatment. For over thirty years now, Fritz has enjoyed a private, non-public medical practice. He lives with the self-satisfaction that comes from seeing people's misery, pain, and suffering turn to joy, happiness, and elation. He embodies all the good and pure attributes of a physician whose only goal is to see his patients cured of their afflictions.

When I met Fritz several years ago we became instant friends. But our friendship almost ended when I expressed my interest in writing a book that would reveal and expose this secret obesity cure protocol. We talked for hours; he shared his concerns. He told me about the powerful corporations, associations, governments, and special interest groups that do not want this cure publicized. He let me know that writing such a book would cause me to be personally ridiculed, criticized, debunked, and persecuted in the public and in a very vicious way. He said this could ruin me financially. He expressed deep concern because of the ruthlessness of these groups.

I thought long and hard about writing this book. When I wrote my first book, *Natural Cures "They" Don't Want You To Know About,* everything he said would happen already did happen. I was viciously and mercilessly publicly humiliated, criticized, discredited, and debunked. I was attacked by the news media, the government, the FDA, the FTC, attorneys general, the drug companies, and various lobbying groups. My legal bills were in the millions of dollars—all because I wrote a book telling the truth about how there are natural non-drug and non-surgical ways to prevent and cure disease. I said the unthinkable, that the drug companies, being publicly traded corporations, have only one goal, which is to get more and more people to take more and more drugs on a regular basis. They do not want to cure or prevent disease because doing so would put them out of business. I blew the whistle and exposed the truth about the unholy alliance between the drug industry, the news media, the food industry, the Food and Drug Administration, and the Federal Trade Commission. I blew the whistle and exposed the truth about how natural non-drug and non-surgical methods of preventing and curing disease are being suppressed and hidden from the public. I exposed the truth about how the drug companies lie about the safety and effectiveness of their drugs. I blew the whistle and exposed the truth about how non-prescription and prescription drugs are the number one cause of illness and disease. I blew the whistle and exposed the truth about how the food industry is purposely creating food and putting chemicals in the food that increase our hunger and appetite, get us physically addicted to the food like a drug, and make us fat. From personal, direct knowledge I exposed these secrets.

Yet, with all the personal attacks and persecution I, like Fritz, have lived with the feeling of self-satisfaction from the tens of thousands of letters from people all over the world who read my first two books and have been cured of their pain, illness, disease, and affliction without drugs or surgery.

Exposing the hidden secrets that they don't want you to know about is worth it. Millions of people are suffering needlessly because these secrets have not been made public. I decided that writing this book and publishing it for wide scale distribution, exposing the truth about the Simeons "weight loss cure protocol" was desperately needed by the growing millions who are suffering from obesity. I knew I had to become "the whistle-blower" once again, and I was willing to face the consequences!

CHAPTER FOUR

The Cure Suppressed

*All truth passes through three stages. First it is
ridiculed. Second it is violently opposed. Third
it is accepted as self evident.*
> —Arthur Schopenhauer,
> German Philosopher

In my first book, *Natural Cures "They" Don't Want You To Know
About,* I reveal the natural non-drug and non-surgical ways to
cure and prevent disease. In my second book, *More Natural
Cures Revealed: Previously Censored Name Brand Products
That Cure Disease,* I list the specific products that have been
proven to be more effective than drugs, inexpensive, and with no
side effects. In both books I, as a former insider, expose the
secrets of how multinational corporations, in conjunction with
governments and the news media, suppress the truth about these
inexpensive natural alternatives to drugs and surgery. I detail
how this occurs and *why* this occurs. The suppression of truthful
information relating to natural inexpensive products that cure
and prevent disease is not some kind of conspiracy theory. It is
purely economic. Every publicly traded corporation is legally
obliged to increase shareholder value. That's the law. The officers and directors of these corporations have only one responsi-
bility and goal: increase shareholder value. This means every
publicly traded corporation must increase profits and growth. It
is publicly disclosed, and reported on in financial newspapers
around the world, that these corporations must continue to sell
more and more of their products to more and more people. This
is not a secret, but no one ever thinks about it. In order to sell
more and more products to more and more people, corporations

always do two things: they lie about the effectiveness and safety of their product, making them appear better than they are; secondly, they must crush any competitor's products. This happens in every business; it happens in politics as well. Political candidates tell you how wonderful they are and how horrible the other candidates are. Companies always say how wonderful their products are and how horrible the competitor's products are.

Corporations employ thousands of lobbyists who get lawmakers to pass laws crushing competitors. In many cases these lobbyists and corporations use illegal tactics, bribes, and payoffs to achieve this result. This is common knowledge today. Hundreds of lawmakers around the world have been convicted of accepting bribes and payoffs from lobbyists and corporations to give them competitive advantages in the marketplace. In America, an unknown lobbyist by the name of Jack Abramoff recently admitted to paying off over sixty congressmen and senators so that his corporate clients could make more money.

Multinational corporations, specifically in the drug industry and food industry, indirectly control the boards of most of the media outlets. This means television networks, radio networks, newspapers, and magazines are no longer bastions of free speech and independent journalism. The media no longer independently reports objective truthful information. The media outlets today are, in effect, propaganda machines used by multinational conglomerates to spread information that ultimately increases sales of their products while simultaneously crushing competitors.

Remember, every publicly traded food company only wants to get more people to buy more food. This is achieved by purposely producing food that gets us physically addicted to the food like a drug, increasing hunger, and making us fat. The food produced today containing genetically modified substances, high fructose corn syrup, monosodium glutamate, artificial sweeteners, antibiotics, and over 15,000 other man-made chemicals has been specifically engineered to make the hypothalamus operate abnormally, thus making us fat.

Remember, the food industry and drug industry are, in fact, controlled by the same group of international billionaires. Food is produced specifically to increase obesity and disease. This increases food sales and also increases drug sales. Simultaneously, commonly used drugs such as cholesterol lowering drugs, high blood pressure medication, pain medication, cough syrup, sleep aids, anti-inflammatories, and antidepressants all have an adverse affect on the hypothalamus and other internal organs, increasing hunger and obesity. The fact is every non-prescription and pre-scription drug can be, in part, responsible for increased appetite and weight gain.

The weight loss industry is generally nothing more than a sub-industry, owned and controlled by the drug industry and food industry. It is estimated to be close to a $150 billion a year market. It is one of the fastest growing market segments in the world. The multinational corporations are excited about this growth poten-tial. It is important to understand that the multinational corpora-tions involved in the drug industry, food industry, and diet industry are looking at billions of dollars in profits as long as people continue to get fat! These industries absolutely want more and more people to become fatter and fatter all around the world. This means astronomical profits for these companies poised to take advantage of this trend. Any company or person that could threaten the increase in obesity must be stopped.

The economics of obesity come down to this: there is huge money to be made as long as people continue getting fatter. Diet aids and products can be sold as long as they don't work! Any true obesity cure must be debunked, discredited, and outlawed.

Another major reason why any effective permanent weight loss cure would be suppressed is the fact that every major drug company has invested hundreds of millions of dollars trying to patent an expensive drug, or surgical procedure, that the FDA will approve for the treatment of obesity. You see these outra-geous, dangerous, and expensive surgical procedures all over television. The drug companies are currently making billions in profits on these insane surgical procedures. The drug companies never want a non-patentable, inexpensive cure widely used or accepted. If an inexpensive natural cure for obesity was available and used by the masses, these drug companies stand to lose bil-lions of dollars in profits every year. To the drug companies, this is a war. Being publicly traded corporations, they are not inter-ested in what is best for mankind. They are legally obliged to be only interested in their own corporate bottom line profits. This is the major conflict of interest that drug companies and every other publicly traded corporation has to deal with. When doing what is best for mankind adversely affects their profits they must choose profits over what is best for individual people.

The Simeons "weight loss cure protocol" is the only known cure for the obesity condition. Combined with the knowledge of what causes the condition, the patient can achieve a permanent cure to their obesity and overweight condition. The drug companies, food industry, and weight loss industry do not want you to know the truth about this cure.

Simeons's unexpected death remains a mystery. Throughout history people who made spectacular discoveries that ultimately posed major threats to the profits of multinational corporations have all suddenly, and unexpectedly, died under mysterious circumstances or just plain vanished without a trace. If you wonder if large corporations will go to illegal extreme measures to protect their profits, consider the well-known case of the big three auto makers setting up fake corporations to buy and dismantle public transportation in California so that they could increase automobile sales. In court the big three were found guilty, yet due to obvious payoffs and bribes, received only a one dollar fine! Remember, executives at Big Tobacco had the scientific proof that cigarette smoking caused disease yet lied about it for fifty years! Remember, that executives at Ford Motor Company knew that if they did not recall the "exploding Pinto" thousands of innocent people would die, and be injured. They decided it was more cost effective to deal with the potential lawsuits than to recall their flawed automobile. Corporate executives have routinely chosen profits over the safety of human lives. In just the last ten years, thousands of corporate executives, corporations, and high ranking government officials have been found guilty of fraud, deception, and committing illegal acts adversely affecting the public in general. Corruption is widespread—more than you could ever imagine. I know firsthand...I was directly involved!

Years ago, people in the world were called the "public at large," "individuals," "humanity," or "citizens." Today, governments and corporations only refer to people as "consumers." This means that the only people that matter are those that have the ability to consume or buy products. If a group does not have the ability to consume or buy products they are irrelevant and expendable in the minds of corporations and governments. This is most notable in the way pharmaceutical companies are using poor impoverished people in third world nations as human guinea pigs in secret drug trials. Uneducated, impoverished human beings are given experimental drugs unknowingly so that pharmaceutical manufacturers can test levels of toxicity. This practice is causing deaths of hundreds of thousands of people. These deaths are never attributed to the drugs. The entire practice is illegal and is nothing more than a form of genocide. Although a work of fiction, the movie *The Constant Gardner* shows in graphic detail this unconscionable act of corporate greed. Watch the movie and be appalled.

Try to remember that every corporation is only trying to increase profits. They are only trying to get you to buy their product and not buy someone else's product. When you see advertisements on television know that the most sophisticated persuasive techniques are being used to motivate you to purchase the product. Deceptions, lies, and false and misleading advertising are at an all-time high. Remember, it's always all about the money.

The Simeons "weight loss cure protocol" was so effective and permanent that news of its success did, in fact, spread in the 1970s. Wanting to cash in on the potential profits available in the weight loss industry, a group of businessmen started a company called Professional Reducing. These were not doctors, or people involved in the medical profession; they were businessmen who wanted to get rich. Clinics were set up in various cities in the U.S. and around the world providing to the patients the Simeons "weight loss cure protocol." The group made a fatal mistake. They put full-page ads in newspapers around the world advertising their weight loss clinics. This caught the attention of the food industry, the existing diet industry, the drug industry, the government and, of course, the media.

The government's public line was that it wanted to protect consumers from weight loss scams and rip-offs that did not work. In reality, the government is *used* by large corporations to wipe out competition. It is well known today, and has been proven in court, that corporations use lobbyists, bribes, and payoffs to get politicians and government officials in such agencies like the FDA and FTC to do its dirty work in crushing any company or person that could adversely affect these corporations' profits. This is true around the world and has been proven over and over again. The government and its agencies do not protect people; they, in fact, protect the profits of the corporations that are paying the politicians.

The drug companies wanted to debunk and discredit the Simeons cure because it would expose how their drugs were partially responsible for obesity. This could adversely affect sales. The Simeons cure also exposed how the food was being manufactured and sold specifically to increase obesity and disease. Knowledge of this could adversely affect drug company sales and profits. The drug companies were also working on surgical methods and expensive patentable drugs for the treatment of obesity, which they intended on selling, resulting in billions in annual profits. Widespread use of the Simeons cure could dramatically, adversely affect these future profits.

The food industry wanted to stop knowledge and use of the Simeons cure because it would result in thinner people, with normal appetites, resulting in less food sold, and lower profits. They also were afraid of being exposed for purposely creating food that makes people obese and gives them disease. They were terrified of being hit with billion dollar class action suits like the tobacco companies were dealing with. This is why, today, food and drug companies are spending tens of millions of dollars trying to get Congress to pass tort reform, which will make them immune to these lawsuits. The drug and food companies know that their products cause obesity and disease, just like the tobacco companies knew for fifty years that cigarette smoking caused disease. The tobacco companies lied about this knowledge for almost fifty years. The drug companies and food companies are lying to us now.

The diet industry was making billions in profits selling diet products and diet food that not only didn't work, but actually made people fatter in the long run. They did not want Simeons "weight loss cure protocol" in widespread use as it would expose them for the frauds and deceivers that they really are. Use of the

Simeons protocol could have a dramatic negative impact on the profits of these diet and weight loss companies.

One of the most massive and coordinated negative PR and debunking campaigns was initiated in history. These huge, powerful multinational corporations spent tens of millions of dollars, and paid off government officials and news media executives, with the goal of wiping out knowledge and use of the Simeons "weight loss cure protocol," as being marketed by Professional Reducing.

Newspaper articles came out criticizing and debunking Simeons's method and Professional Reducing. Flagrant lies about the treatment were printed; newspapers, magazines, and television reports claimed that the treatment included injections of urine from pregnant women. This is false and a blatant lie. The reports said that the whole Simeons protocol was a money making scam. The reports ignored the thirty years of proven results and research. The U.S. Government even claimed that they conducted a double-blind study at Edwards Air Force Base showing that the Simeons cure was completely ineffective. This was an absolute lie. The study at Edwards Air Force Base did not follow the Simeons protocol at all! It was purposely set up to fail, thus allowing the news media to publicly discredit the true effectiveness of Simeons's cure.

Professional Reducing was put out of business. The cover-up and deception by the government and news media about the effectiveness of this cure terrified doctors around the world who were using the protocol with spectacular results.

The cure went underground once again.

Today, there are hundreds of doctors, physicians, and medical experts who are using the Simeons cure, and continuing to see the spectacular results. Revealing this cure on a widespread basis puts me in great personal jeopardy. I have personally seen thousands of patient records verifying the successful results. I have interviewed dozens of medical doctors who are using this treatment with spectacular results. I have talked to hundreds of patients who have received this treatment and report their spectacular results. Most importantly, I have personally done this treatment myself and can attest that everything about it is true.

If you have struggled with weight, I believe this is the only true permanent answer. If you deal with intense and constant hunger, food cravings, uncontrollable urges to eat when you are not hungry, and inability to lose fat in the problem areas of your body, I believe the Simeons "weight loss cure protocol" can quickly, easily, and permanently correct the abnormal condition.

I am not a doctor. I have no formal medical training. As a journalist, reporter, investigator, and researcher, I am sharing with you this suppressed truth about the cause and cure of obesity.

Get ready to start a whole new life without deprivation, hunger, or frustration. Get ready to start a new life as a normal, thin, energetic, happy person. Now let me reveal for the first time ever on a mass scale, the original proven time-tested Simeons "weight loss cure protocol".

CHAPTER FIVE

The Cure Revealed

Great spirits have always encountered violent opposition from mediocre minds.
— *Albert Einstein*

Dr. Simeons's "weight loss cure protocol" is detailed in his original manuscript, *Pounds and Inches: A New Approach to Obesity*. The complete manuscript is available for viewing at www.naturalcures.com. This manuscript gives the exact protocol that Simeons used in the 1950s and 1960s. Remember, at the time Simeons was treating patients with his method, many of today's man-made causes of an abnormal hypothalamus did not exist. When Simeons used his protocol the main causes of an abnormally operating hypothalamus were genetics, overtaxing of the hypothalamus due to stress or trauma, overtaxing of the hypothalamus due to previous severe dieting, or overtaxing of the hypothalamus by eating an excessively large meal preceded by an extended period of time (approximately twenty-four hours) of little or no food, and the repeated consumption of highly refined, low fiber food. These caused the hypothalamus to operate abnormally, creating intense and constant hunger, food cravings, low metabolism, and the excessive and abnormal storing of fat in the secure abnormal fat reserves known as the problem areas.

Today, however, there are many other direct or indirect causes of an abnormal hypothalamus. These include lack of walking, a clogged liver, Candida yeast overgrowth, a clogged colon, lack of enzymes in food, nutritional deficiencies, an inefficient thyroid, an abnormal pancreas, hormonal imbalance, excessive consumption of super-refined food, high fructose corn syrup, artificial sweeteners, growth hormones and antibiotics in meat and dairy, microwaving of food, irradiating of food, pasteurization of food, monosodium glutamate, non-prescription and prescription drugs, the chemicals in the lotions and creams that we put on our skin, the 15,000 man-made chemicals routinely put in our food, chlorine and fluoride put in the water we drink and bathe in, carbonated drinks, trans fats including hydrogenated oils, a sluggish lymphatic system, heavy metal toxicity, poor circulation, lack of oxygen in the blood, food and environmental allergies, parasites, low muscle mass, cold drinks, air conditioning, lack of sun, lack of sleep, electromagnet frequencies, stress, lack of fiber, genetically modified food, and more.

You can see why today obesity is an epidemic. Do not be dismayed. Doctors are still achieving the same spectacular results using "the weight loss cure protocol" exactly as Simeons administered it. However, doctors have found many additional treatments that can be done before and after the Simeons "weight loss cure protocol" is undertaken that addresses all of these new issues relating to obesity that Simeons did not have to contend with.

Ideally, "the weight loss cure protocol" should be done in four phases.

Phase 1:

Phase 1 takes thirty days to complete. In Simeons's time no one needed to do Phase 1. Today, however, Phase 1 is strongly recommended, but is not required. This phase contains many dos and don'ts which are designed to address the new causes of obesity that did not exist when Simeons developed "the weight loss cure protocol." It is recommended that you do as many of the dos and don'ts during the Phase 1 thirty-day period. The benefits of Phase 1 include increased energy and mental clarity, increasing metabolism, decreasing hunger, decreasing food cravings, alleviating depression, increasing overall health and vitality, and flattening of the stomach. People should lose between five and thirty pounds during Phase 1. Ideally, do this phase for at least thirty days. You can do this phase for a shorter or longer period if you so desire. When you complete this phase immediately begin Phase 2.

These results are achieved by cleansing the liver, cleansing the colon, reducing Candida yeast overgrowth, handling nutritional deficiencies, correcting the thyroid, pancreas, and hormonal imbalances, cleansing the body of toxins, hydrating the cells, reducing heavy metals, reducing parasites, increasing muscle mass, stimulating the lymphatic system, and reducing stress. All of these factors have been now proven to create an abnormally operating hypothalamus contributing to your over-weight condition. Doing Phase 1 will have tremendous long-term benefits. It will make your fat and weight loss during the Simeons protocol happen faster and you will lose more weight and fat than if you do not do Phase 1. Phase 1 accelerates the entire process and helps guarantee that the weight will not come back.

Phase 2:

Phase 2 is the exact Simeons "weight loss cure protocol" as outlined in the manuscript *Pounds and Inches: A New Approach to Obesity*. It is the exact protocol being used by medical doctors around the world with spectacular results. This phase is designed to stimulate the hypothalamus to release the secure fat deposits in the problem areas at an accelerated rate. This phase must be done for a minimum of three weeks and a maximum of six weeks. During this phase you should lose approximately one pound per day. You will be losing the secured abnormal fat reserves. You should notice a dramatic reshaping and re-sculpting of your body. Energy levels will be high, hunger and appetite low, and many people see an improvement of other medical conditions and symptoms.

Phase 3:

Phase 3 lasts three weeks. This phase should be done immediately upon completing Phase 2. This, combined with Phase 2, is the original Simeons "weight loss cure protocol." This phase is designed to reset the hypothalamus and bodyweight set point. This is an important phase that keeps the weight off permanently. Successful execution and completion of this phase resets your metabolism higher, resets your hunger lower, and resets your hypothalamus so that in the future it does not store fat in the abnormal problem area secure fat reserves. This phase helps guarantee that your body is corrected from the abnormal condition which caused the obesity.

Phase 4:

This phase is for the rest of your life. It contains the simple, easy to follow dos and don'ts that make sure that the hypothalamus does not get overtaxed and go back to the abnormal state, creating low metabolism, high hunger, food cravings, and the abnormal storing of fat in the problem area fat reserves leading to a return of the weight and the obesity condition.

"The Weight Loss Cure Protocol"

Phase 1

Although this phase is not required, based on today's conditions, it is highly recommended. This phase consists of a series of dos and don'ts. It may be difficult for most people to do all the steps in this phase with strict adherence. Do as many as you can for the thirty days prior to starting Phase 2. The more you do in this phase will result in losing more weight faster during Phase 2. This phase addresses and corrects many of the new underlying causes of obesity that Simeons did not contend with in the 1950s and 1960s. If you skip this phase, or do it halfheartedly, you will still achieve spectacular results in Phase 2. However, this phase will accelerate the fat and weight loss in Phase 2, and make the whole protocol easier to complete. The more you do in this phase also will greatly increase your ability to keep the weight off permanently and eliminate food cravings in the future. Here are the steps in order of importance.

1. **Water.** Fat people are dehydrated. Drink one large glass of water immediately upon arising, and one-half to one gallon throughout the day. Recommended waters include Volvic, Fiji, and Evian. Spring water is best. If spring water is not available, drink water filtered by reverse osmosis. The last choice is distilled water. Never drink tap water as it is loaded with chlorine, fluoride, and other contaminates.

2. **Walk.** In the 1970s, two prominent physicians authored *The Neuropsychology of Weight Control.* They discovered that walking outside at a slow steady pace for one hour per day reset the body's weight set point, making people lean and

thin. Of all the steps in Phase 1, this may be the most difficult one to do on a daily basis. However, this will have the
most profound long-term effects. Walking should be done
outside. Use a treadmill only as a last resort. Walk for one
hour nonstop. Keep the pace steady and do not overexert
yourself. Slow, rhythmic movement is the key. You should
be able to maintain a conversation while walking. Getting
your heart rate up to a level of aerobic should not be done
during your walking. Ideally, this should be done every day.
If this is not achievable, any amount of walking will still
have a dramatic effect on resetting your body's set point and
making you lean.

3. **Extra Virgin Raw Coconut Oil**. This is now easily available
   in most stores. Use this as your fat of choice in cooking.
   Take two teaspoons per day. This is proven to stimulate
   metabolism, improve digestion, and help release fat cells. It
   also gently stimulates the thyroid.

4. **Colonics**. Go to a licensed colon therapist, and under their
   supervision and guidance receive fifteen colonics during the
   thirty-day Phase 1 period. Colonics are similar to a high
   enema. They gently flush the colon with water eliminating
   impacted fecal matter and toxins. Cleaning the colon is
   absolutely vital for weight loss and good health. When the
   colon is cleansed people notice a dramatic flattening of the
   stomach. Colon cleansing this way allows most people to
   lose five to twenty pounds of excess weight! A clean colon
   dramatically reduces food cravings, gas, bloating, and constipation. A clean colon means improved digestion, better
   absorption of nutrients, increased energy and mental
   clarity, and a general overall improvement of health.

5. **Apples**. Eat a minimum of two organic apples every day.
   This will help regulate blood sugar, reduce appetite, and
   increase cleansing of the liver, gallbladder, and colon.

6. **Grapefruit**. Eat a minimum of two organic grapefruits daily.
   Enzymes in grapefruit are proven to help release fat. These
   also help regulate blood sugar, reduce food cravings, and
   stimulate cleansing of the liver, gallbladder, and colon.

7. **Raw Organic Apple Cider Vinegar.** Take one tablespoon three times a day. Use as your vinegar of choice in salads and cooking. This stimulates the metabolism and cleansing of the internal organs. It is also very powerful in helping release stored fat cells.

8. **Colon Cleanse.** In addition to the colonics it is recommended that you take a colon cleanse product during this phase. Four recommended products are The Almighty Cleanse, The Seven-Day Miracle Cleanse, Dual Action Cleanse, and The Pure Body Institute Cleanse. You will lose weight and fat by doing these cleanses. You will feel better and have more energy. Your skin, hair, and nails will look radiant and younger. Your hormonal imbalances can be corrected. All organs and glands in the body will operate more efficiently; your health will dramatically improve. www.tryalmighty-cleanse.com, www.qnlabs.com, www.drnatura.com, www.dr-schulze.com, or www.pbiv.com.

9. **Eliminate/Reduce Candida Yeast Overgrowth.** Candida is a major cause of poor digestion, gas, bloating, constipation, allergies, hormonal imbalances, fatigue, and food cravings. It must be addressed and corrected. Recommended products are ThreeLac. Take as directed. If you do not address Candida, food cravings will persist. www.123candida.com.

10. **Insulin.** The majority of overweight people have some form of diabetes or pre-diabetic condition. The pancreas secretes insulin abnormally. This must be corrected. When this is corrected the person easily loses weight and hunger is also diminished. The recommended product to take is Eleotin. In studies, almost every person who takes Eleotin has a decrease in appetite and begins to naturally lose weight. The Eleotin product is an all-natural combination of herbs that promotes a healthy pancreas. It should be taken for a minimum of ninety days. Eleotin tea is preferred over the capsules. Take as directed. www.eastwoodcompanies.com.

11. **Drink Green Tea.** Ideally, drink a minimum of one cup per day. Organic green tea stimulates cleansing of the cells, increases metabolism, and helps regulate hunger. The

recommended green tea is Wu Long tea. Available at www.wulongforlife.com.

12. **Whole Food Supplement.** Everyone has nutritional deficiencies. For the body to operate normally these deficiencies must be corrected. Take each day a whole food supplement which will supply your body with the needed nutrients for health and weight loss. Recommended products include Garden of Life Living Multiple, Mega Food, and Healthy Habits Maximum Health Maxis. Check out www.qnlabs.com.

13. **Coral Calcium.** Research has proven that most people are deficient in calcium. Calcium supplementation has been shown to have major health benefits and increase weight loss. Ideally, use a coral calcium that comes in a sachet that is added to the water you drink daily. Recommended products include Ericssons Coral Calcium, and Coral Calcium Daily, available at www.ericssonscoral.com, or www.trycorcal.com.

14. **Probiotics.** All people benefit from taking probiotics. This friendly bacteria, when reintroduced into the body, stimulates metabolism, improves digestion, and helps with cleansing. Recommended products include Probiotics Plus, available at www.mercola.com, or similar products available at www.qnlabs.com.

15. **Heavy Metal Cleanse.** Ridding the body of heavy metals and improving circulation is vital for health, increased energy, and increasing metabolism. Take Pectasol Chelation Complex, available at www.advancedbionutritionals.com, or similar products at www.scienceformulas.com, www.qnlabs.com, or www.rxvitamins.com.

16. **Organic Yerba Mate Tea.** Drink at least one cup per day. This tea increases energy without creating nervousness or jitters. It reduces appetite and stimulates releasing of fat cells.

17. **Eat Breakfast.** Eating a large breakfast is important at resetting the body's weight set point, increasing metabolism, and decreasing appetite throughout the day. An ideal breakfast

would include organic eggs from cage-free chickens, wild smoked salmon, organic rye toast (making sure the bread is made with only rye flour, water, yeast, and salt), organic raw butter or organic raw extra virgin coconut oil, organic asparagus, organic tomatoes, organic beef, chicken or turkey sausages, organic beef, turkey or chicken in any fashion, wild (not farm raised) fish in any fashion, organic potatoes cooked in any fashion, organic oatmeal, organic coffee or tea, organic apples, pears, grapefruit, strawberries, plums, peaches, kiwis, mangos, papayas, blueberries, raspberries, nectarines, or melon. A *large* breakfast is recommended.

18. **Eat Six Times Per Day.** It is important to eat throughout the day in order to reset your metabolism high and release abnormal fat reserves. Knowing that during this phase you should be eating a minimum of two organic apples and two organic grapefruits daily, having snacks in between meals should be easy to do. Ideally, you should have a large breakfast, a snack consisting of an organic apple or organic grapefruit mid-morning, a full lunch, a snack consisting of an organic apple or organic grapefruit in mid-afternoon, a full dinner, and an evening snack consisting of an organic apple or an organic grapefruit. Doing this will start the process that allows the body to begin releasing abnormal fat reserves, as well as normalizing hunger and increasing metabolism. You should eat six times a day even if you are not hungry.

19. **Eat Dinner Before 6:00 p.m.** Ideally, you should finish eating your dinner three and one-half hours before you go to bed. This is very important at helping reset the hypothalamus so as not to store fat.

20. **Eat Protein Before Bed.** Eat 100 grams of organic beef, veal, chicken, turkey, or fish right before bedtime. This helps stimulate the mobilization of fat cells and decreases water retention. It also stimulates metabolism and actually helps you burn fat while you sleep.

21. **Take Acetyl L-Carnitine.** This amino acid helps turn fat into fuel. It promotes the increase of lean muscle tissue and

helps prevent muscle tissue from being lost. It speeds the burning of fat cells and increasing metabolic rate.

22. **Eat Hot Peppers.** Organic hot peppers and hot salsa stimulate an increase in metabolism and reduce appetite. It is very effective at helping reset the body's weight set point, metabolic rate and, additionally, helps release fat stores. Use organic hot salsa and organic hot peppers liberally as often as possible.

23. **Use Cinnamon.** Cinnamon helps regulate insulin and blood sugar. This helps stimulate the hypothalamus into being reset to a normal state. Cinnamon normalizes appetite and helps release fat reserves.

24. **Eat Salad With Lunch and Dinner.** In addition to whatever you choose to eat for lunch and dinner, add a big salad made with fresh organic ingredients; include such things as lettuce, onions, radishes, cucumbers, spinach, broccoli, cauliflower, garlic, tomatoes, asparagus, mushrooms, carrots, celery, herbs, fresh lemon juice, extra virgin olive oil, raw organic apple cider vinegar, sea salt, hot peppers, etc. Eating these raw organic vegetables before your meal stimulates digestion, adds important fiber which regulates blood sugar and appetite, and helps reset the body's weight set point. It also adds vital enzymes and nutrients that stimulate the release of stored fat.

25. **No Trans Fats!** Man-made trans fats absolutely, 100% will make you obese. They also lead to heart disease, cancer, arthritis, and diabetes. The most common trans fat is hydrogenated or partially hydrogenated oil of any kind. You cannot eat food with trans fats. Read the labels on food. If it says hydrogenated or partially hydrogenated oil of any kind, do not eat it. Learn to shop at a store such as Whole Foods, Wild Oats, or Trader Joe's. Read the food labels.

26. **No High Fructose Corn Syrup.** You cannot eat any food with any man-made sweeteners. Read the food labels. If it says high fructose corn syrup, corn syrup, sucrose, dextrose, or malto dextrose, do not eat it. These man-made super high

processed sugars have been designed to overtax the hypothalamus and make you fat. If you buy 100% organic products you can find any type of food you want without these
man-made sugars.

27. **No Artificial Sweeteners.** Do not consume any food that
has NutraSweet, Splenda, aspartame, sucrolos, or saccrin
on the label. These artificial sweeteners absolutely make
you fat. They all adversely affect the hypothalamus and
create the conditions for obesity. These artificial sweeteners are also highly chemically addicting and cause depression and anxiety.

28. **No Monosodium Glutamate (MSG).** MSG is a flavor enhancer
and preservative. It is called an excitotoxin. It adversely
affects the hypothalamus, as well as being chemically
addicting. It will make you fat and leads to depression. Read
the labels.

29. **Eat Only Organic Meat And Dairy.** Beef, chicken, turkey,
milk, cheese, and all dairy products that are not certified
organic are loaded with growth hormones, antibiotics, and
other drugs. These products lead to obesity. It is perfectly fine
to eat meat, poultry, and dairy products as long as they are
certified organic, ideally grass fed, and have not been injected
with growth hormone, antibiotics, or other drugs. Consuming
meat, poultry, and dairy products that are not organic means
you are putting in your body massive amounts of animal
growth hormone, powerful animal antibiotics, and other
animal drugs. This will create hormonal imbalances in the
body leading to weight gain, abnormal storing of fat, menstrual
cycle problems with women, PMS, and depression.

30. **No Nitrites.** Read the labels. If nitrites are listed do not buy
the product. Nitrites cause hormonal imbalances and will
lead to weight gain, allergies, and food cravings.

31. **No Farm Raised Fish.** Farm raised fish live in cesspools of
poison water. They are fed massive amounts of drugs and
chemicals to increase growth and production. Much of the
fish is injected with chemical food dyes to make them

appear fresher longer. The chemicals and poisons found in these fish cause hormonal imbalances leading to weight gain and depression.

32. **No Microwaving.** Throw your microwave oven away. Any food that has been microwaved has been chemically altered into an unnatural state. Research shows eating any food that has been microwaved adversely affects blood cell counts and is linked to depression. Microwaved food causes hormonal imbalances leading to weight gain.

33. **Limit Carbonated Drinks.** Carbonated drinks block calcium absorption and lead to nutritional deficiencies. They adversely affect digestion and the pancreas. They clog the liver and lymphatic system. These should be avoided. If you absolutely must have a carbonated drink, never drink a "diet" carbonated beverage. Try to choose a 100% organic carbonated beverage. If this is unavailable, choose a regular soda. The problem is that the major soda manufacturers have changed from sugar to high fructose corn syrup, making their beverages lethal when it comes to weight loss. Drink water, tea, freshly made juice, or coffee.

34. **Limit Ice Cold Drinks.** Drinking beverages that are very cold slows metabolism and actually increases hunger. These should be limited or avoided altogether. If you are drinking your one-half to one gallon of water per day, and several cups of the recommended teas, you should have no need or desire for any other beverage.

35. **No Fast Food.** All fast food restaurants, as well as national and regional chains, should be avoided. The foods served are loaded with all of the ingredients that I mentioned above that should be avoided. Food from fast food restaurants and regional and national chains are loaded with trans fats, super high processed sugars including high fructose corn syrup, artificial sweeteners, MSG, nitrates, and meat, dairy, and poultry that are loaded with growth hormone, antibiotics, and drugs. Much of the food is irradiated and microwaved. The food is super highly refined with little or no fiber. It is perfectly designed to overtax the hypothalamus

and do everything perfectly in the body to increase your hunger, make you physically, chemically addicted to the food, make you depressed, and make you fat! These restaurants did not exist in Simeons's time. They must be avoided.

36. **Eat 100% Organic Food.** Ideally, all the food you buy and consume should be labeled 100% organic. This means the food has not been genetically modified and has little, if any, man-made chemicals, preservatives, flavor enhancers, herbicides, pesticides, growth hormone, antibiotics, or other drugs. One hundred percent organic means 100% organic. The next best is when the label says "organic." This means the product is approximately 80% organic. The next best is when the label says "made with organic ingredients." This means approximately 30% of the product is organic. If the label says "all natural," it means nothing! You need to read the ingredient list. If there is something in the ingredients that you can't pronounce, don't buy it! Eating real food will keep you thin. Eating man-made processed food will make you fat because that's what the food manufacturers have designed the food to do.

37. **Use Natural Sweeteners.** If you need to use a sweetener, choose stevia as your first option. This is an all-natural herb which helps regulate blood sugar and stimulate weight loss. Other good options include raw organic agave nectar, raw organic honey, or raw organic sugar cane. Remember, science is not better than nature. Natural sweeteners are always better than artificial chemically made sweeteners.

38. **Infrared Saunas.** Sweating in a sauna increases metabolism and stimulates the release of fat cells. The skin is the largest organ in the body. Sweating in the sauna helps stimulates the release of accumulated toxins, increasing metabolism, bettering overall health, reducing appetite, and increasing metabolic rate. The two basic types of saunas are conventional saunas and infrared saunas. Both are very good. Based on the current theories, infrared saunas seem to be the better choice. Sweating for twenty minutes a day in a sauna can be difficult to do with people's busy schedules. It is highly

recommended, highly beneficial, and will increase weight loss, and elimination of toxins.

39. **Get Sun.** Lack of sunlight on the body has been shown to lead to depression, overeating, increase in appetite, low metabolism, and weight gain. Ideally, twenty minutes in the sun over a naked body each day is recommended. Do not use any lotions, sunscreens, or sunglasses. For more information on the benefits of the sun go to www.solarhealing.com. Exposure to the sun in this method also increases the release of endorphins, eliminating depression and suppressing appetite. The sun is also the best source of Vitamin D, thus has been shown to prevent cancer.

40. **Get Some Sleep.** Researchers have concluded that lack of proper sleep leads to obesity. Ideally, you should go to bed at 10:00 p.m. and arise at 6:00 a.m. This is ideal. Getting eight hours of sleep is best. The body releases certain healing hormones between 11:00 p.m. and 2:00 a.m. Being in a deep sleep during this time promotes healing in the body, longevity, youthful appearance, eliminating depression, and helps the hypothalamus to stay in a state of operating normalcy.

41. **Krill Oil.** This oil comes from marine animals in Arctic waters. It has one of the highest concentrations of omega-3s. Taking this supplement increases circulation, increases oxygenation in the body, and promotes normal hormone levels. It has been shown to alleviate depression, decrease appetite, and is beneficial to the liver and pancreas. It is a tremendous aid to longevity and health as well as weight loss. Krill oil is available in health food stores and at www.mercola.com and www.qnlabs.com.

42. **Vitamin E.** All-natural Vitamin E promotes proper circulation, has heart healthy benefits, and improves liver and gallbladder function. It is a powerful aid in weight loss, as well as promoting beautiful young-looking skin, and keeping your arteries open. I know of only two sources of Vitamin E that are truly all-natural. Do not buy Vitamin E in a health food store as all brands observed have some synthetic nature to them. The only two brands I recommend are 4 Spectrum E, available

by calling (800) 581-8906, and Unique E available at www.acgraceco.com or www.qnlabs.com.

43. **Digestive Enzymes.** People who are overweight lack the ability to produce enough enzymes to digest food properly. This is caused by eating super high refined foods, pasteurized foods from bottles, cans and cartons, nutritional deficiencies, clogged liver and colon, and non-prescription and prescription drugs. To help bring the body back to normal it is suggested that during Phase 1 you take digestive enzymes with each meal. There are many good brands available including Garden of Life Q-Zyme Ultra. Additional sources are available at www.naturalcures.com and www.qnlabs.com.

44. **No Lotions Or Creams.** Look at all the products that you put on your skin. These include lotions, creams, soap, moisturizers, shampoos, bath gels, etc. People, fifty years ago, did not put these types of products on their skin. Remember, the skin is the largest organ in the body. Whatever you put on your skin is absorbed into the bloodstream. When you put toxic, poisonous chemicals on your skin, they enter the bloodstream and adversely affect the organs and glands. These products also block the pores of the skin, reducing the body's ability to naturally detoxify, thus creating internal imbalances. This all leads to health problems, lower metabolism and, ultimately, obesity. The three most deadly ingredients you should avoid are mineral oil, propylene glycol, and sodium laureth sulfate. These are all deadly poisons. Read the labels on the products you currently have. It is advised that you reduce the amount of products you put on your skin. If you do choose to continue putting various products on your skin, choose 100% organic products. Many doctors around the world believe that for good health—if you can't eat it, don't put it on your skin!

45. **Rebound.** Exercise in any form is beneficial. A simple, fun and easy exercise is rebounding, or gently jumping on a mini-trampoline. Gently jumping on a rebounder stimulates the lymphatic system, releases beneficial endorphins and other hormones, and is the only exercise in the world

that actually stimulates and exercises every cell in the body simultaneously. Rebounding stimulates muscle tone, muscle strength, flexibility, oxygenates the blood, improves circulation, and stimulates the release of toxins. Set up a rebounder in front of your television. Five to ten minutes, once or twice a day, will have almost miraculous physical and mental health benefits.

46. **Massage**. Getting as many massages as possible, as often as possible, is highly encouraged. Vary the type of massage you receive. Try Swedish massage, Thai massage, deep tissue massage, and Shiatsu. During Phase 1 receiving one to two massages per week is encouraged. The more the better. Massage will get everything moving in the body and speedup the weight loss process.

47. **Yoga**. Yoga can be done by any person no matter what your flexibility or physical condition. Yoga stimulates all the internal organs and promotes internal health. It increases flexibility and blood flow through the body. It strengthens and tones the muscles; it improves posture. It also unblocks the energy meridians through the body, dramatically increasing physical energy and emotional wellbeing. During Phase 1 doing as many yoga sessions as possible is highly encouraged.

48. **Shower Filter**. Remember, your skin is the largest organ in the body. The water your shower in is loaded with fluoride, chlorine, and hundreds of other contaminants. Research has proven that when you take a shower your body absorbs more toxins than if you drank eight glasses of the same water. In hot showers steam is created filling your shower with poisonous gas from the contaminated water, which is inhaled into the lungs and, again, absorbed into the skin. Getting a shower filter will allow you to bathe and shower in pure, fresh water. Dry skin caused by the chlorine will disappear. You will never have a bad hair day again! Energy levels and a feeling of wellbeing also increase. Shower filters that I personally use are available at www.ewater.com, and www.wellnessfilter.com.

49. **Electromagnetic Chaos Eliminator.** We are bombarded by invisible electromagnetic energy every day. This did not exist fifty years ago. Today, however, with satellites, radio transmissions, cell phones, wireless devices, high-definition TVs, and an array of electronic products, every cell in our body is being smashed with trillions of bits of unnatural electromagnetic chaos. Researchers have now proven that this adversely affects the cells in our body, which in turn, adversely affect our health. This also leads to glandular abnormalities including that of the hypothalamus. This in turn leads to increased appetite and lower metabolism, thus contributing to obesity. It is recommended that you obtain a device that neutralizes these electromagnetic frequencies. I personally wear a Q-Link and E-Pendant. I also use a Biopro device on my cellular phone. Use of these devices will lead to increased energy, better mental clarity, better body function and reducing of depression. Check out www.ewater.com, www.clarus.com, and www.bioprotechnology.com.

50. **Breathe.** Interestingly enough, the majority of people in America do not breathe fully and deeply, thus have a body that is deficient in oxygen. This is caused by many factors including the stresses we deal with on a daily basis. Several researchers showed that when overweight people did nothing else but deep breathing ten minutes, two times a day, they all lost weight. This is because increased oxygen to the body increases metabolism, lowers appetite, and releases beneficial hormones alleviating depression. Lack of oxygen in the body also leads to a host of diseases including cancer. It is recommended that during Phase 1 and beyond that you engage in a daily practice of deep breathing. You can do this while driving in your car, watching TV, or sitting in front of your computer. For specific breathing techniques and methods, check out www.u-cure.com, www.breathe2000.com, www.oxycise.com, www.tbfinc.com, www.breathing.com, and www.bestbreathingexercises.com.

51. **Reduce Air Conditioning.** This is a mystery. Researchers have shown that people who spend long hours in air conditioning gain weight faster than those who don't. There are

many theories to why this is true. I would encourage you to limit or reduce the amount of air conditioning you are exposed to.

52. **Fluorescent Lights.** Being exposed to florescent lights should be avoided or eliminated. Florescent lighting causes chemical reactions in the brain that product fatigue and depression. This leads to food cravings. Florescent lighting also negatively affects the cells of the body, suppressing the immune system and lowering the metabolism.

53. **Chamomile Tea.** Reducing stress is vitally important for resetting the hypothalamus and achieving permanent weight loss. Organic chamomile tea should be consumed daily to help relax the body. One cup or more per day is recommended.

54. **AlphaCalm.** It is recommended to take one capsule of AlphaCalm two times a day. This is a powerful and effective product at reducing stress, promoting profound relaxation without causing drowsiness. It is a revolutionary break-through product for anxiety, stress, and mental fatigue. This promotes lower appetite and also helps in relieving depression. It is available by calling (800) 554-6051.

55. **De-stressing CDs.** I cannot emphasize how important stress reduction is in reducing hunger, increasing metabolism, alleviating depression, and promoting long-term permanent weight loss. Listening to a stress reducing CD once per day has profound emotional, mental, and health benefits. The recommended CDs are available at www.u-cure.com.

56. **Add Fiber.** Adding fiber to your diet during Phase 1 will help speed up the weight loss process dramatically. It will reduce appetite, relieve constipation, improve digestion, help cleanse the body of toxins, help increase energy, and help correct years of eating super highly refined food. One of the best fiber blend products contains organic flax seed, oat bran, and acacia. It's called Organic Triple Fiber Max, available at www.advancednaturals.com, or call (800) 690-9988.

57. **Parasites**. Eliminating parasites is important for weight loss. Virtually everyone has parasites that are partially responsible for a host of medical symptoms including inability to lose weight. These are also responsible for food and environmental allergies, asthma, skin disorders, constipation, gas and bloating, and can lead to ulcers, diabetes, and even cancer. During Phase 1, it is not recommended to do a complete parasite cleanse. Ideally, you should consider doing a parasite cleanse AFTER you complete Phase 1, Phase 2, and Phase 3 of "the weight loss cure protocol."

58. **Liver Cleanse**. In virtually all obese people tested, a clogged or sluggish liver exists. This leads to improper metabolism of fat, slowing of digestion, increased appetite, low metabolism, and is partially responsible for food cravings. This also creates an overtaxing of the body's immune system and is partially responsible for the onset of many medical symptoms, conditions, and diseases. When the liver is cleansed and operating properly, every organ and gland in the body can work more efficiently. This increases energy, decreases depression, increases metabolism, lowers hunger, and dramatically increases an overall sense of wellbeing. It is recommended that you do a liver AFTER you complete Phase 1, Phase 2, and Phase 3 of "the weight loss cure protocol."

59. **Lift Weights**. Doing any kind of resistance training, such as weight lifting or using the machines available at exercise studios such as Curves, is encouraged and beneficial. It will increase muscle mass, which will increase long-term improvement in the metabolism. Resistance training also releases hormones in the body that have anti-aging benefits, including improved skin and a youthful appearance. Strength increases, which leads to increased energy and vitality.

60. **Drugs**. ALL non-prescription, over-the-counter, and prescription drugs and medications of every kind absolutely, 100%, are proven to lead to weight gain and obesity. All non-prescription, over-the-counter, and prescription medications and drugs absolutely, 100%, cause illness and disease. This is proven. No drug, including even a common

aspirin, is safe. Every time you take even the smallest amount of even the most common medications you are causing severe damage to the human body, leading to additional medical symptoms, conditions, and obesity. The drug manufacturers themselves state this in their own printed literature. It is advised, only under the supervision of a licensed health care practitioner, that you avoid any and all non-prescription, over-the-counter medications, and prescription drugs. If you are taking a drug for such things as acid reflux, high blood pressure, high cholesterol, chronic pain, etc. you should know that there are all-natural non-drug alternatives that are proven to work better and have no negative side effects, but rather only health benefits. You can learn about these at www.naturalcures.com or by reading my first two books, *Natural Cures "They" Don't Want You To Know About* and *More Natural "Cures" Revealed Previously Censored Brand Name Products That Cure Disease*. In Dr. Simeons's day, less than 5% of the population took any kind of drug or medication on a regular basis. Today, it's an astonishing 70% of Americans who take medication or drugs on a regular basis. If you continue to take non-prescription and prescription medications and drugs, your health will continue to deteriorate and weight loss will continue to be a challenge.

This list may seem overwhelming. Certainly the average person may find it difficult to do everything on this list for the entire thirty-day Phase 1 period. If I operated a clinic where people came to receive "the weight loss cure protocol," every person would do everything on this list for thirty days. During the thirty days each person would feel better than ever before with increased energy, decreased depression and moodiness, and a constant feeling of fullness without any feelings of deprivation. At the end of the thirty days every person would have lost between five and thirty pounds! Everyone would look younger and healthier. Everyone would feel more energetic, be sleeping better, and have massive reductions in appetite and food cravings. This would occur, and has occurred, when people do everything suggested in Phase 1.

However, you live a hectic, busy lifestyle; therefore, you may only be able to do some of the things in this phase. Remember, during this phase you are not reducing the quantity of food you are consuming. You are to eat as much food as you want. If you want ice cream, cake, or cookies, eat them. Just make sure they are 100% organic without the forbidden ingredients listed above.

Many of the above items are very easy to do. Drinking water, eating apples and grapefruits, eating breakfast, taking Eleotin, drinking Yerba Mate, Wu Long, and Chamomile tea, taking coral calcium, adding hot peppers and cinnamon, and eating a big salad with lunch and dinner are all very easy to do. Avoiding the forbidden ingredients such as artificial sweeteners, high fructose corn syrup, and MSG is also easy to do. Simply shop at a market such as Whole Foods, Trader Joe's, or Wild Oats, and read the ingredient list on the label!

Remember, this thirty-day Phase 1 was not part of the original Simeons "weight loss cure protocol." When Simeons developed and administered his weight loss cure the conditions that people deal with today did not exist. If you skip this entire phase and go right to Phase 2, which is the original Simeons "weight loss cure protocol," you will still see spectacular results. Doing Phase 1 in ANY degree has been shown to make everything work faster and most importantly, help guarantee that permanent weight loss will be achieved and hunger and food cravings will be permanently eliminated. In actual fact, if a person did everything in Phase 1, the research shows that there is a similar resetting of the hypothalamus that is achieved by Simeons "weight loss cure protocol." The problem is that it takes approximately ninety days to achieve the results.

Therefore, if you truly want to increase metabolism, lower hunger, eliminate food cravings, release secured problem area fat deposits, and correct and reset the hypothalamus permanently so you never gain the weight back, it is strongly encouraged that you do as many items listed in Phase 1 for thirty days prior to starting Phase 2. You will be glad you did!

Phase 2:

This is the exact Dr. Simeons "weight loss cure protocol" as used by hundreds of thousands of patients around the world over the last thirty years with spectacular permanent results. The entire manuscript that describes this protocol entitled *Pounds and Inches: A New Approach to Obesity,* by Dr. A.T.W. Simeons, M.D., is available for you to read in its entirety at www.naturalcures.com.

THIS PHASE MUST BE DONE UNDER THE SUPERVISION OF A LICENSED HEALTH CARE PRACTITIONER!

Day One:

- Take an injection of between 125-200 units of hCG (human chorionic gonadotrophin) first thing in the morning.

- Drink one-half to one gallon of water throughout the day, ideally with coral calcium sachets.

- Gorge yourself and eat as much food as you can throughout the day.

- Do any of the items from Phase 1 as you choose.

Day Two:

- Repeat Day One.

Day Three:

- Weigh yourself immediately upon arising, after emptying the bladder, without clothes.

- Take an injection of between 125-200 units of hCG (human chorionic gonadotrophin) first thing in the morning.

- Drink one-half to one gallon of water throughout the day, ideally with coral calcium sachets.

- For breakfast have only
  - black coffee (organic preferred), or
  - organic green tea, or
  - organic Yerba Mate tea, or
  - organic Wu Long tea, or
  - organic chamomile tea.
  - You may have as much as you desire.

- Throughout the morning drink as much organic green tea, organic Yerba Mate tea, organic Wu Long tea, and/or organic chamomile tea, and water as you desire. Always make your tea with pure water, never tap water.

- For lunch eat 100 grams (weighed raw) of grilled (no oil or fat)
  - organic grass fed beef or veal, or
  - organic chicken breast (skinless), or
  - wild Chilean sea bass, or
  - flounder, or
  - sole, or
  - halibut

- One large handful of one of the following organic vegetables
  - Spinach
  - Chard
  - Beet greens
  - Lettuces of any kind
  - Tomatoes
  - Celery
  - Fennel
  - White, yellow, or red onions
  - Red radishes
  - Cucumbers
  - Asparagus, or
  - Cabbage

These can be eaten raw, steamed, grilled (without oil), or gently boiled. Do mix vegetables in the same meal.

- One small organic apple, or small organic grapefruit, or a handful of organic strawberries

- You may season any of the food with the juice of half an organic lemon, white or black pepper, organic raw apple cider vinegar, sea salt, organic garlic, organic basil, organic parsley, organic thyme, organic marjoram, or any other organic herb. Absolutely no oil, butter, dressings, or anything else!

- Dinner:
  - The same choices as for lunch. Do not, however, have two meals exactly the same in the same day.

- Black coffee, organic green tea, Wu Long tea, organic Yerba Mate tea, and organic chamomile tea can be consumed in any quantity as often as you wish throughout the day. You should drink at least one cup Wu Long, one cup Yerba Mate tea, and one cup chamomile tea each day.

- No medicines or over-the-counter non-prescription drugs should be taken. (Done under supervision of a physician.)

- No cosmetics other than lipstick, eyebrow pencil, and facial powder should be used.

- No creams, lotions, or moisturizers, or anything should be put on the skin.

- You must eat everything as described. Do not skip meals, and each meal must consist of the protein, the vegetables, and the fruit.

- You may eat the fruit in between meals *instead* of with the meal if you choose.

It is encouraged, but not required, that you do the following activities:

- Drink Eleotin tea three times per day, as the instructions suggest.

- Walk for one hour per day.

- Listen to stress reducing CDs daily.

- Use a rebounder as often as possible.

- Do yoga as often as possible.

- Sweat for twenty minutes in an infrared or regular sauna as often as possible.

- Get colonics as often as recommended by a licensed colon therapist.

- Get twenty minutes of sun daily as often as possible.

- Wear a Q-Link or E-Pendant, and use a Biopro chip on your cellular phone.

- Reduce exposure to air conditioning.

- Do not drink very cold beverages.

- Get one to three Thai massages a week. Thai massages are administered without lotions. You will be fully clothed and the massage consists of a series of assisted stretches. Do not take regular massages where lotions and creams are applied to your skin.

Day Four Through Day Forty-Five:

Follow the **Day Three** instructions every day for the entire course of treatment. In order to achieve permanent results you must continue the treatment exactly as described for a minimum of twenty-one days and a maximum of forty-five days.

Starting Treatment: Women should start the treatment immediately after their menses, or at least ten days before their next menses. During menstruation no injections are to be taken, but the diet is continued exactly as described. Injections are resumed immediately following the menses.

Duration: This phase must last for a minimum of twenty-one days, and a maximum of forty-five days. If you need to lose more weight after the forty-five days of treatment have been completed, you take six weeks off, eating normally with the exception of no sugar and no starch. You then resume Phase 2 for up to six weeks. If at that point you still need to lose more weight, you must take eight weeks off, eating normally with the exception of no sugar and no starch, and then resume Phase 2.

The Simeons "weight loss cure protocol," as you can see, consists of a daily injection of hCG, combined with a very strict and specific food consumption plan. The specific foods used cause chemical reactions in the body, combined with the hCG to activate the hypothalamus into releasing the secure abnormal fat reserves causing dramatic weight loss without the loss of muscle or structural fat. The amount of food consumed is approximately 500 calories. The reason for the very low caloric intake is that the body will only release the abnormal fat reserves after it has burned the consumed calories. Interestingly enough, eating lower amounts of calories do not speed up the process. Eating smaller quantities of food actually stop the

fat releasing mechanism. Dr. Simeons discovered that by changing the food, the fat releasing process is also slowed or stopped.
For example, when Simeons added mushrooms or artichokes,
even though they had the same or less amounts of calories, the
fat releasing was slowed or stopped completely. This is due to
unique chemical compositions in the food.

It is of the utmost importance for this protocol to work, you
must strictly follow the exact procedures to the letter.

The Last Injection Day Injection: On the day you receive the
last hCG injection you must follow the diet program exactly. For
the next two days you also must follow the diet exactly. This is
because your body is flooded with hCG and it should take two
days for it to leave the body.

During the entire Phase 2 you should weigh yourself every
morning at approximately the same time. Keep a daily record of
your weight. You should also take front, side, and rear photos of
your stripped down body on the day you start Phase 2. Take measurements of the thighs, calves, hips, waist, chest, back, and
arms. Upon completion of Phase 2 take another series of photos
and measurements. The weight and inch loss will be absolutely
astounding. The before and after pictures combined with the
weight and inch loss are a vital key to motivating you to continue
with Phase 3 and Phase 4. This will also start reprogramming
your mind with the belief and mental image of the body you
desire. This is a very important component as it will counteract
the programming we have self-imposed, as well as the food company advertising brainwashing we have endured over the years.

During this phase you should lose approximately one pound
per day. This will vary from day-to-day. Hunger will vary for each
individual. Hunger pangs will last no more than five to seven days.
The majority of people have no hunger pangs at all, even from the
first day, or have mild hunger pains that last only one to three
days. The more you did in Phase 1, in many cases, determines
how long the hunger pains last. If you have severe Candida overgrowth, a clogged colon, or have taken large amounts of non-prescription and prescription drugs over the years, your hunger
pains may initially be higher and duration slightly longer. The
vast majority of patients, however, state that hunger pains are

very mild or nonexistent. The major feeling that people deal with in the first few days of Phase 2 is a feeling of emptiness in their stomachs. This is quite different than hunger pains. Weighing yourself daily and seeing the spectacular results will keep your motivation high, allowing you to overcome any short-term hunger.

You may have many questions regarding this phase. You may read Dr. Simeons manuscript *Pounds and Inches: A New Approach to Obesity* at www.naturalcures.com. In the question and answer section of this book I address the most common concerns. At the end of the book I also give you additional references for your review, as well as the names, addresses, and websites of clinics that are currently administering this "weight loss cure protocol."

The most common question asked is that if a person just did this low calorie diet without the hCG injections, wouldn't they still lose weight? Every legitimate double-blind study shows that when people eat this diet without the hCG injections they do, in fact, lose weight. However, they do not lose the problem area secure fat deposits. Their body is not reshaped. They lose muscle and structural fat. They have massive hunger and fatigue. When they stop the diet they immediately gain all the weight back, plus more! Those who do the diet *with* the hCG injections lost *more* weight than the other group, had no hunger or fatigue, and lost fat in the problem areas. Their bodies were completely reshaped. They did not lose structural fat and muscle. Most importantly, when they stopped the diet and hCG injections, *they did not gain the weight back!* Although there are critics and so-called experts that continue to debunk and discredit Simeons's "weight loss cure protocol," the hundreds of thousands of patients achieving these results, combined with the massive amounts of scientific documentation, double-blind studies, clinical studies and observations, are proof beyond a doubt that this is in fact the ultimate cure for obesity. This method has passed the test of time.

Once you have completed one or more six-week rounds of Phase 2 and have lost the weight and reshaped your body to your personal satisfaction, then it is time to go on to Phase 3.

Phase 3

This is an important phase of the treatment. This is also part of the original Simeons protocol. Successfully following the instructions in this phase should result in a resetting of the body weight set point and hypothalamus. This is the phase that resets metabolism to a high normal state, eliminates future intense and constant hunger, and prevents the abnormal future storing of fat in the secure problem area fat reserves in the body.

This phase is relatively simple. For twenty-one days immediately following the last day of the Phase 2 restricted diet you are allowed to eat as much food and any type of food you choose. The exceptions are as follows:

- No sugar, dextrose, sucrose, honey, molasses, high fructose corn syrup, corn syrup, or any sweetener.

- No starch, including breads, pastas, any wheat product, white rice, potatoes, yams, etc.

- No artificial sweeteners, including aspartame, sucrolos, NutraSweet, Splenda, saccharin, etc.

- No food from fast food restaurants.

- No trans fats, including hydrogenated or partially hydrogenated oils.

- No nitrites.

- Limit non-prescription and prescription drug use.

- Limit ice cold drinks.

- Limit exposure to air conditioning.

- Limit exposure to florescent lights.

Additionally, doing as many of the following activities is highly suggested and recommended:

- Drink one-half to one gallon of pure spring water daily, ideally with coral calcium sachets.

- Walk for one hour per day.

- Eat a minimum of two organic apples per day.

- Eat a minimum of one organic grapefruit per day.

- Take a teaspoon of raw organic coconut oil twice per day.

- Take one to three teaspoons of raw organic apple cider vinegar per day.

- Continue to drink Eleotin tea three times per day, as the directions suggest.

- Take ThreeLac as directed.

- Drink organic green tea, organic Yerba Mata tea, organic Wu Long tea, and organic chamomile tea daily in any quantities you desire.

- Use stevia as the sweetener of choice.

- Sleep seven to eight hours per night, ideally going to bed at approximately 10:00 p.m. and arising at 6:00 a.m.

- Eat a large breakfast.

- Eat something six times per day.

- Finish your dinner three and one-half hours before bedtime.

- On occasion eat 100 grams of organic chicken, turkey, veal, beef, or fish before bedtime.

- On occasion take Acetyl L-Carnitine.

- Take digestive enzymes with food.

- Take probiotics daily.

- Take a whole food supplement daily.

- Take Vitamin E daily.

- Take krill oil daily.

- Use a rebounder five to ten minutes twice per day.

- Sweat twenty minutes per day in an infrared or conventional sauna.

- Get twenty minutes of sun daily.

- Get additional colonics as recommended by a licensed colon therapist.

- Do yoga as often as you can.

- Do not use the microwave.

- Continue wearing a Q-Link or E-Pendant and use Biopro on your cellular phone.

- Add hot peppers to food.

- Add cinnamon to food.

- Always eat a big salad with lunch and dinner.

- Avoid lotions, creams, and body care products with propylene glycol or sodium laurel sulfate.

- Avoid monosodium glutamate.

- Avoid farm-raised fish.

- Add fiber from flax seed, oat bran, and acacia daily into your diet.

- Continue to listen to stress reducing CDs daily.

- Do resistance exercise such as weight lifting.

- Take AlphaCalm daily.

- Buy and use a shower filter.

You must absolutely weigh yourself every morning after first emptying your bladder. You must do this daily without fail. As it takes about three weeks after completing Phase 2 before the weight stabilizes, it is important that daily weighing during this phase be adhered to. As long as your weight stays within two pounds of the weight reached on the day of the last injection you are fine. The moment the scale goes beyond two pounds, even by only a few ounces, you must do the following steps:

- The same day you notice the increase you must entirely skip all food until 6:00 p.m. During this time you should drink as much water, up to one gallon, as you can. You must drink a minimum of half a gallon of pure water. In addition to the water, drink as much of the various teas that are recommended. You may use stevia in the teas. In the evening eat the biggest steak you can from grass fed organic beef.

The steak can be grilled or fried with oil and seasoned with pepper and herbs, but no salt. You may have either a large organic raw tomato or large organic raw apple.

It is of the utmost importance that these steps of skipping meals occur on the same day as the scale registered an increase of more than two pounds from the weight you achieved on the last day of injections. You must not postpone this protocol until the following day. Weighing yourself daily is vitally important. Because the hypothalamus is now corrected from its abnormal condition, when you gain weight the body will not store the excess in the secure abnormal fat reserves. This means that weight gain will now result in storing of fat evenly throughout the body in the normal or structural fat areas. This means that by looking in the mirror, or by feeling how your clothes fit, will be misleading. You can actually gain ten to fifteen pounds and never notice it. This is why daily weighing is so important.

During the three weeks in Phase 3 monitor and be aware of your appetite. Many people out of habit put large amounts of food on their plate. During this time you will notice you get full very quickly. Take note of the feeling of fullness and loss of appetite and stop eating! It is very important that you eat a full breakfast, lunch, and dinner, and have three snacks, ideally consisting of an organic apple or an organic grapefruit, however, during each meal it is advised that you eat slowly, consciously be aware of chewing your food thoroughly, and stop eating when you are full.

Many fat people have the fear that if they don't continue to eat during mealtime they will be hungry later on and feel miserable. This three-week Phase 3 is important as it helps change behavioral habits that played a part in your weight problem. Some basic guidelines that will help change past behavioral habits that lead to obesity include the following:

- Sit at a table and be relaxed when eating a meal.

- Do not eat in front of the TV, in the car, or standing up.

- Eat slowly and consciously chew food thoroughly.

- Play relaxing music while eating, ideally baroque classical music or other types of music that are known to relax the body at the biological level.

- Put smaller amounts of food on your plate, and don't go for seconds.

- Be conscious about whether you are really hungry or full. Stop eating when you are no longer hungry and are full and satisfied.

You should never gain more than two pounds during this phase without immediately correcting this situation by doing the skipping meals and steak protocol. Surprisingly, Simeons discovered that it is equally undesirable for you to lose more than two pounds after the last injection. This is because any loss of weight after the last injection is usually a loss of muscle, or structural fat.

Simeons noted that some patients become overly enthusiastic after the success they achieved during Phase 2. These patients do not believe they can eat normal amounts of food six times per day without regaining weight. They disregard the advice to eat anything they please (with the short list of exceptions) and want to play it safe. They try, more or less, to continue the low calorie diet from Phase 2 with minor variations. To their horror they find that their weight actually goes up. They then follow the instructions of skipping breakfast and lunch, but are afraid to eat the steak for fear of gaining more weight and instead have something such as a small salad. They become hungry and weak. The next morning they find they've increased yet another pound! They feel terrible and even the dreaded swelling of their ankles comes back. Dr. Simeons explained these phenomena in these terms. During Phase 2 the patient is just above the verge of protein deficiency, but because of the hCG injections protein is being fed back into a system from the breakdown and release of the secure problem area fatty tissue. Once the treatment is over, there is no more hCG in the body and this process no longer takes place. Unless an adequate amount of protein is eaten as soon as Phase 2 is over, protein deficiency is bound to develop. This inevitably caused a marked retention of water, increased weight, which many times results in swelling of the ankles, huge hunger, tiredness, and irritability.

It is advised that you follow these instructions exactly as described. Never do this or any weight loss program without being supervised by a licensed health care practitioner. You are encouraged to go to www.naturalcures.com and read Dr. Simeons entire manuscript *Pounds and Inches: A New Approach to Obesity*. It is suggested that you invest some time for viewing the various scientific documents, abstracts, double-blind studies, and patient testimonials that are available from the sources listed at the end of this book.

Remember, I have personally done this protocol myself. I have talked to the medical doctors who are treating patients with this protocol. I have reviewed patient files and records. I have talked to numerous patients who have utilized Simeons's method. The results are 100% verifiable and true. The safety is without question. The long-term success is unrivaled.

I have also talked to skeptics and naysayers who claim that the Simeons method is dangerous and does not work. None of these people have any hard legitimate evidence to backup their claim. Recently I called the Food and Drug Administration and talked to a senior officer about the use of hCG in the treatment of obesity. I was provided information from the FDA and the National Institutes of Health. The government literature states, "Although hCG has been prescribed to help some patients lose weight it should NEVER be used this way. When used improperly hCG can cause serious problems." Remember, this is "the weight loss cure" THEY don't want you to know about. Remember, I discussed earlier how the FDA and other government agencies have an unholy alliance with the food industry and drug industry to keep the truth about this real weight loss cure from the public.

I inquired with dozens of government agency officials as to WHY they claim hCG should never be used to help patients lose weight. They could never give me a legitimate answer! I asked, what are the "serious problems" that hCG has been *known* and *proven* to cause? No one in any government agency could supply ANY documentation or substantiation proving that using small doses of hCG and the Simeons "weight loss cure protocol" has EVER caused any serious problems in any patient even though the government makes this erroneous claim in their own literature. The drug companies, the food companies, the government, and the media do not want you to know the truth about this obesity cure breakthrough.

When you successfully complete the twenty-one days of Phase 3, you are ready to begin your new life as a normal, thin, energetic, happy, healthy person who is no longer a slave to hunger, food cravings, and food. Your hypothalamus will be reset and corrected from its abnormal operating state. Your metabolism will be high. Your hunger and food cravings will be low. You will no longer abnormally store fat in the abnormal secure fat reserves. You will have been cured of the main causes of obesity. Now let's make sure that you keep this corrected condition permanently and don't screw up your hypothalamus again!

Phase 4

When you start this phase it will be the first day of the rest of your life. It will be a whole new life. Your life now will be different than before. Your hunger will be normalized and will no longer be intense and constant. You will eat normal, small amounts of food and be perfectly satisfied and full. You will no longer have uncontrollable urges and desires to eat. You will no longer have food cravings, causing you to eat when you are not hungry. Your metabolism will be high so you easily burn for fuel the food you consume. You will not gain any more weight. Your body will no longer abnormally store fat in the secure problem area fat deposits around your body. Your energy levels will be high. You will sleep deeply and soundly. Your skin, hair, nails, and eyes will be youthful and radiant, glowing with vibrant health. You will be happy and no longer suffer from depression, stress, or anxiety. You will find yourself more energetic, doing things and exercising more than you ever imagined. You will be more social and your relationships with other people will be better.

Up until now you have been a slave to food. You've been an addict, programmed by the food industry to be a compulsive overeater. You were plagued with a low metabolism, fatigue, and constant and intense hunger. You also developed many dangerous habits that helped create the weight problem you have had to endure. Those days are gone and the bright, sunny, beautiful days are now your present and future.

Phase 4 is for the rest of your life. This phase will consist of some basic and easy to follow dos and don'ts that will become your new, exciting habits. These new success habits will replace some of your old failure habits. These new healthy habits will begin to replace many of your old unhealthy habits. These new habits will give you a feeling of empowerment; they will make you feel in control; they will give you confidence, peace, and security.

Remember who the enemy is. The food companies, including fast food, regional and national chain restaurants, and all manufacturers and sellers of everything we eat are doing everything in their power, through deceptive advertising and other coercive techniques to get you to buy their food or eat in their restaurants. Remember too that they are purposely creating and making food that will get you chemically and physically addicted, increase your appetite, and make you fat. They are the enemy.

The simplest rule to follow is to eat anything you want, as much as you want, as often as you want. The only caveat is only eat 100% organic food. If you do this you will never be consuming all of the things that are designed to overtax your hypothalamus and create the conditions of obesity. In real life, in the real world, eating only 100% organic food can be next to impossible. Basically then, what you work to achieve is to avoid, as best you can, the man-made ingredients that cause obesity. Remember, obesity and weight gain is generally not caused by calories, fat, simple or complex carbohydrates, foods with a high glycemic index rate, or sodium. Obesity and weight gain is caused by the man-made ingredients, chemicals, and food processing techniques employed in the growing, producing, and manufacturing of food. To keep the weight off permanently, and to achieve vibrant dynamic health, here is a list of dos and don'ts:

1. Eat only 100% organic food. Although this is the ideal scene, in real life this can be next to impossible. Do the best you can. You don't have to count calories or be concerned with fat, carbohydrates, protein, or sodium. As we've learned so far, real food without man-made chemical ingredients and food processing techniques, that are not super highly refined, do not create the conditions for obesity. As you go throughout your life following this rule will not only prevent weight gain, and give you dynamic, vibrant health, it will

also allow you to fully indulge in the most delicious food without deprivation.

2. No "brand name" food. The rule here is not to eat food produced by publicly traded corporations. Remember, large publicly traded food companies are the enemy. They are producing food that is genetically modified, loaded with chemicals, growth hormone, drugs, trans fats, and other ingredients specifically and purposely created to increase your appetite, get you chemically addicted to the food, and make you fat. You cannot trust any of the mass-produced food they sell. They are using deceptive advertising techniques and sophisticated brainwashing techniques in their advertising to create mental triggers that cause us to have compulsive urges and cravings for their food. Staying away from any brand name heavily advertised product is the best course of action. Knowing that every publicly traded large food company will use every deceitful and misleading technique, and fancy food label, to get us to buy their product and make us fat is reason enough to avoid supporting them by never buying their products.

3. No fast food, regional or national chain restaurants. This is the same as the previous rule. Virtually all the food available from regional and national restaurant chains and fast food companies is specifically designed to increase appetite, get us chemically addicted to the food, and make us fat. This is a new phenomenon. It did not exist in Simeons's day. If you go back to eating food from these unscrupulous companies you will get fat again.

4. Do a Candida cleanse. In Simeons's day Candida yeast overgrowth was almost nonexistent. Today, over 80% of the U.S. population has some degree of Candida yeast overgrowth. This condition creates massive food cravings, gas and bloating, depression, increased hunger, poor digestion, and fatigue. In order to make your weight loss permanent and to ensure no food cravings or feelings of deprivation, it is vital that you do a Candida cleanse as soon as possible. A good beginner cleanse is the ThreeLac program, available at www.123candida.com. The most complete and powerful

Candida cleanse is the LifeForce Program available at www.lifeforceplan.com. There are many other Candida cleanse and programs available. Consult with a local licensed health care practitioner who uses non-drug and non-surgical methods to cure and treat disease. A list is available at www.naturalcures.com.

5. Clean your colon. Hopefully, you have done this step in Phase 1. Since it is impossible for you to eat perfectly for the rest of your life, it is necessary for you to clean your colon at least once per year. I generally do some form of colon cleanse three to four times per year. Good colon cleanses include a series of five to fifteen colonics in a thirty-day period. Other good colon cleanses can be found at www.drnatura.com, www.tryalmightycleanse.com, www.pbiv.com, www.qnlabs.com, and www.dr-schulze.com.

6. Do a liver cleanse. Cleansing the liver will dramatically improve digestion, increase metabolism, and make permanent weight loss very easy. Several liver cleanse products and programs can be found at www.drnatura.com, www.liverdoctor.com, www.dr-schulze.com, and www.qnlabs.com.

7. Drink one-half to one gallon of pure water daily. This is vital to keep the cells hydrated and continually flush toxins from the body. Ideally, drink water with coral calcium sachets.

8. Do a parasite cleanse. After you have done a colon cleanse and a liver cleanse, it is wise to use a parasite cleanse product or program. In addition to promoting long-term weight regulation, the benefits also include dramatic increase in energy and alleviating of a multitude of medical symptoms and conditions. It has been shown that a majority of people have parasites which are partially responsible for the development of many degenerative diseases. For a list of recommended parasite cleanse products and programs go to www.naturalcures.com, www.qnlabs.com, www.drnatura.com, www.drstockwell.com, and www.paradevices.com.

9. Do a heavy metal cleanse. The best known method is intravenous chelation performed by a licensed health care practitioner. Products that can be taken at home that help

remove and help the body cleanse heavy metals can be found at www.rxvitamins.com, www.advancedbionutritio-nals.com, www.scienceformulas.com, www.qnlabs.com, and www.drnatura.com.

10. Walk for one hour, outside, every day.

11. Eat! Always eat breakfast, eat something six times per day, and finish your dinner three and one-half hours before you go to bed. Avoid eating a huge meal as this overtaxes the hypothalamus.

12. Eat protein before bed. On occasion eat 100 grams of orga-nic beef, veal, chicken, turkey, or fish right before bed.

13. Take Acetyl L-Carnitine. This helps turn fat into fuel.

14. Eat a minimum of one organic apple every day.

15. Eat organic grapefruits as you desire.

16. Have a big salad with lunch and dinner (made with organic ingredients).

17. Add organic hot peppers and cinnamon as often as possible.

18. Use organic virgin coconut oil as often as possible.

19. Use organic raw apple cider vinegar as often as possible.

20. Sleep eight hours per night; ideally, between 10:00 p.m. and 6:00 a.m.

21. Drink organic Yerba Mate tea, chamomile tea, Wu Long tea, and green tea liberally.

22. Every day take a whole food supplement, probiotics, Vita-min E, and krill oil.

23. Use stevia as your sweetener of choice.

24. Get sun on a regular basis.

25. Use an infrared or conventional sauna as often as possible.

26. Use a rebounder as often as possible.

27. Do yoga as often as possible.

28. Do resistance training, such as weight lifting, as often as possible.

29. Take digestive enzymes with food.

30. Take AlphaCalm as needed.

31. Listen to stress reducing CDs often.

32. Reduce exposure to florescent lights and air conditioning.

33. Limit ice cold drinks.

34. Get massages often.

35. Use a Q-Link, E-Pendant, and/or Biopro for neutralizing electromagnetic chaos.

36. Limit carbonated drinks.

37. Limit non-prescription, over-the-counter, and prescription drug use.

38. Use deep breathing techniques on a regular basis.

The following items must be avoided at all costs as they will quickly and easily make you gain weight:

39. No super highly refined sugars. These include high fructose corn syrup, corn syrup, sucrose, and dextrose.

40. No genetically modified food. If it doesn't say 100% organic, it is probably genetically modified.

41. No artificial sweeteners. This includes NutraSweet, Splenda, aspartame, sucrolos, and others.

42. No trans fats. This includes hydrogenated or partially hydrogenated oils.

43. No monosodium glutamate.

44. No food with nitrites.

45. No meat, poultry, or dairy that is not 100% organic. All meat, poultry, and dairy that is not 100% organic is loaded with growth hormones, antibiotics, and other drugs. These absolutely cause weight gain and other physical and emotional problems.

46. No farm raised fish.

47. No propylene glycol or sodium laureth sulfate. Make sure your shampoos, conditioners, moisturizers, soaps, lotions, and creams do not contain these deadly poisonous chemicals.

48. Do not use a microwave.

49. Drink fresh cantaloupe and watermelon juice. Juicing experts Jay Kordich and Jack LaLane suggest drinking freshly made juice from cantaloupes and watermelons can speed cleansing of toxins and promote weight loss. Use a Juiceman juicer or a Jack LaLane Power Juicer.

50. Do a full body fat cleanse. The best known cleanse that releases toxins from the fatty tissue in the body is called the Purification Program. I, and many of my friends, have done this program with spectacular results. Cleansing toxins out of the fatty tissue is vital in reducing or eliminating food cravings and urges. Check out www.pruification.org, and www.clearbodyclearmind.com.

This list may seem overwhelming and difficult to implement in real life. I can tell you it is relatively easy. The key is to shop in stores which carry the types of products that do not make you fat. Shop at your local farmers market, your local health food store, or stores such as Whole Foods, Wild Oats, or Trader Joe's. You still must read the ingredient list on the label. I recently went into a major supermarket chain to do some investigating. I looked at mustard, ketchup, and bread. Every single jar of mustard had high fructose corn syrup in it! Every single bottle of ketchup had high fructose corn syrup in it! Most amazingly, every single loaf of bread had some kind of super highly refined processed sugar such as high fructose corn syrup, corn syrup, dextrose, malto dextrose, honey, molasses, etc. This is why obesity is an epidemic today. I then went to Whole Foods. I easily found many brands of mustard, ketchup, and bread that did not have any high fructose corn syrup or any other super refined highly processed sugars. You see, it's not that mustard, ketchup, bread, or any other type of food is fattening, it is the ingredients and food processing techniques of that food that make it fattening! Understanding this means you can eat virtually any *kind* of food you want and not gain weight. You can still eat mashed potatoes and gravy, cheeseburgers, French fries, pizza, pasta, cheese, butter, eggs, pot roast, cake, cookies, ice cream, etc. The key is reading the ingredient list. All of these foods are available without the forbidden fat inducing man-made ingredients. They are all available with 100% organic whole food, non-refined, real ingredients as nature intended. This kind of food actually tastes much better, is more filling, and much more satisfying than the man-made mass-produced counterparts that are sold by the large publicly traded international food conglomerates.

It is impossible for the average person to eat this way all the time. This is why doing a colon cleanse, liver cleanse, heavy metal cleanse, and parasite cleanse once or more per year is strongly suggested. The Candida cleanse usually only needs to be done once. Always consult a licensed health care practitioner before and during your cleanses.

As you can see, today's environment is quite different than in the 1950s and 1960s when Simeons was treating patients. Today, virtually everything we eat, combined with our sedentary lifestyle, is working perfectly to make us fat. There are more causes for obesity today than ever before. Now that you know the causes you can avoid them in the future. Avoiding the causes of obesity is a decision.

People ask me if they can still eat the foods they are accustom to. The answer is absolutely yes, but you must change brands! If you like Oreo cookies change to another brand such as Paul Newman organic cookies that are almost identical to Oreos. The Oreos are loaded with trans fats and super highly refined sugars and ingredients that make you fat. Paul Newman's cookies have no trans fats, organic ingredients, and no super highly refined sugars and ingredients. They taste better, and are more filling; they do not give you the sugar crash and increased hunger associated with Oreos. In normal amounts they will not make you fat.

If you have successfully completed Phases 1, 2, and 3, implementing the suggestions in Phase 4 should be easy. You should have renewed energy, enthusiasm, and confidence for keeping the weight off permanently. As you read this, you probably have not started "the weight loss protocol" yet. It may seem hard to do. I can assure you that the protocol outlined in Phases 1, 2, 3 and 4 will be easy and enjoyable.

When I first learned of the Simeons "weight loss cure protocol" I thought it was very strict and would be very hard to follow. I was fearful that I would have to use superhuman willpower to stay on the protocol. I believed I would be hungry, tired, grumpy, and feeling deprived throughout the course of treatment. I believed I would be giving up all the pleasures of eating. This fear made me come up with every excuse to delay starting "the weight loss cure protocol." It took over one year before I actually got started. I can tell you all of my fears and apprehension was totally unjustified. I was never hungry, I had tons of energy, my disposition was bright and pleasant, I did not have to use any willpower, and my motivation to stick with the protocol was very high. I, like every other patient I talked to, found this approach to obesity very easy to do. I only wish I had done it a year earlier. I encourage *you* to do this protocol exactly as Simeons outlined it.

At this point there are several items I want to address and clarify. The next chapter is entitled "Frequently Asked Questions." It is important that you read everything in that chapter as well as everything in this entire book. Many important and vital questions and issues must be handled before you start "the weight loss cure protocol." You may be skeptical or apprehensive of Simeons's approach to obesity. There are many groups, associations, government agencies, companies, alleged watchdog groups, alleged consumer advocacy groups, and doctors who are critical of Simeons's method. We are tapping into the $150 billion per year diet and weight loss industry. The money at stake is so big that I am sure the news media, the American Medical Association, the FDA, the FTC, state attorneys general, and other groups will do everything in their power to debunk and discredit me, this book, and Dr. Simeons's work.

Remember, this approach has passed the test of time. It has been successfully used for over thirty years. Hundreds of thousands of patients have achieved successful results. There is not one known patient who has had any serious negative effects by doing the protocol *exactly* as Simeons described. The scientific research is overwhelmingly conclusive showing the effectiveness and safety of this protocol. The clinical trials, double-blind studies, and thousands of doctors, and patients' observations over the last thirty years prove conclusively that this protocol is absolutely, completely safe, and absolutely works! The hundreds of thousands of patients, including members of royal families, celebrities, and the super wealthy, who have used this protocol safely achieving spectacular results, cannot all be wrong! Will you be the next success story who says, "The Simeons "weight loss cure protocol" absolutely, 100%, works. It's easy and safe. I should know, because I used it myself!"?

Read on to learn more inside secrets to this technique, and how and why everyone will try to convince you *not* to use it!

CHAPTER SIX

Frequently Asked Questions

The thing that bugs me is that people think the FDA is protecting them. It isn't. The FDA is protecting the profits of the corporations that pay us and the politicians!

—Herbert Ley, M.D.,
Former FDA Commissioner

This is an important chapter. In order for you to safely achieve the results from "the weight loss cure protocol" it is essential that you fully understand all of the specifics and nuances of this protocol and do it exactly and precisely as directed under the supervision of a medical doctor. Make sure you have read this book cover-to-cover and fully understand every concept and instruction without any confusion. If you have any questions or need clarification on anything described in this book, or any health matter, you may go to www.naturalcures.com. Members of the www.naturalcures.com web community have access to trained specialists who can answer all your questions. You are also strongly encouraged to read Dr. Simeons's manuscript *Pounds and Inches: A New Approach to Obesity,* which is available online in the weight loss section of www.naturalcures.com.

This chapter will cover the most common questions that people have regarding "the weight loss cure protocol." It will also cover additional important issues and situations that can come up during the process.

Question: Where do I get hCG?

Answer: HCG is a natural substance that is produced in the human body during pregnancy. Pharmaceutical companies extract this substance from the urine of pregnant women. It is purified and made into pharmaceutical grade hCG. Although it is a natural substance, it is classified as a "drug" and available by prescription only. You must get hCG from a medical doctor with a prescription. In countries around the world doctors may prescribe hCG for a number of conditions. In most countries medical doctors are allowed to prescribe hCG for use in the treatment of obesity. In America hCG is one of the only pharmaceutical compounds that the FDA has specifically said should not be used in the treatment of obesity! There is much debate of whether a medical doctor in America has the legal right to prescribe hCG to be used with the Simeons "weight loss cure protocol." I suggest showing your medical doctor this book and have them read Simeons's original manuscript *Pounds and Inches: A New Approach to Obesity*. I am not suggesting, or recommending, that you in anyway break any federal or state law. I am suggesting that in America you have a constitutional right to do what you feel is best for your own body. It is ludicrous that people around the world have easy access to hCG, under the supervision of a medical doctor, and are fully able to do the Simeons "weight loss cure protocol" and Americans must continue to suffer.

HCG and the Simeons "weight loss cure protocol" can also be procured from doctors outside of the United States and legally brought back into the country for personal use. This is provided you have a valid prescription from a licensed medical doctor in that country. I, myself, went to Germany, got a prescription, and received enough hCG injections to do the entire six-week protocol. I then legally returned to the United States with the prescription and the hCG, and finished the protocol in America. It is my understanding that this is a legal option.

Question: What if I just did the diet in Phase 2 without the hCG injections?

Answer: Many double-blind studies have been conducted that give the answer to this question. If you just do the diet in Phase 2 without the hCG injections, you will, in fact, lose weight. The problem is, during the diet you will be hungry and tired; most importantly, you will be losing muscle and structural fat; you will not lose any of the abnormal fat deposits in the problem areas. Your body will not be reshaped and re-sculpted. When you finish the diet your metabolism will be lower than before and your hunger higher than before. You will not have achieved the results you want.

Question: Can I start the program with Phase 2 without doing any of the things in Phase 1?

Answer: Yes. However, if you do not do Phase 1 to at least some degree, you will not be handling and addressing many of the new causes of your overweight condition. Doing as much as you can of the Phase 1 steps will accelerate the process and make permanent weight loss easier to achieve. In today's world, the steps outlined in Phase 1 absolutely are recommended if you want to eliminate food cravings, increase metabolism, reduce hunger, and keep the weight off forever.

Question: Do I have to do Phase 3?

Answer: Yes. Phase 2 and Phase 3 are, in fact, the original Simeons "weight loss cure protocol." Phase 3 is necessary to stabilize your weight and reset the hypothalamus so that the weight does not come back. It is vitally important that you follow Phase 2 and Phase 3 exactly as described. You must strictly adhere to Simeons's instructions in Phase 2 and Phase 3.

Question: What if I cannot get hCG and cannot do Phase 2?

Answer: If hCG is completely unavailable to you there is an option. First, do ALL the steps in Phase 1 for thirty days. Then, you replace Phase 2 with the *The Turbo Protein Diet* as described in the book written by Dieter Markert. This protocol uses a product called Almased, available at (800) 256-2733 or www.almased.com. Do this protocol for up to six weeks. Then, continue with Phase 3 and Phase 4 exactly as described. This protocol is not as effective as the Simeons "weight loss cure protocol" with hCG. However, it is the next best alternative. If you do this protocol you must do all the steps in Phase 1 and you must do the Candida cleanse, liver cleanse, and parasite cleanse in Phase 4 in order to achieve the same results.

Question: What does the FDA say about hCG?

Answer: The FDA, the National Institutes of Health, and even the manufacturers of hCG themselves state, "HCG has no known affect on fat mobilization, reducing appetite or sense of hunger, or body fat distribution." They further state, "HCG has not been demonstrated to be an effective adjunct therapy in the treatment of obesity and does not increase fat losses beyond that resulting from caloric restriction." They even say specifically that, "HCG should never be used in the treatment of obesity because serious problems can occur." These statements are blatantly and flagrantly false. There is absolutely no documentation or substantiation backing up and proving that these negative statements are true. The studies that the government uses to backup these lies were conducted as part of the massive cover-up of the truth about the Simeons "weight loss cure protocol." In these studies the researchers purposely caused the results to be negative. First, they did not follow the Simeons protocol exactly as instructed. Dr. Simeons was very clear that if the protocol was not followed exactly and precisely as described, the results would not be achieved. The researchers changed the specific mentioned food items to other items claiming that the calories were similar; therefore, would not affect the results. This was a fatal flaw. Most importantly, the researchers mixed the hCG solution weeks in advance before giving the daily injections to the patients. Simeons was very clear that hCG should be mixed daily. It cannot be mixed and stored for later use. Once hCG is mixed it begins to lose potency very quickly. Within twenty-four hours the potency of the hCG is completely gone. Therefore, the injections were completely useless. In effect, the test subjects were receiving no hCG at all. The studies showed that all people on the diet lost weight, therefore concluding that the hCG injections had no positive effects.

The truth is that in all properly conducted studies, people on the diet without hCG and people on the diet with hCG did, in fact, both lose weight. However, in these properly controlled studies, the group receiving the hCG with the diet lost more weight, had no hunger, and more importantly, lost dramatically more inches. The hCG group saw a dramatic reshaping and re-sculpting of their bodies. The hCG group lost fat in the problem areas. The FDA, the National Institutes of Health, and the drug companies are simply lying to us in order to protect the profits of the food companies, the pharmaceutical companies, and the diet industry.

Question: Is hCG legal for use in a weight loss regime?

Answer: It all depends on what country you live in! In America the FDA makes the erroneous statement that hCG should never be used in the treatment of obesity. They are adamant about this. I have talked to dozens of officers at the FDA, the National Institutes of Health, and various other government agencies. I asked why they were so adamant about making sure people did not use hCG in the Simeons "weight loss cure protocol." No one could give me a straight answer. No one could provide me any documentation or substantiation proving that the Simeons "weight loss cure protocol," used exactly as described, was unsafe. This is a great cover up as to the true causes and cure for the obesity epidemic. The FDA and other government agencies are protecting the profits of the pharmaceutical companies as they work to get approval on a number of expensive, ineffective surgical procedures and patented drugs to be sold for the treatment of obesity. As the past commissioner of the FDA, Dr. Herbert Ley, stated, "The FDA is not protecting people. It protects the profits of the pharmaceutical companies." In 1962, the *Journal of the American Medical Association* warned people against the Simeons protocol stating, "Adherence to such a drastic regime is potentially more hazardous to the patient's health than continued obesity." This has been proven to be a false, unsubstantiated statement. In 1974, the Food and Drug Administration required producers of hCG to label the drug with a warning against using it for weight loss or fat redistribution. Interestingly enough, no one has ever come out with a clear definitive statement that the use of hCG as part of the exact Simeons protocol was ineffective or dangerous. It is true that hCG should never be used to treat obesity alone. It must only be used as part of the exact Simeons protocol. According to the FDA, it is in fact legal for doctors in America to prescribe medications for purposes that are not approved by the FDA. This suggests that doctors in America can prescribe hCG to be used as part of the Simeons protocol, even though this purpose has not been approved by the FDA.

Question:	My doctor says this won't work and is not safe.
Answer:	Find another doctor. If your doctor has not personally treated patients using the Simeons "weight loss cure protocol" exactly and precisely as instructed, how would he know whether the protocol was effective and safe? Thousands of medical doctors around the world over the last thirty years have treated hundreds of thousands of patients. The success rate is almost 100%. There has never been a single patient that has been reported to have any negative side effects during or after the Simeons "weight loss cure protocol" was administered. The safety and efficacy of this protocol is absolutely without question. There is not one bit of evidence showing that even a single patient has had any negative side effects as long as they have done the Simeons "weight loss cure protocol" precisely and accurately as described. Thousands of medical doctors all can't be wrong. Hundreds of thousands of patients all can't be hallucinating about their successful fat reduction and weight loss. I personally did this program and, like hundreds of thousands of other successful patients, can attest that everything about it is true.
Question:	Are there doctors and clinics using this treatment now?
Answer:	Yes. I have personally talked to numerous medical doctors around the world who are currently treating patients with the Simeons "weight loss cure protocol." Because of the overwhelming desire by the pharmaceutical industry, food industry, and various government agencies to suppress the truth about this obesity cure, most of these doctors asked not to be mentioned by name in this book. Doing so would subject them to persecution and possible prosecution for curing obesity in patients. At www.naturalcures.com I will be listing doctors and clinics around the world that are administering the

Simeons "weight loss cure protocol." One fearless doctor using this method is Dr. Daniel Belluscio, M.D. For most of Dr. Belluscio's medical career, he has been devoted to the study of hCG and the Simeons method for weight loss. He spent many years at the Bellevue Klinik in Switzerland, an institution with one of the most impressive records of using hCG in the treatment of obesity. He has traveled extensively, lecturing on HCG and obesity in the U.S.A., Sweden, Italy, Germany, and Israel. He has published several reports on the method for health care practitioners and articles on the subject for the general public. In 1987, Dr. Belluscio founded the hCG Research Clinic, an institution for obesity research. Records show that the clinic has used the hCG approached on over 6,500 patients to date. This reliable and effective method for obesity management has been validated by appropriate double-blind studies. Information on this clinic is available at www.hcgobesity.org.

Question: Isn't 500 calories a day too low to be safe?

Answer: No. Research now confirms that eating very low calorie diets actually increase overall health, have anti-aging effects, and increase lifespan. This was reported recently in *The New York Times*. Most importantly, however, is when you are doing the diet combined with the hCG injections, your body is being flooded with over 2,000 calories of nutrition from the releasing of the abnormal fat reserves. This is one of the reasons that during Phase 2, consisting of the diet and hCG injections, you are not hungry and generally have an increase in energy levels.

Question: During the diet in Phase 2 will I have vitamin, mineral, or other nutritional deficiencies due to the low food consumption?

Answer: No. During the three- to six-week Phase 2 period your body is releasing massive amounts of stored nutrition from the fat cells that are being synthesized. Extensive studies have been conducted on patients throughout the protocol proving that no nutritional deficiencies develop. Therefore, during Phase 2 you should not be consuming anything other than those listed in the instructions. This includes no vitamin, mineral, or food supplements.

Question: Have any changes been made to the original Simeons "weight loss cure protocol"?

Answer: Phases 2 and 3 are, in fact, the original instructions as described in Simeons's manuscript *Pounds and Inches: A New Approach to Obesity.* There are two exceptions. Simeons used 125 IE of hCG. He suggested that taking larger amounts do not improve results, but rather have the opposite effect. Doctors in the 1970s and 1980s began dealing with patients who had many more issues and causes of abnormal hypothalamus activity than Simeons dealt with. Therefore, after Simeons's death in 1970, doctors began researching with slightly higher amounts of hCG. It was found that between 175 and 200 IEs were the optimal daily doses. Remember, this is an incredibly small amount of hCG. During pregnancy women are flooded with over 300,000 IEs of hCG on a daily basis. Doctors routinely administer 6,000 or more IEs of hCG to patients with various medical conditions. Taking 125 to 200 IEs daily for three to six weeks is an incredibly small amount. How much you should take should be determined between you and your doctor. The minimum is 125 IEs, as Simeons originally instructed, and the maximum should be no more than 200 IEs.

The second modification to Simeons's original protocol is the exclusion of melba toast, or an Italian grissino breadstick with lunch and dinner. It has been found that by eliminating the small melba toast or grissino breadstick from the lunch and dinner meals speeds up the fat burning process.

Simeons also did not include Phase 1 or Phase 4 of the current protocol. This is because all of the issues that are addressed in Phase 1 and Phase 4 did not exist in the 1950s and 1960s when Simeons was treating patients.

Question: Why was the Simeons "weight loss cure protocol" kept a secret and why don't food companies, drug companies, and the government want us to know the truth about its effectiveness and safety?

Answer: It was kept secret because the doctors who are using the treatment successfully know full-well that they will be criticized, debunked, persecuted, and prosecuted for curing people of their obesity. Remember, the more overweight, fat, and obese people there are, the more money the drug companies, the food companies, and the diet industry companies make. It's pure economics. It's all about money and profits. These companies will go to the greatest lengths of deception and fraud to increase their profits. A prime example of the deceit and fraud these companies partake in is the recent initiative brokered by former president Bill Clinton with soft drink manufacturers and school systems. President Clinton announced that he had brokered a deal with the soft drink manufacturers that would help fight obesity and promote health in school children. His announcement was that the soft drink manufacturers would no longer be selling soft drinks in schools through vending machines and at school lunch programs. This was supposed to help reduce the large consumption of sugar contained in soft drinks. This sounds like a wonderful thing. It was made to appear that the soft drink companies were losing profits and were sincerely interested in helping fight obesity in school age children. This is a great lie and deception. What they didn't tell you is that the number of soft drink vending machines in the schools continues to increase. The number of soft drink dispensers in school lunch programs continues to increase. The most significant thing they did not tell you was that diet sodas will continue to be sold and served to our children! This is a huge profit windfall for the soft drink manufacturers. Soft drink companies want to sell more diet sodas than regular sodas. Why? Diet sodas are cheaper to make and are more profitable. Diet sodas contain artificial sweeteners, including NutraSweet and Splenda, that are physically, chemically addicting. Diet sodas also increase depression and obesity. Diet sodas are being called the new crack. Soft drink manufacturers are popping the Champagne over this initiative. They are like crack cocaine dealers, selling their product to young school children, getting them physically and chemically addicted and creating a life-long consumer who cannot stop consuming their products. The drug companies, the food companies, and the diet industry companies do not want you to know the truth about the safety and effectiveness of the Simeons "weight loss cure protocol" because it absolutely will cost them huge profits. They are so fearful about this information becoming accepted that they are paying lobbyists tens of millions of dollars to get lawmakers to enact legislation that will stop this information being disseminated and used by the masses. Additionally, this information is blowing the whistle and exposing the dirty secrets about how the food industry is purposefully designing and creating food that makes us physically, chemically addicted, increase our hunger and appetites, and actually make us fat! Exposing how the food companies are purposefully creating the obesity epidemic, it is putting great fear in the executives who could face massive multibillion class action suits from angry citizens who have been duped, lied to, and deceived by these multinational publicly traded corporations.

Question: What are your sources for the information in this book?

Answer: I have traveled over five million miles researching non-drug and non-surgical ways to cure and prevent disease. My research and investigations have been going on for over twenty years. I am not a medical doctor, and have no formal medical training. I am simply reporting to you the facts as an investigative journalist. I have interviewed over 5,000 medical doctors and health care practitioners around the world. I have read over 1,000 books on various health subjects. I have interviewed hundreds of authors who have focused on various areas of health care. I have dozens of inside sources at the FDA, the Centers for Disease Control, the FTC, the National Institutes of Health, and other state and federal agencies who provide me inside, top secret information. I have inside sources at dozens of pharmaceutical companies, food companies, and diet industry companies that have supplied me with massive amounts of secret documents. I have personally been involved, on a covert basis, with pharmaceutical companies and government agencies around the world. I have interviewed thousands of patients who have gone through these various protocols. I have reviewed hundreds of thousands of pages of scientific documents, studies, and doctor/patient records. I have personally done this protocol myself and have the best firsthand experience on reporting it to you.

Question: Isn't obesity just caused by overeating?

Answer: No. Dr. Simeons states in his manuscript that most obese patients do not suffer from compulsive overeating; they suffer genuine hunger. This real, gnawing, torturing hunger has nothing to do whatever with compulsive overeating. Sudden desires for sweets are a result of Candida yeast overgrowth and from the subconscious knowledge that highly refined food will relieve the hunger faster than any other kind of food. Compulsive overeating differs fundamentally from the obese patient's actual genuine hunger and real greater need for food. Compulsive overeating can be a frightening, ugly spectacle to behold. The mechanisms causing this reaction are entirely beyond the patient's control. These eating frenzies are also caused by the mental triggers and hypnotic suggestions implanted in our minds by the food companies' coercive television, radio, and print advertising. The solution to this condition is the LifeForce Plan, comprehensive Candida cleanse, a complete and comprehensive colon cleanse, liver cleanse, parasite cleanse, and heavy metal detox. The Purification Program is also a required course of treatment that will help alleviate the physical and biological causes of this disorder. www.purification.org or www.clearbodyclearmind.com. Handling nutritional deficiencies via whole food supplementation is also required. Stress reduction by taking AlphaCalm and listening to stress reducing CDs also are needed. Deprogramming the mind by reading books that expose the coercive nature of advertising is an effective solution to the hypnotic triggers that we carry with us. In Simeons's time people suffering from compulsive eating disorders constituted less than 2% of patients. Today estimates vary between 30% and 50% of all obese individuals suffer from this disorder.

Question: Could it be that I actually have a fear or reluctance of losing weight?

Answer: Dr. Simeons stated that some patients are consciously or unconsciously deeply attached to their fat and cannot bear the thought of losing it. Some people have subconsciously worked out a pattern in life in which their obesity plays a determining role, and then become subconsciously reluctant to upset this pattern and face a new kind of life which will be entirely different when their bodies have become normal and very attractive. This condition can be corrected. One known recommended technology for this and other mental and emotional issues, as well as psychosomatic illness, is Dianetics. www.dianetics.com.

Question: Does the weight loss protocol get rid of cellulite?

Answer: In most cases, absolutely yes! If you are very strict and fully commit to all of the dos and don'ts in Phase 1, complete a full course of treatment in Phases 2 and 3, and partake in all the suggestions in Phase 4, cellulite can vanish completely in a one- to six-month period of time.

Question: How do I prepare and inject hCG?

Answer: HCG is available by prescription only. It is a pure substance extracted from the urine of pregnant women. The form that is to be used in this protocol is human chorionic gonadotrophin, not any animal form. It should come as a highly soluble powder. These preparations are carefully standardized, and any brand made by a reliable, approved pharmaceutical company is acceptable. The hCG should be extracted from the urine and not from the placenta. It must be of human and not animal origin. In fake, false, and misleading studies done around the world, animal hCG or hCG from the placenta was used, which will, of course, not work. The powder should be sealed in small ampoules where the amount is stated in international units. Be sure to check the date of manufacture and expiry. Once the date of expiry has passed, the hCG becomes useless. A suitable solvent solution is always supplied in a separate ampoule in the same package. Once the hCG powder is mixed with the solution it must be used within a few hours. Some say that the hCG will stay fully potent for two to three days after mixing. There is debate about whether this is true. Ideally, take the injection of hCG immediately upon mixing it into a solution. HCG, when injected, produces little if any tissue reaction. It is completely painless, and in the many thousands of injections Simeons has given he has never seen a negative reaction at the site of the injection. The injection is done deep intragluteally in the outer upper quadrant of the buttocks. Ideally the injection should not be given into the superficial fat layers, but should reach the muscle. It is important that the daily injection be taken at the same time each morning. Always do these injections while under the care and supervision of a medical doctor.

Question: Must I gorge for the first two days in Phase 2?

Answer: Yes. Dr. Simeons states that a person will not be comfortable on the 500 calorie diet unless his normal fat reserves are reasonably well stocked. It is for this reason that in every case a person must eat to capacity the most fattening food they can get down for the first two days in Phase 2. It is a fundamental mistake to start the 500 calorie diet as soon as hCG injections are started as it seems to take about three injections before abnormal fat deposits begin to get released and circulate, thus becoming available to the body as fuel.

Question: How do I measure the 100 grams of protein?

Answer: Use a highly accurate small kitchen scale. Always weigh the protein raw.

Question: Can I substitute smoked fish, pickled fish, or deli meats?

Answer: Absolutely not. Nothing smoked, dried, or pickled. Never use deli meats. The meats must be of the leanest variety, trimming off any and all visible fat. The meat must be 100% organic otherwise it will contain growth hormone, antibiotics, and other animal drugs which slowdown or stop the fat burning process.

Farm raised fish should never be used as these are loaded with man-made chemicals and food dyes which will slow down or stop the fat burning process. Simeons was very specific that grass fed beef and veal be used, otherwise the animals were fed genetically modified grain and animal parts, creating an abnormally high fat content and fat marbling of the beef and veal. Eating beef and veal that is not grass fed and 100% organic will slow down or stop the fat burning process. The amounts must be extremely accurate. One hundred grams is 100 grams!

Question: Can I mix vegetables?

Answer: No, with one exception. You can make a salad consisting of various organic lettuces, organic cabbage, organic spinach, organic celery, organic onions, organic cucumbers, organic radishes, and organic tomatoes. Season with organic raw apple cider vinegar, or the juice of one-half an organic lemon. Add sea salt, black pepper, crushed garlic, in any amounts of dried or fresh organic herbs. It's delicious and filling!

Question: Can't I change some food items on the diet?

Answer: No. You must be very strict in following the diet exactly if you want to achieve results. Simeons was very particular in his research about how even the smallest change or variation would slow down or stop the fat burning process completely. He said that the diet used in conjunction with the hCG injections must not exceed 500 calories per day. He also stated that the way these calories are made up is of the utmost important. He pointed out that if a patient dropped the apple and had a little more protein he would not be getting any more calories, but he would not lose weight. There are a number of foods, particularly fruits and vegetables, which have the same or even lower caloric values than those listed as permissible. However, when substitutions are made Simeons found that they interfere with the regular loss of weight under hCG. This is due to the nature of their chemical compositions. Simeons also noted that beef in Europe was quite different than beef from America. If it's not on the list do not eat it.

Question: Can I eat lamb, pork, shellfish, duck, or venison while on the 500 calorie Phase 2 diet?

Answer: No.

Question: Will I be hungry during this protocol?

Answer: During Phase 1 you can never be hungry because there is no restriction on the amount of food you eat. In Phase 2 you may have slight hunger between one and seven days. This will depend on how much of Phase 1 you did. During Phase 3 you cannot be hungry because there is no limit to the amount of food you consume. In Phase 4 you can never be hungry because the hypothalamus has now been reset, lowering your natural hunger and there are no limits to the amount of food you consume. Do not be fearful of this program because you are horrified at the thought of enduring torturous hunger. Like the hundreds of thousands of other people who have gone through this protocol, you will find the process enjoyable and relatively easy.

Question: Can I use artificial sweeteners while on this protocol?

Answer: No. You should never use any artificial sweeteners ever again for as long as you live. All artificial sweeteners, including NutraSweet and Splenda, should never be consumed. They increase depression, are physically, chemically addicting, and they make you fat.

Question: Can I use MSG (monosodium glutamate)?

Answer: No. You should never eat anything with MSG in it ever again as long as you live. It is a deadly, dangerous excitotoxin. It increases depression, increases appetite, and makes you fat.

Question: Can I swim or use hot tubs?

Answer: Although swimming is fantastic exercise, I do not recommend it because almost all swimming pools today are loaded with deadly chlorine. All tap water is loaded with chlorine and fluoride. Swimming pools and hot tubs have additional chlorine and other poisonous chemicals added to them. The skin is the largest organ in the body. Being in a swimming pool or hot tub means you are flooding your bloodstream and body cells with deadly chlorine, fluoride, and other poisonous chemicals. These chemicals, once on your skin and in your body, create hormonal imbalances leading to a host of problems including depression, PMS, digestive disorders, and obesity. I have a swimming pool and hot tub; however, no chlorine or any chemicals are used. The water has been filtered through ultraviolet light, granular activated charcoal impregnated with silver, and other organic filtering material. It is kept clean, with infusing of ozone and oxygen. It is actually super healthy to drink the water, never mind swim in it! Swimming in the ocean or lakes is highly beneficial and recommended. Watch out, however, as certain natural water sources can be heavily polluted.

Question: While on the protocol can I use gum, mints, lozenges, or cough syrup?

Answer: No, no, no, no!

Question: If I'm not hungry while doing Phase 2, do I still have to eat everything as described?

Answer: Yes. Whether you're hungry or not, you must eat the lunch and dinner in their complete form. You cannot have one big meal per day. You may take the apple from either lunch or dinner and eat it at breakfast. No other changes or substitutions are allowed as they slow or stop the fat burning process.

Question: What if I cheat on the diet during Phase 2?

Answer: If you do cheat for a meal or for one or two days in a row, all it means is that the weight loss process will stop for a few days or a temporary slight increase in weight may occur. Immediately start the diet again at the next meal and carry on. If you cheat on a meal every other day, you are wasting your time.

Question: What if I have low energy or hunger during Phase 2?

Answer: Some patients may be dealing with insulin resistance or low blood sugar. The solution is to make sure you are drinking Eleotin tea as the instructions dictate. Make sure at breakfast you drink organic Yerba Mate tea. Drink several cups of organic Yerba Mate tea throughout the day. Also, take the apple from either the lunch or dinner meal and eat it for breakfast. Low energy could also be caused by a hypoactive thyroid, Candida yeast overgrowth, poor circulation, or parasites. If you did the steps in Phase 1, low energy should not be a major concern. It is extremely rare that low energy persists for more than a day or two during Phase 2. It has never been reported that low energy ever reaches the point of being de-habilitating. If you are experiencing low energy, know that the condition is temporary and will be addressed by following Phases 3 and 4.

Question: Can I drink juices while doing the protocol?

Answer: During Phase 2, since juices are not on the list, you cannot drink them. However, in Phases 1, 3, and 4 you may drink juices. Ideally, you want to drink made fresh at home with a juice machine such a JuiceMan, or Jack LaLane Power Juicer. Use organic fruits and vegetables and drink the juice within an hour after juicing. There are "magic juices" that I recommend called goji, mangosteen, acai berry, noni, and aloe vera. Note that almost all juice purchased that comes in a bottle, carton, can, or any container should be 100% organic. Most of these juices have been pasteurized. This means they have been heated to over 180 degrees for thirty minutes, killing all the living enzymes and concentrating the sugar levels making them highly refined or super highly refined. Many juices have sugar added even though they claim on the label that there is no added sugar. Drinking juices purchased from the supermarket, therefore, is not ideal.

Question: What about human growth hormone, testosterone, or other hormone treatments?

Answer: Receiving any hormone replacement therapy such as injections of human growth hormone or testosterone can produce increased muscle mass, increased energy, and fat reduction. There are many anti-aging benefits. However, once you start taking hormones your body shuts down its normal hormone production. This means you are actually making the condition worse in the long run. You will be a slave to taking the hormone injections for the rest of your life. This is serious business and you should strongly consider all options before taking such drastic measures. There are, however, homeopathic substances which stimulate the body to produce human growth hormone naturally. One such product is called Renewal, available at www.alwaysyoung.com.

Question: Can I take apple cider vinegar tablets instead of the liquid?

Answer: Organic raw apple cider vinegar in liquid form is the best. However, it is better to take apple cider vinegar tablets than taking nothing at all. I personally take apple cider vinegar tablets on the occasions where it is inconvenient to take the liquid form. Remember, organic raw apple cider vinegar has almost miraculous health enhancing effects, as well as helping reduce fat deposits in the body.

Question: Must I eat breakfast as well as eating six times per day?

Answer: Yes. Dr. Simeons stated that one of the causes of obesity was eating infrequently and having extremely large meals. The human body's digestive system is designed to eat smaller meals every few hours. The body is designed to handle food that is raw or unrefined. The human body's digestive tract is similar to primates; it best operates with continual nibbling. It is not suited for gorging followed by long periods of time without food. Thus, skipping breakfast, eating a light lunch, and a huge dinner places a great unnatural burden on the digestive system and intestinal tract. In today's society we eat large meals which contain more food than the body requires at the moment in order to tide us over until the next meal. This food has been produced to be easily digestible, is highly refined, and floods the body with nourishment and calories for which it has no immediate need and cannot physically handle. The body must store this surplus somehow somewhere, thus creating fat deposits. This is why experts agree that eating breakfast, a snack mid-morning, lunch, a snack mid-afternoon, dinner, and a snack in the evening, is one of the healthiest, best long-term approaches for weight management and better health.

Question: Can I eat salt?

Answer: During all the phases salt may be consumed, however, always choose sea salt or Himalayan salt. Ideally, use salt in minimal amounts and use approximately the same amount of salt each day. A sudden increase in salt intake during Phase 2 will be followed by a corresponding temporary increase in weight. It does not influence the loss of fat however. It will only create retention of water, which will show up as increased weight on the scale. Therefore, during

Phase 2 keep your salt intake close to the same every day.

Question: The instructions in all the phases call for a large consumption of water and teas. Is this necessary?

Answer: During all the phases you should drink a minimum of one-half gallon of water per day, up to a maximum of one gallon. In addition to the water intake you should be drinking several cups of the recommended teas. This is, in fact, a large amount of liquid. It is important in the treatment of the obesity condition. The importance and benefits of adhering to the water and tea intake cannot be overemphasized. It is absolutely vital in order for the protocol to work effectively.

Question: Must I eliminate cosmetics, moisturizers, lotions, and creams during Phase 2?

Answer: Yes. Dr. Simeons stated that most people find it hard to believe that the fats, oils, creams, and ointments applied to the skin are absorbed into the body and interfere with the weight reduction by hCG just as if those ingredients were eaten. This almost incredible sensitivity to even such very minor increases in nutritional and caloric intake is a peculiar feature of the hCG method. Simeons found that persons who habitually handle fats, such as workers in beauty parlors, masseuses, butchers, etc. never show a satisfactory loss of weight when using hCG unless they avoid all contact with the skin of such fats and various products. Simeons illustrated this important point with two cases. A lady who was following the protocol perfectly suddenly increased half a pound. No dietary error was made and she used no face creams of any kind. Menses was not an issue as she was already past menopause. This puzzled the doctors. Finally, she realized that she had bought herself a new set of makeup, pots, and bottles. She used her fingers to transfer her large assortment of cosmetics to the new containers. This was enough to create absorption through the skin, which in turn adversely affected the hCG weight reduction results. Another case concerned a man Simeons treated who was twenty pounds overweight. From the first day of Phase 2 he did not lose weight at a satisfactory level. He followed the program exactly, but still without the anticipated one pound per day weight loss. In questioning, the patient explained to Simeons that he had a glass eye. He changed and cleaned the eye daily, putting a very special ointment into his eye socket. The patient was told to stop using the ointment immediately. From that day forward his weight loss became satisfactory and consistent.

Many modern cosmetics contain hormones which interfere with endocrine regulations in the body and must be avoided. Remember, whatever you put on the skin is absorbed into the body just as though you ate it.

Question: What about abdominal exercises and aerobics?

Answer: Aerobic exercise has many health benefits. In terms of resetting the body weight set point, walking one hour per day outside is much more effective. In terms of increasing metabolism and flushing the body of toxins, yoga and rebounding is more effective. In terms of increasing muscle mass, strength, and tone, as well as getting the body to release anti-aging hormones, resistance training such as weight lifting is more effective. Aerobic exercise is extremely healthy and beneficial and should be engaged in by everyone at any level you desire.

Abdominal exercises or fancy abdominal exercise machines do, in fact, strengthen and tone the abdominal muscles. They will not, however, burn fat around the waist, midsection, or stomach. They will not eliminate the "love handles." They will never flatten the stomach. I have been in the TV infomercial and direct response industry for over twenty years. I know most of the people selling these abdominal products. The joke in the industry is that "These products are for selling, not for using!" The advertisements for these products are all false and misleading. I should know because I was involved in the production of many of them. If you want to get a flat stomach and eliminate the fat around the waist and midsection you must do "the weight loss cure protocol" in its entirety. If you want stronger, more defined abdominal muscles, then abdominal exercises are effective. But, you'll never see those defined abdominal muscles unless you get rid of the layer of fat that is covering them!

Question: What if I have problems sleeping?

Answer: Getting seven to eight hours of deep sleep is important for health and makes you lose weight. This research comes from Dr. Neal Kohatsu from the California Department of Health Services. He states, "Even a modest increase in sleep duration has shown to have a clinically significant affect on weight." Sleep disorders are caused by nutritional deficiencies, MSG, and other excitotoxins, artificial sweeteners, the massive amounts of caffeine and other stimulants consumed on a daily basis, trans fats, toxic ingredients in the products you put on the skin, chlorine and fluoride in the water you shower and bathe in, parasites, and several other factors. If you do all the steps in Phase 1 and Phase 4, your ability to fall asleep and sleep fully and deeply the entire night should be normalized within ninety days. Studies show over 50% of Americans deal with some kind of sleep problems at least two to three times per week. Another cause of sleep disorders is non-prescription and prescription drug use. Most common over-the-counter non-prescription and prescription drugs actually cause sleep issues.

Non-prescription and prescription sleeping aids are one of the most profitable market segments for drug companies. Like obesity, the food companies and drug companies are specifically designing products and food that cause sleep disorders. This is done purposely so that more sleeping pills will be sold and corporate profits will continue to sky-rocket. Isn't it interesting that fifty years ago virtually no one had a hard time falling asleep and staying asleep? Isn't it bizarre that today almost everyone has a hard time falling asleep even though they are physically exhausted? This condition has been created by the food companies and the drug companies themselves! When you go through all four phases of this protocol your sleep disorders will be corrected.

Question: What about all these diet pills, patches, and products that claim to burn fat, reduce hunger, increase metabolism, block carbs, etc.?

Answer: Repeat after me...scam, scam, scam, scam! They are rip offs and do not work! Remember, I know most of the people who sell these worthless products! For years I was involved in the production of the labels and advertising of these products. Everything about these products is false, misleading, and deceptive. They absolutely, categorically do not work. Do not waste your money. In some cases they will temporarily, slightly reduce hunger or increase metabolic rate. However, when you stop taking the product your hunger comes back stronger than ever before, and your metabolism is lower than before! You will gain all the weight back, plus ten pounds! None of these products allow you to burn or release the secure problem area fat reserves. When you use them, any weight you lose will be either muscle or important structural fat. If a product is ever invented that actually works I will personally endorse it and give all my endorsement royalties to charity!

Question: What about all these doctors and celebrities who endorse weight loss products or various food products?

Answer: Celebrities, doctors, and everyone who endorses products does so for three reasons. Money... money... and money. It's always all about the money. These endorsers will say anything about the product as long as they get the check. I should know because I hired celebrities and doctors to endorse products I was involved with over the last twenty years. I can tell you that if you heard what these people say about what they truly think of these products it would make you sick. When you see them on television looking so sincere, and telling you how wonderful their life is because of this product, drug, or food, you must know that they are simply reading a script. They are professional actors doing what they do best...acting! If you saw the outtakes, and heard their comments after the filming is completed, you would see that you are being mislead and lied to. In most cases the celebrities and doctors endorsing products do not even use the products they are endorsing. Remember, these doctors and celebrities are paid millions of dollars to endorse, recommend, and help companies sell their products. This is nothing more than deceptive and fraudulent advertising at its highest.

Question: After I do Phases 1, 2, and 3 should I continue weighing myself every day?

Answer: Yes. Because you have dealt with the obesity condition for so long, it is important to weigh yourself every day to make sure that you are maintaining your new lower weight. This will help keep you focused on doing the steps in Phase 4, thus making sure your bad habits do not return and the weight stays off permanently.

Question: Will this protocol restore structural fat that may have been lost during years of severe yo-yo dieting?

Answer: Yes. Dr. Simeons discovered a curious condition that was common among patients who have engaged in severe on and off dieting for years. These patients had sagging skin and an unbearable pain in their heels which they feel while standing or walking. When the heels of the feet were examined the patients were found to have less than normal structural fat around the bones. This created great pain while standing or walking. This showed that the patients lost important structural fat during their past dieting episodes. Even when these patients ate to capacity and gained weight, these structural fat deposits did not return to normal. Even with rapid and large weight gain, there was no improvement in the painful heels. In all patients tested, Simeons found that within twenty days of the hCG protocol, as outlined in Phase 2, the pain completely disappeared. In follow-up over many years, no reoccurring pain ever was recorded. This Simeons believed was further proof that the hCG, plus specific diet protocol, not only removes abnormal secure problem area fat deposits, but actually permits the body to replace important structural fat in needed areas. This occurs in spite of the low caloric intake of food.

Question: Will I gain the weight back?

Answer: If you go back to eating fast food, restaurant food, and food containing trans fats, high fructose corn syrup, super highly refined food, artificial sweeteners, meat, poultry and dairy with growth hormone and antibiotics, etc., etc., etc., you will, in fact, mess up your hypothalamus again and regain the weight. If, however, you follow the dos and don'ts in Phase 4, the weight should never return. It is interesting to note that Simeons's patients of the 1950s and 1960s very rarely, if ever, gained the weight back. This is because fast food, trans fats, high fructose corn syrup, etc. was not in widespread use. Today, however, because the food industry is on a mission to create an obese world, it is more difficult to avoid all of the new things that cause obesity. Follow the steps in Phase 4 and you should be able to keep the weight off forever.

Question: If the weight comes back can I do this protocol again?

Answer: Yes. If you lose a substantial amount of weight and a year later find you have gained some weight back, do the protocol as often as you desire. I know of many people that have lost sixty pounds or more who find themselves gaining ten to fifteen pounds over a year's time. Rather than let their weight gain get out of hand, they do Phase 2 of the protocol for three weeks each year to lose the weight because they have found it is the easiest and most effective way to lose abnormal fat and has the best long-term effects.

Question: What if the food label says "all natural"?

Answer: Today, the phrase "all natural" means absolutely nothing! Major food manufacturers have lobbied congress allowing new laws to be passed defining what can legally be called "all natural." Even if the food contains thousands of chemicals and is heavily processed, it is still legal to use the phrase "all natural." This is deceptive. If the food is labeled "all natural" the company is trying to deceive you. You must read the ingredient list on the food. Look for 100% organic.

Question: Should I buy food that says "diet," "lite," "low fat," "low carb," "fat free," etc.?

Answer: No. These are marketing ploys and scams designed to deceive you. Always read the ingredient list on the product labels. Always look for 100% organic.

Question: What if I'm skeptical and nervous about using this protocol?

Answer: Dr. Simeons found that patients were often skeptical about the claims that this protocol could be done without hunger and would deliver fast and long-term results. He overcame this by letting new patients spend some time in the waiting room with patients who were currently engaged in the protocol. The existing patients would always explain to the potential new patients, with evangelical zeal, the ease and spectacular results they were achieving. When new potential patients heard firsthand and saw with their own eyes the results, skepticism, apprehension, and anxiety was always relieved. I would encourage you to visit www.hcgobesity.org and view before and after photos of actual patients who have engaged in this protocol. Also go to www.naturalcures.com and look under the weight loss section. Read Dr. Simeons's manuscript *Pounds and Inches: A New Approach to Obesity* for yourself. Read actual patient testimonials from real people who have done this protocol. Do not listen to doctors or the news media that have a direct financial interest in keeping the truth about this protocol hidden. Do not listen to any government official, medical doctor, journalist, reporter, or individual who has not personally done the exact original Simeons "weight loss cure protocol" exactly as outlined. If they haven't actually done it themselves they cannot possibly give a legitimate opinion!

Question: Do I really need to eat organic grass fed beef, organic poultry, and organic milk, cheese, and dairy products?

Answer: Yes. Unless it is 100% organic, the animals and dairy products will be loaded with growth hormones, antibiotics, and other animal drugs. When you consume meat, poultry, and dairy you are, in fact, consuming these animal growth hormones and drugs. This causes health problems in the body, depression, and leads to obesity. If the animals are not 100% organic and grass fed, they are fed genetically modified grain, man-made chemical food products, and ground up dead animals. This creates meat, poultry and dairy products that are unnatural and will, in fact, lead to obesity and other diseases.

Question: Why are fast food, and regional and chain restaurants so bad?

Answer: All restaurant food is designed to make you fat. The worst offenders are fast food chains. All regional and national chain restaurants should also be avoided. Virtually all restaurants have their food produced by the same small group of multinational food companies. Almost all restaurant food comes premade, premixed, preseasoned, freeze dried, frozen, or in jars and cans. Restaurants today do not cook food from scratch. They are not using fresh organic ingredients. Most food served in these kinds of restaurant are simply reheated! The food sold in fast food restaurants, regional and national restaurants, and most other restaurants are loaded to the highest degree with the specific ingredients that cause obesity. These include super highly refined sugars, such as high fructose corn syrup, corn syrup, sucrose, and dextrose; trans fats, such as hydrogenated or partially hydrogenated oils; artificial sweeteners, including aspartame and sucrolos; meat, poultry, and dairy loaded with growth hormone, antibiotics, and other animal drugs; virtually no food with any fiber; food that is super highly refined and extremely high on the glycemic index; monosodium glutamate and other excitotoxins; and meals that are massively high in calories. This situation permeates American culture and is spreading all around the world. Wherever these kinds of restaurants spring up, and this kind of food is sold, obesity springs up as well. We know that smoking cigarettes causes cancer. The tobacco companies lied about this known fact for fifty years. We now know that eating food from fast food restaurants, regional and national chain restaurants, and most other restaurants, absolutely causes obesity. These companies have done this purposely and are lying to us now about this true fact.

Question: Will you be setting up clinics around the world offering this protocol?

Answer: I am assisting medical doctors around the world in setting up clinics where this protocol can be taught and administered. For a list of doctors who administer this protocol, and clinics that offer this protocol, go to www.naturalcures.com. Look under the weight loss section.

Question: Do you have any recipes that work with this protocol?

Answer: Yes. I intend on coming out with a cookbook in the future. I am not a chef. I do, however, cook simple, delicious meals almost every day. Fantastic meals can be made from scratch in less than an hour and, in most cases, in less than thirty minutes. If I can cook, anybody can cook! I should have a show on the *Food Network*! Call or e-mail them and let them know you think so as well. For current recipes and DVDs with cooking instructions go to www.naturalcures.com.

Question: What if I show no weight loss four days in a row while on Phase 2?

Answer: Dr. Simeons discussed at length daily weight fluctuations or reaching weight plateaus. He explained that at times there may be no drop of weight at all for two or three days, which is then followed by a sudden large drop which reestablishes the normal daily average of about one pound per day during Phase 2. Weight fluctuations occur more so in women than in men. If a person weighs themselves and notices that the weight stays the same for four days in a row, the patient is told that after weighing on the fourth morning, to only eat six organic apples for that day. The patient is told to drink nothing except a small amount of water, just enough to quench their thirst when needed. Two cups of corn silk tea should be consumed. The next morning there should be a drop in weight. If not, do not be concerned. It is important to note that because this protocol is synthesizing and releasing so much abnormal fat, the body may retain excess water in order to rid the system of this excess released fat and accompanying toxins. This at times results in no apparent weight loss on the scale, however, you must know that the body is still being reshaped, and massive fat loss is still occurring.

Question: Can I do Phase 1 for longer than thirty days?

Answer: Yes. You can do the items in Phase 1 for as short or as long as you want. Doing if for a minimum of thirty days immediately before starting Phase 2 is ideal. Some people have done the steps in Phase 1 for forty-five, sixty, even ninety days before starting Phase 2. This was mainly due to the fact that Phase 1 has no restrictions on the amount of food you can consume. Patients found doing Phase 1 was easy and they saw consistent weight loss; therefore, because they were apprehensive about doing Phase 2, they simply continued with doing the steps in Phase 1. This is entirely acceptable. In actual fact, if you were to do all the steps in Phase 1 with strict adherence for ninety to 120 days in a row you would actually begin to reset the body's weight set point and correct the abnormal hypothalamus condition. Weight loss would be slow, but you would in fact be releasing abnormal secure fat deposits. This is another alternative for those who do not want or are unable to do the hCG protocol. If you do Phase 1 for an extended period of time you should do the LifeForce Plan Candida cleanse (www.lifeforceplan.com), as well as a liver cleanse and a parasite cleanse, to achieve the full results of resetting the hypothalamus.

Question: Can I take higher doses of hCG?

Answer: Simeons said never go above 200 International Units of hCG a day. He also said do not take a larger amount and increasing the duration between injections. Therefore, do not take a weekly injection, for example. You must take only between 125-200 IUs, and this must be taken every day during the protocol.

Question: Can I stay on Phase 2 longer than six weeks?

Answer: Simeons found that the body has a tendency to create an immunity to hCG. Therefore, staying on Phase 2 for longer than six weeks is not advised. You must take at least a six-week break before you start the injections and protocol of Phase 2 again. This is important, as once your body starts developing immunity to hCG you will no longer be burning abnormal fat reserves, but rather start burning structural fat and muscle. Therefore, if you complete six weeks of Phase 2, and still desire to lose more weight, you must then do Phase 3 for six weeks. Then, do Phase 2 again up to a maximum of six weeks. If you still have more weight you wish to lose, then do Phase 3 for eight weeks. Then, do Phase 2 again for up to a maximum of six weeks. If you still have more weight you wish to lose, do Phase 3 for ten weeks. Then, do Phase 2 again for a maximum of six weeks. Continue adding two weeks to Phase 3 for as long as you need. When you have reached your desired weight during Phase 2, continue by doing Phase 3 for three weeks, then continue to Phase 4.

Question: What if I'm a vegetarian?

Answer: If you are a vegetarian and cannot do the diet in Phase 2, then it is advised that you not do the Phase 2 Simeons protocol of diet and hCG. Instead, do the Turbo Protein Diet as your Phase 2. Available at www.almased.com.

Question: What if I'm really stressed?

Answer: Stress plays havoc with your hormones and will lead to obesity and other health problems. Good methods of stress reduction include laughing, giving and receiving hugs, playing with pets or children, singing, dancing, drinking small amounts of alcohol, playing a musical instrument, massage and other types of body works, reflexology, acupuncture, listening to stress reducing CDs, walking outside, coral calcium, B-complex, and AlphaCalm. The more you reduce stress the easier weight loss will be.

Question: Is buying food in bulk a good idea?

Answer: No. Research shows that buying in bulk causes people to eat more frequently, and larger quantities of food. Ideally, keep little food in your home. Buy food on a daily basis for daily consumption. This allows you to buy fresher, more nutritious food, as well as reducing the quantity and frequency of food you consume.

Question: What about homogenized dairy products?

Answer: The best dairy products are 100% organic and raw. Raw means the dairy products have not been pasteurized or homogenized. Pasteurization and homogenization of dairy products changes their chemical compositions, making them hard to digest and creating excess mucus in the body. If you can only get homogenized and pasteurized dairy products, limit their use.

Question: Why are the majority of children today fat starting at birth?

Answer: There are many factors causing the majority of children to be classified as overweight, fat, and obese. During pregnancy the mother is releasing secured fat reserves which nourish the child. Because of all the toxins consumed by the mother before conception, these fat reserves are loaded with toxicity, which is transferred to the unborn fetus. What the mother eats transfers to the unborn fetus as well. This means the unborn fetus is being flooded with residues of non-prescription and prescription drugs, herbicides, pesticides, trans fats, artificial sweeteners, and thousands of other chemical compounds. When the child is born, the likelihood that the hypothalamus has already been overtaxed is very high. Not breast feeding and using formula that has been microwaved worsens the condition. Early and massive use of vaccines and antibiotics also cause the hypothalamus to become abnormal, thus creating obese children. School lunch programs and "kids meals" are loaded with the highest amounts of super highly refined food and sugars, lack of fiber, high fructose corn syrup, trans fats, nitrites, and MSG. The kids don't have a chance. Obesity will continue to rise as this is what the food industry wants.

Question: Any suggestions for eating in restaurants?

Answer: Eating in restaurants is a nightmare. The food is heavily processed, loaded with trans fats, high fructose corn syrup, MSG, and lacks fiber. It is almost never fresh. The portions are outrageously huge. The environment in restaurants creates massive overeating, and eating food that is specifically designed to make us fat. On one occasion I was in a restaurant eating breakfast. It noticed on the menu a "fresh fruit salad." I asked the waitress if the fruit salad was fresh. She said yes. When it arrived it was obvious that it was canned, loaded with heavy sugary syrup. I told the waitress that the fruit salad appeared to be canned. She said yes. I was surprised. I asked her, "Didn't you say it was fresh?" She replied, "It is fresh; we opened the can this morning." On another occasion I asked if the chicken wings on the menu came premade and frozen. The waitress said yes, but they were "all-natural." I asked if I could see the bag so I could read the ingredient list.

There were over seventy-five ingredients in these chicken wings, including monosodium glutamate, high fructose corn syrup, and trans fats. It's hard to eat restaurant food. This is why you must consistently do the various cleanses throughout the year to get poisonous toxins out of your system. An effective technique that I use when eating in restaurants is this: knowing that the portions will be enormous, I normally tell the waitress to take half of my food and put it in a "to go bag," and only serve me a half-size portion. This is always more than enough food and makes it so I don't have to use willpower to stop eating. I also order one main course and share it with my dinner companion.

Question: What if I have only ten pounds to lose?

Answer: If you do all the steps in Phase 1 you may lose all the weight you need to. However, the Simeons "weight loss cure protocol" is designed to reshape and re-sculpt the body and release abnormal fat deposits. If you are on Phase 2 and lose all the weight you need before the minimum three weeks has been completed, simply double the amount of food on the diet.

Question: When the FDA, AMA, or FTC says a medical treatment or drug is effective and safe, or ineffective and dangerous, aren't they usually correct in their statements?

Answer: No. These organizations have repeatedly said that thousands of drugs are safe and effective. Later, these drugs, like Vioxx, need to be pulled off the market because so many people are dying or developing major medical conditions. The FDA's history of emphatically claiming a drug is safe, then pulling it off the market because it becomes proven to be unsafe, is full of thousands of such cases. Whistleblowers who work for the FDA claim that the FDA's statements of safety and effectiveness of drugs and surgical procedures can never be trusted. Conversely, when the FDA says that something is not effective and unsafe, they are often proven in court to be lying or making such statements without any substantiation or documentation. There are hundreds of examples where courts have proven that the FDA and various medical boards make statements claiming that certain natural products and procedures are dangerous when there is absolutely no substantiation. Statements made by the AMA, FDA, FTC, and various medical boards can never be trusted. This comes directly from whistle-blowers who are working, or who have worked, directly for these agencies.

Question: Do medical boards, the AMA, FDA, or other organizations really suppress effective cures that could help people?

Answer: Yes. This has been proven in hundreds of documented cases all around the world. The most recent example is two Australian medical doctors who claimed to have discovered that bacteria lives in the stomach which can partially be responsible for ulcers. For over 100 years, the established medical community has known the fact that bacteria does not, and can not, live in the stomach. These medical doctors were ridiculed, harassed, discredited, and almost lost their licenses. After ten years of persecution, "science" finally proved that these two doctors were correct with their discovery. The entire medical establishment was wrong for over 100 years. The doctors received a Nobel Prize for their discovery. Suppression of effective, safe cures is widespread around the world.

Question: Weren't you sued by the Federal Trade Commission and called a habitual false advertiser?

Answer: The U.S. Government has said in their own internal documents that agencies are encouraged to sue, debunk, discredit, and make false allegations against anyone and any company that it deems has taken any action that could expose internal corruption, conflicts of interest, or adversely affect profits of the corporations who are in effect paying the politicians. The FTC has sued and made false accusations against hundreds of individuals and companies that expose the truth about inexpensive, safe and effective, natural cures for medical conditions. I was sued twice by the FTC for allegedly making false, misleading, and unsubstantiated statements in advertising. This is the standard method that the FTC uses to crush whistle-blowers. All of these allegations have been proven in court to be totally false. The FTC was forced to drop all charges against me and sign official court documents stating that after a full investigation, "There is no finding of any wrongdoing by Mr. Trudeau or any of his companies." I have never paid any fines to the FTC. The attacks on me started when I became a whistle-blower exposing the corruption and conflicts of interest in the FTC, FDA, and other state and federal agencies. It is interesting to note that the FTC has never sued a pharmaceutical or food corporation, even though it has been proven in court that they routinely engage in false and misleading advertising and make unsubstantiated claims. U.S. government agencies routinely lie, deceive, and mislead the public in an attempt to protect the profits of large conglomerates. The most obvious example of this is when the United States Supreme Court ruled that the tomato, which is scientifically a fruit, be legally called a vegetable so that additional tax revenue can be generated by the government! I am currently suing the Federal Trade Commission and other government agencies for their blatant and flagrant violations of the U.S. Constitution against me and other citizens. Remember, insiders at these agencies have said themselves that these bureaucracies do not protect citizens, but rather do everything in their power to protect con-glomerate profits.

Question: Should I read your first two books?

Answer: Yes. *Natural Cures "They" Don't Want You To Know About* has sold over six million copies. It exposes in great length the unholy alliance between the drug companies, food companies, media, and government agencies. It gives you the inexpensive, safe and effective, all-natural, non-drug and non-surgical ways to cure and prevent virtually every disease. There are inexpensive, natural alternatives to virtually every drug on the market. This exposé blows the whistle and exposes information that "they" don't want you to know about.

More Natural Cures Revealed: Previously Censored Brand Name Products That Cure Disease picks up where the first book left off and contains information that was actually censored out of the first book by the U.S. Government. Both books give information that is not available anywhere else. They are fast, entertaining, and exciting reads. They are available at www.naturalcures.com and everywhere where books are sold.

Question: Do thoughts play a role in obesity?

Answer: Yes. Remember, you become what you think about. The pictures you have in your mind, what you think about, and what you say with your mouth all have powerful effects on the physiology and can contribute greatly in creating obesity or creating a thin, lean, healthy body. Two effective techniques that can help you use these facts to your advantage are as follows. Write down the phrase "I weigh _____ pounds." Put your goal weight in the blank. Put this card everywhere you can see it, such as on your computer screen, on your TV, on the dashboard of your car, on the mirror in your bathroom, on your refrigerator, etc. Carry it with you at all times. Look at this card as many times as possible throughout the day and say the words out loud. This will help program your mind to create your ideal weight. Another effective technique is to use a computer software program to put your face on a picture of the body that you desire. Put this picture, or pictures, everywhere you can see it throughout the day. Look at this picture as many times as possible. This will help create the picture in your mind that will cause it to be attracted into your life. Thoughts are, in fact, *things*!

Question: Is the media really biased?

Answer: The media is very biased and has major conflicts of interest, which means it can never have objective journalism. All major television networks are owned by multinational corporations that in turn own thousands of companies around the world. The large corporations, therefore, use the television networks to promote their other business holdings. A perfect example is Fox News Network. Fox News is owned by News Corp., which is owned by Rupert Murdock. News Corp owns Harper Collins book publishers. All of the Fox News TV anchors get books published by Harper Collins. They are told to use their television shows to promote their books. Fox also uses its TV network to promote other books sold by Harper Collins. It also uses its network to bash and discredit books published by other publishing companies, such as mine. This happens with every television network. TV news shows are nothing more than commercials promoting products sold by the group's other companies, and discrediting products sold by competitors. Because I expose the drug companies and the fast food industry, most news shows will never have me on as a guest. Because I expose what the news channels are doing and how they deceive the public, I am constantly bashed and discredited by news organizations. Another example is the *Larry King Show* on CNN. I was scheduled to appear on *Larry King* because I had the biggest selling nonfiction book in America. Every major author has been invited as a guest on *Larry King*. When the executives at CNN heard that I was going to be a guest, they immediately ordered Larry King to cancel my appearance. They gave no rational explanation. My insiders at CNN tell me that the executives are petrified that I will expose the CNN news network, its drug company sponsors, and food company sponsors. Because the *Larry King Show* is live, I could not be edited. The major advertisers and senior executives do not want me to educate the public about their unhealthy products. As you can see, there is no objective journalism.

Question: Do electromagnetic frequencies really affect our cells and cause weight gain?

Answer: Yes. All wireless devices, and all electrical wiring, create electromagnetic fields which adversely affect the cells in the body, creating hormonal imbalances leading to fatigue, depression, and weight gain. If you've ever been in your home when the electricity went out you would notice how amazingly quiet everything becomes. You will notice that you begin to feel calmer and more relaxed almost instantly. This occurs when people go camping and sleep in a tent or log cabin without electricity. Without all the electromagnetic fields, the body dramatically relaxes and normalizes. This is why you need some kind of device that can neutralize EMFs.

Question: Do governments and corporations really work together to make us fat?

Answer: Yes. This is not a conspiracy theory. This is pure economics. Governments are pressured by corporations to write laws and do things that protect and increase corporate profits, even at the expense of citizens. Governments around the world have passed laws making corporations legal entities with all the same rights and privileges as human beings! In America, in airports and interstate highways, governments passed laws allowing only fast food restaurants like McDonald's and Burger King to be the exclusive food providers for travelers. Virtually nothing is homemade. This unholy alliance between governments and corporations is not new. Big Tobacco has paid off politicians, allowing cigarettes and other tobacco products to be the only item in America where the ingredients do not have to be listed! This was done because the tobacco companies did not want to show the hundreds of poisonous chemicals put in cigarettes. Ingredients do not have to be listed on food sold in restaurants for the same reason. Some of you may have watched the movie *The Aviator*. I recommend the movie. It shows how Pan American Airlines was paying off politicians to get laws passed giving Pan Am a monopoly for transatlantic travel. The bill that was promoted by the senator from Maine was actually written by the executives of Pan American Airlines! This goes on all the time. A company called Halliburton received massive construction contracts from the government without any other company allowed to bid. It is estimated that Halliburton has overcharged the government in excess of $100 billion in just the last few years! Corruption between corporations and governments continues to rise. One tragic example is when corporations and the super wealthy of the world paid off U.S. politicians to write laws allowing stocks to be bought and sold without exposing the owners. This was because the corporations and super wealthy wanted to be able to buy and sell stocks on inside information without their identities being revealed. The day before the 9/11 tragedy these secret individuals or entities bought massive amounts of airline stocks hoping their value would go down. When 9/11 happened, the airline stocks crashed, and these anonymous individuals and corporations made hundreds of millions of dollars in profits. They obviously knew that the World Trade Center would be attacked by airplanes in this terrorist activity. The government could have easily required that the identities of those who profited be revealed. The government will not do so because it is more concerned about protecting the profits of these corporations and individuals than in protecting American citizens.

Question: Can you define "homemade" or "made from scratch"?

Answer: Making things from scratch means you start with single basic ingredients. Some people are confused about what making something from scratch means. As an example, I had a friend who said she was going to make a pie from scratch. She went out and bought a premade pie crust, bought canned pie filling, and bought Cool Whip topping. This is not making something from scratch. Making a pie from scratch means using flour, water, eggs, salt, and butter to make your crust. It means getting fresh fruit, organic raw sugar, cinnamon sticks, and fresh lemon juice squeezed from a real lemon to make your filling. It means getting fresh organic raw cream and whipping it into whipped cream for your topping. This is making something from scratch. Cookbooks today teach people how to open up cans of soup, use premixed products, and making them believe they are cooking from scratch. These cookbooks are a joke. Because it's so hard to get good food in real life, I suggest doing what I do. I almost always make my own lunch, put it in a lunch bucket, and take it with me. It's easy, it's cheaper, and makes you feel fantastic knowing you're eating food with the best quality organic ingredients, made from scratch!

Question: Do food companies really lie to us about their products just to make money?

Answer: Yes. McDonald's said they were taking trans fats out of their food; they have not. They lied to us for years about the fact that they were using beef fat to make their French fries. They lie to us now about the fact that they put sugar on their French fries. One food manufacturer had a pudding it called "lite." The label proudly said "One-third the calories of our regular pudding!" They were deceiving everyone, because what they didn't tell you was it was the exact same pudding, but the containers were one-third the size! Arby's makes a sandwich with something it calls roast beef. It is not roast beef at all. They actually had to payoff politicians to rewrite the laws which allowed them to call their artificial man-made product "roast beef." Companies deceive us with labels that say such things as "Made with real juice." We are led to believe that the product is real juice. It is not. The product is made WITH real juice. This means they can put in a drop of juice and the rest can be chemicals! The examples go on and on. Companies like Arthur Daniels Midland Company makes billions of dollars selling genetically modified, manufactured food products around the world. One of the largest privately held corporations is the international food giant Cargill, which is trying to monopolize how food is manufactured, sold, and distributed around the world. Their goal is to make local farms, fresh fruits and vegetables, and fresh meat and poultry a thing of the past! They want everything mass-produced, preseasoned, prepackaged, and made in such a way that these food products can be stored for years and years. In restaurants and in the food we buy, the ingredients listed are bad enough, but imagine all of the things that are not listed, such as over 15,000 chemicals, herbicides, pesticides, chlorine, and fluoride. These do not have to be listed on the label. The food can be genetically modified, pasteurized, microwaved, irradiated, gassed, or filled with other poisons, none of which have to be listed on the label. All of these things lead to obesity.

Question: Do drugs really make us fat?

Answer: Yes. All nonprescription over-the-counter and prescription drugs cause disease and obesity. As an example, all decongestants, even those found in cough syrups, create high blood pressure. High blood pressure itself leads to obesity. High blood pressure medication creates dehydration and dry mouth syndrome. This also leads to obesity. All drugs have a cumulative effect by continually leaving trace toxic residue in fatty tissues in the body. This leads to obesity and other health conditions. This is why cleaning these toxins out of the fatty tissue by doing The Purification Program is so vitally important.

Question: You're not a doctor. How can I feel good about your dos and don'ts in Phases 1, 2, 3, and 4?

Answer: Every single do and don't in all four phases of this protocol come directly from medical doctors and credentialed experts. Thousands of licensed health care practitioners around the world use these dos and don'ts with spectacular results. No negative side effects are experienced. These are not my recommendations. I did not create or invent them. I am simply reporting on what doctors around the world are using successfully. All the backup references are in the Appendix of this book, and in the books listed in the bibliography, and each of those books' respective bibliographies.

You may have other questions regarding this protocol. Information about this method is being constantly updated. Visit www.naturalcures.com under the weight loss section often to view new information and updates as they become available. You may also submit questions at www.naturalcures.com, which will be answered by a trained specialist. You may also visit www.hcgobesity.org for additional information about the use of this method.

Now, let's fully address, in full detail, compulsive overeating, food cravings, emotional eating, and uncontrollable urges to eat even when you are not hungry! The solutions to these tortuous, debilitating issues are simple, easy, and miraculous in their effectiveness!

Curing Food Cravings, Emotional Eating, and Uncontrollable Compulsive Eating

Every fat person is familiar with severe intense cravings for food or certain kinds of food. Every fat person is intimately aware of the sometimes sudden uncontrollable, almost insane urges to eat food even when they are not hungry. Fat people know too well that emotions drive them uncontrollably to eat food. Most fat people have had the occasion when "something snapped" and they went on a compulsive nonstop food eating binge. People who have never had a weight problem have no comprehension of how tortuous, how debilitating, and how uncontrollable these food cravings and urges can be. Almost every fitness guru, weight loss guru and author has never experienced these feelings or had to deal with this ever-present condition.

I know what you have gone through. I have lived with this condition most of my life. Like you, I have experienced the seemingly never-ending compulsion and focus on eating. I, too, was once a slave to these uncontrollable internal mechanisms.

It appears that the causes of these conditions are now known. There is a way out, and there is a cure. To go into great detail about the causes of these conditions would take hundreds of pages. My intent is to cut to the chase and give you the bottom line causes, and the simple, easy to follow methods that cure this disorder.

All food cravings, compulsive overeating, binging, uncontrollable urges to eat when you're not hungry, and "emotional eating" are caused by one or more, or a combination of the following:

- Candida yeast overgrowth.

- Parasites.

- Food and environmental allergies.

- A clogged liver.

- A clogged colon.

- Artificial sweeteners.

- Monosodium glutamate and other excitotoxins.

- Man-made trans fats in food.

- Bovine growth hormone and animal drugs in meat, poultry, and dairy products.

- Hormones, sodium laureth sulfate, propylene glycol, mineral oil, and other toxins in soaps, shampoos, cosmetics, moisturizers, lotions, creams, and anything else you put on your body.

- Fluoride and chlorine in the water you drink, bathe, and shower in.

- Super high refined sugars, including high fructose corn syrup.

- Genetically modified food.

- Microwaved food.

- Hormonal imbalances.

- Common non-prescription, over-the-counter drugs, and prescription medications. These include pain relievers, cough suppressants, allergy medications, sleep aids, antidepressants, high blood pressure medications, cholesterol lowering drugs, blood thinners, nasal decongestants, etc.

- Stress.

- Exposure to electromagnetic chaos from cell phones and all wireless devices.

- Programming from the misleading and hypnotic suggestions in TV, radio, and print advertising for food and
drugs. This cannot be overemphasized!

- Environmental toxins such as air fresheners and common
cleaning products.

- Excessive exposure to air conditioning and florescent lighting.

- Lack of sun.

- Oxygen deficiencies in the body due to poor breathing
habits.

- Dehydration of the cells in the body.

- Heavy metal toxicity.

- Nutritional deficiencies.

As you can see, it is virtually the same list of items that
causes most disease and illness, low metabolism, high hunger, an
abnormal operating hypothalamus, an abnormally high storing
of fat in secure problem areas in the body that cause these
uncontrollable physical and emotional food cravings and compulsive eating disorders. Psychologists give us a bunch of psycho-
babble and mumbo-jumbo about eating disorders. I have never
met a patient who was treated by a psychologist or a psychiatrist
that was ever cured and totally free from these internal, overwhelming, and compulsive food cravings and urges. They may
have these cravings and urges "under control," but they are still
always there.

Doctors around the world who clear and correct all the above
conditions find that their patients are completely free from food
cravings, emotional eating, and uncontrollable urges to eat when
they are not hungry. The method of clearing and wiping out the
causes of food cravings is to do "the weight loss cure protocol" in
its entirety! Doing all the steps in Phases 1, 2, 3, and 4 addresses
and corrects all the causes for food cravings and compulsive
overeating.

Doing the LifeForce Plan and/or ThreeLac Candida cleanse
wipes out the main cause of sugar and carbohydrate cravings.

Doing a full parasite cleanse, liver cleanse, colon cleanse, and heavy metal cleanse will also dramatically reduce, or wipe out completely, cravings for certain types of foods. Eliminating from your diet artificial sweeteners, MSG, trans fats, high fructose corn syrup, genetically modified food, microwaved food, and meat, poultry, and dairy with growth hormone and antibiotics also frees the patient from excessive binging tendencies, food cravings, and uncontrollable desires to eat. Drinking pure spring or filtered water, and using a shower filter, thus eliminating chlorine and fluoride, dramatically reduces food cravings as well. Eliminating sodium laurel sulfate, propylene glycol, mineral oil, and other various hormones and toxins from the products you put on your skin eliminates the causes of some hormonal imbalances which lead to insane, crazy food cravings. Taking coral calcium, Vitamin E, krill oil, and whole food supplements address nutritional deficiencies, thus eliminating the body's survival mechanism of making you crave certain foods. Drinking pure water addresses dehydration of the cells, thus stopping additional food cravings. Doing the Purification Program as described in Phase 4 cleanses the fatty tissues in the body of toxins, thus eliminating that mechanism from creating additional urges to eat when you are not hungry. Walking, rebounding and/or doing yoga reduces stress and normalizes hormonal imbalances, dramatically reducing non-hunger related cravings to eat food.

While all of these items play a role in food cravings, the number one most important cause of carbohydrate cravings is Candida yeast overgrowth. If you want to eliminate carbohydrate and sugar cravings, you absolutely must do a complete extensive Candida cleanse. There are many good Candida cleanses that can be found online, in your local health food store, from licensed healthcare practitioners, or at www.naturalcures.com. A good beginner Candida protocol is called ThreeLac, available at www.123candida.com. The most comprehensive and complete Candida cleanse is the LifeForce Plan, available at www.lifeforceplan.com. The LifeForce Plan was created by a longtime friend, Dr. Jeff McCombs. It is the only program I know of that cleanses the body of not only the Candida yeast, but also the fungus that the Candida turns into and which is spread throughout the body. Doing the complete

LifeForce Plan will be a profound life-changing experience. Not only will sugar and carbohydrate cravings be gone forever, but you will experience a dramatic increase in energy, almost miraculous relieving of anxiety, stress, and depression, develop beautiful radiant young looking skin, hair, eyes, and nails, eliminate constipation, gas, and bloating, and see a dramatic flattening of your stomach. Sleep will also dramatically improve. Metabolism will skyrocket.

If you do not do a Candida cleanse you will always be a slave to sugar and carbohydrate cravings.

The single most significant cause of "emotional eating" or uncontrollable urges to eat when you are not hungry, is a combination of stress and anxiety patterns locked in the body, as well as the hypnotic triggers that are in our minds due to the subliminal, and highly advanced, suggestive advertising we are bombarded with on TV, radio, and print media put out by the food companies. Every person reading this has been purposefully and systematically hypnotized, given posthypnotic suggestions and bombarded by subliminal suggestions by the food companies in their advertising to specifically create uncontrollable cravings to eat specific food even when they are not hungry. Combine this with the fact that the food you are craving is loaded with chemical agents to create drug-like physical addiction and you can now see why you are screwed when it comes to trying to lose weight! There are several solutions to this dilemma.

1. Don't eat the forbidden foods as listed in Phase 4 as they create drug-like physical addictions. This is absolutely essential. When I say never, I mean never. Would you consider thinking that you could on occasion smoke some crack cocaine or shoot-up some heroin and not become addicted? The food at fast food restaurants, and the ingredients that I suggest be forbidden, can be as physically chemical addicting as heroin or crack cocaine.

2. Do not watch advertising for restaurants and food products. Avoid listening to ads on the radio, or reading ads printed in magazines, for food companies, fast food restaurants, any restaurants, or any food products. I can assure you from personal inside experience that all of these ads are being

produced with either subliminal messages, hypnotic methods, misleading information, or are designed to simply make you buy their product at all costs. If you think for a moment, right now, can you recall any ad or jingle for a restaurant or food product? I bet everyone can finish this... "Two all beef patties, special sauce, lettuce, cheese..."! Think about it. This ad for McDonald's Big Mac hasn't run in over ten years. However, it is still programmed into our brains! Not watching, listening to, or reading advertisements for food is unrealistic. If you really want to win, then hit them where it hurts the most. Do not buy any food product that is heavily advertised! Do not go to any restaurant that is heavily advertised! The best companies producing the best products spend the majority of their budget on the quality of their ingredients. These large multinational food conglomerates spend the majority of their money on advertising and packaging.

3. Deprogram yourself from all the posthypnotic suggestions and subliminal messages that are stuck in your brain. The best way to do this is to read books and watch DVDs that expose the truth. Doing this will counteract the posthypnotic suggestions and subliminal messages that will be triggered in the future creating uncontrollable urges. If you don't think posthypnotic suggestions and subliminal messages are being used in the advertising of food, just watch how children react when they want certain food items. Children become insane, like crazed drug addicts needing a fix, demanding food from certain fast food restaurants, cereals, or sweets such as cookies, cakes, and candies that are heavily advertised. When the child is told no, these posthypnotic suggestions and subliminal messages are triggered, causing anger, fear, and anxiety in the children if they do not get the food product they are after. These advertising techniques have been documented in several books and documentaries. Corporate insiders and whistle-blowers have come forward exposing what is being called a heinous crime against children and humanity. Ideally, you should read immediately upon arising at least one page from one of

the recommended books, and read at least one page just before retiring. You are being bombarded daily with these messages; therefore, you should counteract them and deprogram yourself on a daily basis as well. Remember, these food companies are spending millions of dollars and using every dirty trick in the book to get you to buy their products, have uncontrollable urges to eat their product, and get you physically chemically addicted to the product like a drug addict. Books include:

- *Natural Cures "They" Don't Want You To Know About*, by Kevin Trudeau

- *More Natural "Cures" Revealed: Previously Censored Brand Name Products That Cure Disease*, by Kevin Trudeau

- *Sweet Deception: Why Splenda, NutraSweet, and the FDA May Be Hazardous to Your Health*, by Dr. Joseph Mercola and Dr. Kendra Degen Pearsall

- *Don't Eat This Book: Fast Food and the Supersizing of America*, by Morgan Spurlock

- *Fat Land: How Americans Became the Fattest People in the World*, by Greg Critser

- *The Hundred-Year Lie: How Food and Medicine Are Destroying Your Health*, by Randall Fitzgerald

- *Chew On This: Everything You Don't Want to Know About Fast Food*, by Eric Schlosser and Charles Wilson

- *The End of Food: How the Food Industry is Destroying Our Food Supply—And What We Can Do About It*, by Thomas F. Pawlick

DVDs include:
- *Supersize Me*
- *Who Killed The Electric Car?*
- *Iraq For Sale: The War Profiteers*
- *The Corporation*
- *The Constant Gardner*
- *Tucker*

- *Sister Kenny*
- *The Smartest Guys in The Room: The Story of Enron*

4. De-stress. Today's lifestyle is incredibly stressful. The enormous amounts of violence and graphic images on television and movies dramatically increase stress. Cell phones and constant instant electronic communications dramatically increase stress. Interestingly enough, the advertising produced by the food companies is, in many cases, specifically designed to increase stress and create a subconscious belief that eating their food will reduce stress. There are many ways to reduce stress: meditating or praying, massage, exercise, singing, dancing, walking outside in the sun, playing with pets or children, laughing, playing a musical instrument, listening to baroque classical music, or having a glass of wine or other alcoholic beverage all are some effective ways to reduce stress. All are encouraged and recommended. Two particularly effective stress reducing methods include Dr. Coldwell's stress reducing CDs, available at www.u-cure.com. The U-Cure CDs are some of the most effective and powerful stress reducing and health enhancing products every developed. Listening to these CDs help alkalize the body's pH, dramatically increasing health, vitality, and energy. Another effective product for stress and anxiety is AlphaCalm, available by calling 1-800-554-6051.

There is one other incredibly powerful and effective technique that can reduce stress and anxiety, and eliminate uncontrollable urges to eat when you are not hungry. This technique also has been proven to cure post-traumatic stress disorder and phobias in virtually five minutes! The technique was developed by Dr. Roger Callahan, Ph.D. Dr. Callahan was a practicing psychologist who found, after years of research, that standardized psychological and psychiatric treatment methods were totally ineffective at addressing emotional, and mental, stress and phobic disorders. He found that all known treatments used by mental health practitioners for addictions were useless. Moreover, he discovered that psychiatric drug therapy and other treatments actually harmed the patient. He then discovered that stress, anxiety, phobias, and uncontrollable "addictive" urges could be eradicated by a method of tapping with the fingers certain acupressure points on the body in a specific sequence. His technique was so effective that he toured the world, appearing on numerous television and radio shows demonstrating how in less than five minutes he could cure someone of phobias, stress and anxiety, uncontrollable addictive urges, and even post-traumatic stress disorder. On talk show after talk show he was challenged by the journalists and reporters who gave him the most difficult cases. People who were massively phobic of spiders, snakes, elevators, or heights were one after the other instantly and permanently cured of their phobia. This was proven with follow-up studies of these individuals. Imagine a person who was deathly afraid of heights his whole life, being cured of this debilitating condition in less than five minutes, and able to walk on the ledge of a tall building without any fear or apprehension whatsoever. One patient who was phobic of snakes her whole life was shown a snake locked in a fish tank. She immediately screamed with fear and started to hyperventilate. Her phobia and fear of snakes was a lifelong condition. Within five minutes of using the Callahan technique, this woman was holding the snake, laughing with glee. She was totally and permanently cured of her fear, anxiety, and phobia of snakes. This type of result occurred virtually every single time.

Callahan also worked with people with severe, compulsive, overwhelming addictive urges. This included heroine addicts, cocaine addicts, cigarette smokers, and compulsive overeaters. In all cases the results were virtually the same. When the patient had the overwhelming urge, they used the Callahan technique. In less than five minutes the urge was completely gone. The patient no longer wanted the heroine, cocaine, cigarette, or food. In most cases, the thought of consuming the substance became repulsive.

It is highly recommended that every person who engages in this "weight loss cure protocol" become familiar with the Callahan technique for reducing and eliminating urges.

Once you are fully aware of how to use the technique you are to use this technique EVERY TIME you have an overwhelming urge to eat food. This means, during the entire Phase 1, 2, 3, and 4, EVERY TIME you have a strong urge to eat something, or any food craving, you are to use the Callahan technique. What you will find is that the urge or craving will be greatly reduced or

eliminated altogether. You may find that you have urges or cravings many times throughout the day. Use the Callahan technique
each and every time! By using the Callahan technique each and
every time you have a strong urge to eat, or a food craving, you
will be releasing stored energy patterns. As these energy patterns
get released, the severity and number of strong urges and food
cravings will go down dramatically. By the time you reach Phase
4 there is an excellent chance that food cravings and strong urges
will have been totally eliminated.

In one particular patient strong urges and food cravings
occurred ten to fifteen times per day. The patient was told that
the next time they felt the strong urge to eat or a food craving,
they were to use the Callahan technique. The patient took less
than two minutes to apply the technique. Instantly, the patient's
body completely relaxed from head to toe. The patient noticed
all the muscles in his face and throughout his body became completely relaxed. The patient's breathing dramatically deepened
and became much easier and fuller. The strong urge to eat and
food craving was 100% gone. The patient was told to use the
Callahan technique the next time a strong urge or food craving
came up. The patient fully expected that he would get another
urge or craving within an hour or two. Amazingly, the rest of the
day passed without any urges or cravings whatsoever. Six weeks
later the patient still had not had a return of any strong urges to
eat, or food cravings! The patient did have a reoccurrence of food
cravings upon hearing news of his sister's sudden death. The
stress of this traumatic incident triggered strong urges and cravings. The patient applied the Callahan technique. In less than five
minutes the patient was completely relieved of his stress, anxiety,
and trauma. His strong urges and food cravings were completely
eliminated. It has been five years since, and the patient still has
yet to have a reoccurrence of strong urges and food cravings.

Most people may need to use the Callahan technique several
times each day. In many patients, one or two treatments is all
that is needed and lasts months or years before urges or food
cravings return and another simple treatment is needed. For
many patients the process is more gradual. For the first several
days or weeks the patient may be using the Callahan technique

many times each day. Usually, as days and weeks go on, the number of times that the patient needs to use the Callahan technique goes down dramatically.

When I first learned of this powerful, effective technology, I tried it on almost everyone I met! It was instantly curing people who were phobic of elevators, escalators, spiders, snakes, and who had fear of heights.

On one particular instance I was traveling to Canada on a fishing trip. My good friend Bill was coming up from Florida to meet me at the airport. I didn't know it, but Bill had a fear of heights and, specifically, flying his whole life. I was a little surprised that he did not fly from Florida to meet me at the airport in Canada. He actually drove the entire way. When he met me at the airport he thought we would be driving to the fishing lodge. Little did he know, we were about to get on an old four-seater, pontoon float plane that would take off and land on the lake, and take us to the lodge. He nearly crapped his pants when he saw the plane. I had no idea he was being serious when he told me he did not want to fly. We got on the plane. I quickly realized that he had a most severe fear and phobia of flying. He was at the verge of hyperventilating. He grabbed onto the seat so tightly his knuckles turned white. He was sweating profusely and appeared to be mumbling some sort of prayer. I actually became excited because I thought this would be a good test for the Callahan technique. I immediately applied the technique. Virtually, within two minutes, Bill completely changed. He stopped griping the seat, his breathing completely relaxed, and he stopped sweating. I think he had already finished the prayer at this point. He looked at me and said he couldn't believe how good he felt. He was amazed that he felt totally relaxed, confident, and in control. He looked out the window with childlike amazement. He was laughing. He told me this was the first time in his life that he had looked out the window of an airplane. That was over ten years ago, and his phobia and fear of flying has never returned.

On another occasion I was visiting a health spa in Utah. At this health spa and resort many celebrities would come for beauty treatments, relaxation, and a desire to lose weight through traditional diet and exercise. I met a famous celebrity whose name I will not mention. We struck up a friendship and she explained that she was desperately trying to lose weight. I was not aware of the Simeons weight loss protocol at the time. I asked her if she had any particular foods that she craved. Her eyes brightened up, and a big smile came across her face. She looked up and said, "I'm addicted to Häagen-Dazs ice cream." It was obvious that she truly loved and craved this food. I asked her if there was a particular flavor that she enjoyed. With passion she exclaimed, "Butter Pecan is by far my favorite. I eat it every day." Knowing that she had been on a strict diet for the last few days, I assumed she was dealing with hunger and feeling deprived by not being able to eat the food she enjoyed. I asked her if she would like to have some Butter Pecan Häagen-Dazs ice cream right now. The look of anxiety and depression came over her face as she said, "I would love, love, love some, but I need to lose weight, I need to stick to this diet." She obviously had a strong desire, urge, and craving for this Butter Pecan Häagen-Dazs ice cream. I asked her if she would be excited if she could eliminate the overwhelming, almost uncontrollable urge and craving for this ice cream. She said yes. She loved the idea of no longer being a slave to this uncontrollable food craving. I said, let's make this test real. I'll be right back. I ran out the door, hopped in my car, and drove to the store to get some Häagen-Dazs Butter Pecan ice cream. Ten minutes later I was back at the spa dining room with my super star celebrity friend. I went to the kitchen and scooped out a large bowl of the luscious and delicious Häagen-Dazs Butter Pecan ice cream. I was excited to see if the Callahan technique could cure this desperate woman from her overwhelming addiction and compulsive food craving for this ice cream. I was slightly apprehensive knowing that if the Callahan technique did not take her cravings away my little experiment may trigger a massive food binge. But I had seen this work in virtually every instance on *Good Morning America, CNN, Evening Magazine, Phil Donahue, Jenny Jones,* and *Regis and Kelly.* Dr. Callahan's techniques virtually worked 100% of the time with even the most severe cases. I was optimistic and confident.

I went back to the dining room and put the bowl of ice cream in front of my new friend. I watched as her face contorted, her breathing quickened, and she obviously became highly agitated. She stared at the ice cream with a fixed intention that would not waiver. I asked her on a scale of one to ten what was her desire for the ice cream. While keeping her fixated stare at the bowl of ice cream in front of her she said, "Eleven." She never looked at me; she was consumed with the thought of the ice cream. I then applied the Callahan technique. It took less than three minutes. Immediately her breathing relaxed and deepened; her tense and rigid body relaxed dramatically. She looked around the room as if she was coming out of a trance or a deep sleep. It was almost as if she didn't know where she was. She was not looking at the ice cream. I told her to look at the ice cream and tell me what her desire to eat it was now. She gazed at the ice cream and seemed confused and befuddled. She looked up at me with a strange expression as if dumbfounded by what she was about to say. After a long pause, she said slowly and as if she didn't believe her own words, "I don't want it at all." My insides were jumping with glee. It had worked again! This woman may now be free of a lifelong compulsive eating disorder. I pushed further. I told her to pick up the bowl of ice cream, smell it, and imagine how wonderful and delicious it would taste. She complied with my request. I asked what her desire on a scale of one to ten was now. She again looked confused as she said, "I have no interest or desire in eating this ice cream. I absolutely do not want it."

Three years later I received a call from this super star celebrity. She had lost over fifty pounds and told me that since that day she has never had any desire to eat ice cream!

I could give you dozens more examples of similar situations from my personal direct experience. The point is, this is an incredibly effective and profound technique. I will give you the instructions here for the basic technique; however, there are more advanced techniques available. I recommend you read Dr. Callahan's books *Tapping the Healer Within, The Anxiety Addiction Connection*, and *Why Do I Eat When I'm Not Hungry?* For additional information or personalized, individualized treatment by a fully trained practitioner, go to www.tftrx.com, or www.emofree.com.

The Basic Callahan Technique

This technique should be done EVERY time you have a strong urge to eat or have any food cravings.

1. Ask yourself on a scale of one to ten, how severe is your urge or food craving? This is very important.

2. With two fingers from your right hand tap 15 to 20 times directly under the right eye. About half an inch to one inch is perfect. You do not have to tap very hard.

3. Now tap directly under the right armpit, approximately three to four inches down. Tap 15 to 20 times.

4. Find the collarbone point. This is located approximately one-half inch below the small dip in the front of the neck, and two to three inches over on the right side of the chest. You are looking for the top of the collarbone. Tap 15 to 20 times.

5. Find the "gamut spot" on the back of the left hand. This is located between the little finger and ring finger, approximately one inch below the "V" on the back of the hand. Tap repeatedly on this spot as you do the following:

   - Keep your eyes open for five seconds.
   - Close your eyes for five seconds.
   - Open your eyes for five seconds.
   - While keeping your head still, move your eyes down to the right and hold for five seconds.
   - While keeping your head still, move your eyes down to the left and hold for five seconds.
   - Roll your eyes in a circle to the right.
   - Roll your eyes in a circle to the left.
   - Count to five out loud.
   - Hum a tune for five seconds, out loud.
   - Count to five out loud again.
   - While keeping your head straight, look down as far as you can and slowly move your eyes upward until you are looking up as high as you can.

6. Take three slow, long, deep breaths.

7. Ask yourself on a scale from one to ten what your urge or food craving is now. If the urge or food craving is gone you are finished with the process. If it is the same, higher, or slightly lower, repeat the process one more time.

This basic technique should dramatically reduce, or completely eliminate, the urge, desire, or food craving. Sometimes additional patterns and more advanced techniques are required for complete permanent results. These can be done by talking to a licensed practitioner on the phone who uses a special voice recognition technology that determines what points and sequence should be used. Using this basic technique, however, EVERY time you have an urge or desire will, over time, produce dramatic long-term results.

This is an important ingredient in "the weight loss cure protocol." Do not underestimate its value and deep powerful effects.

As you can see, there are many overlapping and connected causes of food cravings, compulsive eating urges, and uncontrollable desires to eat when you're not hungry. The root causes will be neutralized and corrected by doing all the recommendations in this book. In some people these sensations will be reduced or eliminated very quickly. In other people the causes are deeply entrenched throughout the physiology and will take more time to be significantly reduced or totally eliminated. Doctors around the world state that although each patient reduces or eliminates these cravings and urges over different time periods, every patient can and does dramatically reduce or eliminate these urges and cravings provided they do the recommendations and suggestions as outlined.

You can overcome food cravings, compulsive overeating, binging, and uncontrollable urges to eat when you are not hungry. Do not be dismayed. Instead, be of good cheer. The causes of your condition are now known, and the cure is in the palm of your hand.

CHAPTER EIGHT

The Proof Revealed

Power tends to corrupt, and absolute power corrupts absolutely.

—Lord Acton

Once the media touches a story the facts are lost forever.

—Norman Mailer

The information I am reporting on and revealing in this book may appear to some as unconventional and controversial. The proof and evidence, however, showing that everything in this book is accurate, true, and works, is overwhelming. If the contents of this book were ever put on trial, the evidence is so overwhelmingly clear that any judge or jury would come back with a verdict exclaiming that without a doubt all the concepts, methods, and protocols outlined in this book are accurate, safe, and effective!

Why then are so many trying to debunk and discredit this information? When I first published *Natural Cures "They" Don't Want You To Know About* I was personally ridiculed and discredited on a massive scale through the media. The concepts I exposed and reported on in that book were criticized and debunked as being quackery. They were not my concepts or opinions, I was simply reporting effective non-drug and non-surgical, all-natural methods that were being used successfully by doctors around the world to cure and prevent disease. Yet, the book and the accurate reporting contained in the book were widely criticized by those companies and organizations that had a financial interest in keeping that information hidden. A few years and six million copies later, that book is now being held up as one of the great exposés on the healthcare system in America. The non-drug and non-surgical ways to cure and prevent disease that I reported on and revealed in that book are now being accepted in the mainstream.

The protocols, methods, and causes of obesity outlined in this book are not my opinions and theories. They are factual, evidence-based conclusions made by scientists, researchers, medical doctors, and acclaimed well respected experts in the field. Many of these have been reported on in well respected media outlets, scientific and medical journals, and by acclaimed, well respected journalists and authors. The key points in this book have been discussed in the *New York Times, The Wall Street Journal, CBS News, CNN, Fox News, The New England Journal of Medicine, The Lancet,* and virtually hundreds of other major newspapers, major magazines, radio programs, television networks, scientific and medical journals, best selling books, and documentaries.

There are many sources that provide indisputable evidence and proof that all of the recommendations and steps in "the weight loss cure protocol" are safe and effective; these include published studies, double-blind studies, clinical studies, published abstracts, published articles, and reported observations from scientists, biochemists, medical researchers, medical doctors, and journalists.

The most powerful evidence is always direct, firsthand, eye witnesses! Therefore, the absolute most compelling evidence comes first from the hundreds of medical doctors who have been using these techniques for over thirty years and know firsthand that they are safe and effective. Secondly, the bombshell that blows any criticism out of the water is the hundreds of thousands of actual real people who have used these techniques with virtually no side effects and almost 100% positive results.

It is important that you not take my words blindly. The evidence, proof, documentation, and substantiation being presented absolutely, positively comes to the following conclusions:

1. "The weight loss cure protocol" is absolutely safe and not dangerous in any way.

2. "The weight loss cure protocol" is the fastest, easiest, and most effective way to lose weight, and lose stubborn secure problem area fat and keep the weight off forever.

3. "The weight loss cure protocol" is the fastest, easiest, and most effective way to reduce physical hunger, increase metabolism, correct physical addictions to food, and eliminate or reduce food cravings and uncontrollable urges to eat when you're not hungry.

4. "The weight loss cure protocol" has, in fact, been purposely suppressed, discredited, debunked, and in some cases, outlawed in an attempt to keep this effective cure hidden so that obesity continues to grow globally and profits continue to soar!

Let's read what people like you have to say about "the weight loss cure protocol." These people are real and have not been compensated in any way. These comments have been written in their own words.

> "My ex husband and I were part of a company in the mid states that opened over 250 Medical Weight Loss Clinics. These clinics were medically staffed with RN's to administer the injections. All of our patients had to go through a medical examination with our on staff doctors. Lab work was done on all patients. Our program called for two days of load diet, with higher doses of hCG, followed by lower doses and a 500-calorie diet. HCG had been scrutinized for many years. The FDA contends that anyone on a 500-calorie diet will loose weight. And we agreed.
>
> The significant difference, however, was the fact that with hCG the following occurred:
>
> — HCG released 2500 calories of abnormal fat cells. Therefore your body was using 3000 calories per day.
>
> — Patients never lost the structural fat, only the abnormal fat deposits.

– During the program not only was your weight decreasing at an amazingly fast rate, but your body's skin was shrinking as well.

– A patient never ended up with stretch marks from rapid weight loss. When a patient went from a size 18 to size 6, they appeared to never have had a weight problem. No saggy skin etc.

– The program incorporated a lot of water intake. If your urine was not clear, you were not drinking enough water. A patient was literally flushing out the fat cells through urination.

There is so much more to this program than meets the eye..."

—T.G., Oklahoma

◇ ◇ ◇

"I am currently taking the hCG shots for obesity. I have a condition called PCOS (polycystic ovary syndrome).

As a result, it is very hard for me to loose weight, and I have excess hair growth from the level of testosterone. I have tried methods such as metphormine.

With that I got very sick. I have tried everything short of starving myself to loose the weight, but with no success.

The hCG shots not only have helped my weight issue, but my PCOS symptoms as well. I have lost weight and the excess hair growth has become very slow. My energy level from losing the weight is tremendous. All of which was noticed just within the first week! Which in turn gives someone like me very much hope of being "normal."

My doctor that helps control the PCOS has also been following my success as well and is amazed at the effects the shot has had. He was the one who recommended that I give this a try. I was very wary at first, but seeing the results encouraged me.

I would strongly recommend hCG to anyone who has the same condition. Even if they don't have poly-cystic ovary syndrome and are just overweight. The effects of obesity are way more dangerous then the effects of this shot, if there are any. And believe me, I have done my research!

Thousands and thousands of people die of obesity. Now there is a method of helping them that is as natural as you can possibly get. Let's fact the facts, obesity is an extremely fast growing killer....

So, thank you for the research that you do. It reassures me as well as the population who do take the shots."

—J.K., North Carolina

◇ ◇ ◇

"The 'Fat Chance' special missed the whole point that hCG therapy cured obesity 40 years ago. Dr. A.T.W. Simeons of Rome found the permanent cure for obesity in the early 1960's and the American diet industry suppressed it for 40 years.

Why?

The American diet industry has grown in the last 40 years from $2 billion/year to over $150 billion/year.

That industry would collapse if the fact were widely known that obesity is a permanently curable symptom of a hypothalamus dysfunction.

What is unconscionable is the almost infinite amount of pain and distress and degradation that have been endured by almost three generations of fat Americans, let alone those fat people in the rest of the world, because of the greed of the diet industry. I have used the Simeons weight reduction program. I personally guarantee that it works."

—N.S., La Grande, Oregon

◇ ◇ ◇

"When I used the Callahan techniques the pounds just flew off! I lost 51 pounds and have kept if off for over two years without any effort."

—C.L., North Carolina

"The Callahan techniques helped my clients successfully deal with addictions, stress, grief and fears."
—Dr. C.S., California

◇ ◇ ◇

"I have gotten great results with the Callahan techniques personally, and the results that my patients get are nothing short of miraculous."
—R.M., D.O.M., Pennsylvania

◇ ◇ ◇

"The Callahan technique is the miracle drug without the drug."
—P.F., New Jersey

◇ ◇ ◇

"When I started using the Callahan technique I noticed my food cravings going away. I used to have certain comfort foods, like chocolate, ice cream, Starbucks coffee with extra caramel. I was obsessed by these foods and loved them. I have always been a yo-yo dieter, an emotional eater, and a binge eater. The Callahan techniques are a Godsend."
—F.K., California

◇ ◇ ◇

"I have said it hundreds of times to everyone who is skeptical—that Dr. Simeons's method meets and exceeds the scientific method of proof...

I have written you in the past about the criminal deceit of those who have prevented by slander, allowing the prescribing of the hCG material, and the correct method, etc. Which means I have been angry and outspoken about this for 35 years...

What's missing, to me, is the 'background' of anyone opposing the use of hCG. As a matter of record, the medical profession as a whole has no understanding of the biochemistry, nor means to cure obesity...

The radical treatment using surgery is pretty brutal. [Someone told me those undergoing this surgery will die without it, so...] How can anyone say he/she performed hCG group experiments and thereby 'proved' the treatment of no use...

Their experiment designs were idiotic, apparently— and none of them have found, specifically, the mechanism of hCG in the body. I'll bet money on that. They have proved nothing. I keep telling you things you already know. But I'm interested...

And this is where I would demand that those nice people who write to you and who already know personally that the treatment is excellent, get out there and ask all departments, all top management, anyone they can find to ask who is hostile, or absolutely in power to prevent these people from getting it. Take the fight to the enemy."

—P.J., Iowa

◇ ◇ ◇

"I had exceedingly good results on hCG (injectable) diets many years ago, but the FDA and AMA have since intimidated almost all U.S. doctors into not prescribing it for obesity treatment.

As you may know, United States law allows citizens to import for personal use non-narcotic drugs unapproved by the FDA for sale in the U.S.A.

Since I do not expect to see the FDA ever (at least in my lifetime) approve hCG, in any form, for weight loss (injectable hCG never was so approved) I will have to get it from some other country in any case.

The problem in the U.S., pardon my cynicism, is that there is no major (as in multi-billion dollar) political lobby for hCG weight control products. The AMA, like any good trade organization, is obsessed only with driving up its member income and the big money for doctors in this area comes from the surgery and long-term care for obesity-related disorders, not from writing a prescription for hCG to eliminate obesity. (For this reason, virtually all weight-loss specialists in private practice refuse to join the AMA.)

The other big medical lobby in the U.S., the insurance industry, is not particularly interested in the issue because most policies exclude coverage of obesity disorders and overweight individuals are generally denied life insurance and health insurance coverage completely unless they can afford exorbitantly high premiums for very limited coverage.

Thanks very much."

—E.B., Texas

◇ ◇ ◇

"Almost 30 years ago I had gained 60 pounds that dieting and exercise would not move. I was an active mother of six, and then, as now, I refuse to take any medicines and remain extremely healthy.

When I saw the weight loss others were achieving from hCG, I went to an obesity doctor here and began to receive the needles.

During the first month I received 24 needles and lost 30 pounds! The second month I went on a maintenance diet and received one needle per week...and lost that last 30 pounds! It was not difficult to remain on that diet while getting the shots because the results are so immediately apparent...and you feel great.

...It is my opinion that the thousands of people here who benefited from hCG give the lie to the vague claims that this is a dangerous substance. I feel that fat is a lucrative bu$ine$$...diets, books, videos, gym equipment, weight programs, food programs, operations, etc....

If the medical establishment were really seriously addressing obesity, they would have to bring back human Chorionic Gonadotrophin.

This substance seems to go directly to those areas that will not budge through diets, fasts or exercises. I applaud the efforts of Dr. Belluscio to keep hCG discussion alive and force the medical profession to recognize the value of studies. I would recommend hCG to anyone with a serious weight problem.

On health boards I see desperate people posting about liposuction, stomach and intestines operations, amphetamines, and all sorts of questionable drugs and other weight-loss scams...while the truth about hCG is hidden. Who does this serve?

Obesity is a health issue and we must DEMAND answers as to why this hCG is being kept from us!"

—A.S., Florida

◇ ◇ ◇

"I am a layperson who used Dr. Simeons's hCG technique, starting in 1969. The treatment is perfect, and works the same for all, if Dr. Simeons's technique is used. I respected him a lot and wrote to him in Italy; he sent a gracious reply.

Since then, I have tried to find out who was behind the attacks on this procedure and never got very far. They were, of course, malicious and moronic; distorting every detail of the fat-reducing technique he devised, and the results obtained. I wrote to several obesity researchers, and clipped articles, etc., but had neither the clout nor the connections to go further into the opposition. One who wishes to overcome the flak generated will have to be vocal and influential; smoking out the opposition would be desirable, also.

The campaign against this technique was underhanded and I suspect the motives could not bear the light of day.

Regards,"

—D.J., New Jersey

◇ ◇ ◇

"I am so pleased to be able to share this with anyone and everyone!

My Husband and I have been going to a clinic in Tennessee. We both started this diet (with much doubt). I've tried many diets and failed at most...UNTIL I started this diet using hCG and a VLCD (very low calorie diet)...I have lost 20 pounds in one month! Can you believe it?? And on top of the weight loss I feel GREAT! Full of energy! And that's something that I have not had in years! I am 37 years old, I have 2 very active boys and work a full time job!

Before this wonderful diet method came into my life I couldn't hardly go...but now I'm on the go all the time and have so much energy...its super!!!!.

If anyone out there has doubts about this weight loss method...send me an email and I will send you pictures! Before and after of me and my husband who by the way is also on this diet and feels just as good as I do!

Have a great day..."

—A.B., Florida

◇ ◇ ◇

"Ten years ago I was very over weight and needed to reduce. I tried four other programs before I found the hCG program. The first four helped me lose a total of eight pounds at the rate of about $100/pd.

Then a friend told me about the hCG program. I started at over 200 pounds and finished at 138. I had no side effects and gained self-confidence. The program helped me to like myself and the results kept me going."

—S.L., Ohio

◇ ◇ ◇

"I am very interested in anything concerning hCG. Because I don't understand that it is such a rejected method. After my second child I gained more then 20 kilos and whatever diet (seriously done without cheating myself) no loss of weight.

Negative doctors, til I went to one who I knew did the hCG diet in order to try that. Results: Fantastic.

I remain more or less one year on the same weight, then start gaining again a few kilos and then on my own do the same diet again to lose about ¾ kilos, which I cannot lose with any diet. It's easy, and I feel great during the diet, injecting myself every day...

My hormones are checked seasonally because of menopause, and they are the same as a 38 year old woman. My age is 50! Could be because of hCG????"

—M.B., North Carolina

◇ ◇ ◇

"I was so thrilled to find your web site www.hcgobesity. org. I used the hCG injections in Orlando for several months. I went from a size 14 to size 6.

The results are incredible!"

—W.B, Florida

◇ ◇ ◇

"When I was in Los Angeles, California in 1974 I was treated for obesity with weekly injections of hCG.

I was able, with a controlled diet, to lose 40 pounds in 2 months. It was the most effective method of weight loss that I have ever tried. My energy was up, my mood was up and the weight came off. I know from first hand experience that the injections WORK!!!"

—C.M., Georgia

◇ ◇ ◇

"I now take injections of hCG...It's terrific for weight loss, never have been able to stick to a diet before. I've lost 21 lbs, feel great and blood sugars have lowered...

God bless whoever invented this program..."

—M.B., Texas

◇ ◇ ◇

"I am a past success story of hCG. I lost over 75 pounds about 12 years ago.

Sincerely,"

—S.M., Washington

◇ ◇ ◇

"I have already lost 13.5 kg; my treatment of 45 days ends today and tomorrow I'll start to eat 1,000 cal so my injections are done.

I just feel great and I am very happy, I had no hungry feelings and I am very enthusiastic about the hCG treatment!"

—A.V., Illinois

◇ ◇ ◇

"I have recently, 2 weeks ago, begun the diet using the injection method, with incredible results.
I have already dropped 10 lbs and my goal is 20.
The injections are working incredibly well."

—E.N., New York

◇ ◇ ◇

"I concur with all the letters on the internet that are posted on websites.
It is a shame that the US took hCG away from the doctors. It really works and I never had any side effects.
In fact, I felt better than I had ever felt before and was successful in losing weight.
I know that hCG works."

—K.S., Kentucky

◇ ◇ ◇

"I had started on the hCG injections in January 1981 after the birth of my daughter.
I noticed a SIGNIFICANT loss of weight and inches. I took the injections for 5 months as that was my goal—to lose 50 pounds by my birthday in May. I needed to lose a total of 60 pounds (I felt) but the 50 were enough.
I never had any side effects nor did I notice any side effects. The low calorie diet was enough and the food I was allowed to eat kept me feeling full most of the time.
Thank you very much"

—C.K.M., Toledo, Ohio

◇ ◇ ◇

"I was a patient who took hCG in the early 1970s and not only lost weight, but also experienced the changes in body contour. That was a big issue for me,

and I always believed that hCG was the one diet program that accomplished that.."
                                    —A.S., Minnesota

◇ ◇ ◇

"I am a gynecologist practicing in Miami, FL. Several years ago, I started an hCG weight loss program which has been very effective."
                                    —C.L.G., Florida

◇ ◇ ◇

"I am a doctor in the Philippines and have a weight loss center wherein I have used hCG for my obese patients. I have combined the hCG treatments with a controlled diet and the results have been very gratifying for both my patients and myself."
                                    —J.R.N., Philippines

◇ ◇ ◇

"In 1972 I was treated by a physician in New Orleans for obesity. He was a dermatologist that I had visited for an allergic reaction to a medication that I was taking. He told me about this weight loss program he ran out of his office. I was very interested. I weighed 195 lbs....

Over a period of 6 weeks I lost 37 lbs. I weighed in at 158 lb. after my last injection.

Even at 500 calories a day, this was the easiest diet I ever followed. After the first week I even found myself offering to share my ½ cup of strawberries with my husband one night after dinner.

I never felt hungry, irritable, deprived and had more energy than I've ever had in my life. Just thought I would share this with you."
                                    —J.M., Louisiana

◇◇◇

"I used hCG many years ago and experienced great results."
                                    —K.K., Utah

"3 years ago in Florida, I went to a weight-loss clinic that allowed me to administer hCG shots in combination with a low-fat, low-cal diet. I lost over 30 pounds."
—R.N.J., Florida

◇ ◇ ◇

"In the early 70's I was introduced to hCG by my family doctor. I was on a low caloric (500) daily diet with a shot of hCG daily. I was amazed at the loss in weight and the changes to my body shape also."
—C.F., North Carolina

◇ ◇ ◇

"I was on a weight loss program in Florida that used hCG injections. I was able to successfully shed the twenty pounds I needed to lose."
—A.C., Colorado

◇ ◇ ◇

"In my experience the use of Chorionic Gonadotrophin in the treatment of obesity has an effect on weight loss; however, your article is the first one I have found in which that effect is significant."
—SB, M.D., MS Doctoral Student
School of Nutrition Science and
Policy, Tufts University, Medford, OR

◇ ◇ ◇

"In Florida, back in 1986 I went through hCG shots to lose weight. I lost 26 lbs. in 2 months and felt the best I ever had in my life."
—K.B., Texas

◇ ◇ ◇

"I had used the hCG injections myself for weight loss. I had never had results of any kind from any other weight loss program. I went from 165 pounds to 127 pounds in less than 4 months. I not only lost on the scales, but I lost inches in my bra size, my neck, my arms, legs, waist and hips; everywhere."
—R.H., Missouri

◇ ◇ ◇

"Some years ago, due to a variety of reasons, my wife found herself having gained 45 lbs...she connected to a clinic in So. Calif. (where we then lived) who put her on a program of very low diet and self-injections of hCG. In about 3 ½ months she took off nearly all the weight."
— A. & D., California

◇ ◇ ◇

"A couple years ago, a friend of mine told me about hCG. She had considerable success over an 18 month period. I reviewed the research published by A.T.W. Simeons, M.D. and began a diet program with hCG self injected each day. I completed 3 phases, each a 6 week hCG course followed by 6, 8 and 12 weeks of maintenance. I began at a weight of 237 pounds and I lost a total of 46 pounds after approximately 1 year. I had no side effects, felt great and increased my energy. I was able to begin weight training at the YMCA. I am a very strong and active woman of 45—SCUBA diver, league bowler, traveler and hiker."
— O.M.C., San Jose, California

◇ ◇ ◇

"Fifteen years ago, I was overweight (not obese) and sought medical treatment from a physician in Huntington, West Virginia, USA, in order to lose weight. Part of his program was the injection 3 times per week of hCG. I lost weight quickly and looked and felt fabulous.... Thanks"
— T.M., Wyoming

◇ ◇ ◇

"My sister had an injection of hCG many years ago and lost about 30 pounds in a month, my doctor never even heard of it."
— S.N., San Joaquin Valley, California

◇ ◇ ◇

"About 20 years ago moving from CA to Calgary, the change of climate, lack of friends, different working and living conditions, etc., caused me to gain some 25 pounds over my normal 120. With the hCG treatment I lost the weight, and had good muscle tone, good skin, energy, etc."

—S.S., Calgary, Alberta, Canada

◇ ◇ ◇

"In 1975, I paid for a program to lose weight that included hCG injections and diet. In a very short period of time, approximately two months, I lost around 30 pounds, as well as significant inches over my whole body (neck included).

I was very satisfied with hCG, and other than one morning experiencing something like morning sickness, I felt fine the whole time I was taking the shots. As far as I know, I had no other side effects."

—M.C., Philadelphia

◇ ◇ ◇

"Thank you. I very successfully completed this program about 16 years ago. I lost about 35 pounds, going from 160 to 125, at age 40. I was on the program 2 months. I was not hungry. I did sometimes eat extra vegetables.

However, this is a strict program only for the sincere and serious. It is not possible to have any result at all, zero zip, if a person cheats or makes exceptions....

On the program I felt so very healthy and energetic and just wonderful."

—J.H., Ohio

◇◇◇

"My experience was very positive. I lost 60 lbs. while on this treatment. It would be wonderful to see it made available again to those who would benefit."

—B.H., Arizona

◇ ◇ ◇

"I was treated with hCG and a very low calorie diet at a diet clinic in California almost 30 years ago. It was wonderful! And the only positive dieting experience that I have ever had."

—T.B., Pennsylvania

◇ ◇ ◇

"HCG treatment was the only effective treatment that I have ever encountered the last 30 years of my life."

—P.F., Las Vegas

◇ ◇ ◇

"I used hCG through a clinic in 1972—it was administered in small doses by injection. My results were incredible and I felt wonderful during the treatment."

—S.L., Arizona

◇ ◇ ◇

"I am one of those who used hCG many years ago to lose weight. It was indeed the most effective and successful weight loss program I have ever done."

—A.C., Hawaii

◇ ◇ ◇

"I used the hCG program in the eighties for weigh loss. It worked like a miracle!!! I am an RN now living in Littleton, Colorado."

—M.C., Colorado

◇ ◇ ◇

"I have used this program very successfully for weight loss that's so easy and it makes you feel great. It lowers cholesterol and blood sugar."

—G.M., Florida

◇ ◇ ◇

"Hello again, I just wanted to take the time to thank you for giving me Dr. Walter J. Jagiella's name. My husband and I both went to Rome, and started the diet. We both are in our 5th week. I have lost 25 pounds and my husband has lost 40. I wish there were more doctors out there like you.

Thank you again, God bless."
—D.R., Georgia

◇ ◇ ◇

"I am a 60 year-old man who began the injectable hCG weight loss program 3 years ago. I have arthritis in both knees and one has very little cartilage left...I had tried all the other plans—Jenny Craig, Weight Watchers, Sugar Busters, etc. with NO success.

Under hCG, in 15 months I lost 69 pounds. I have no skin folds from the loss. I went from a tight size 50 to size 42 pants. I can now walk vigorously, play golf and conduct a normal life style.

I no longer need a leg brace or cane to walk. My cholesterol has gone down 40-50 points, BP is 110/64, sugar is 96. I feel like a new man. This program is a life-saver!"
—S.M., West Virginia

◇ ◇ ◇

"I'm on week 11 of the plan. My husband and I were visiting with friends and they noticed I'd lost a few pounds. I don't own a scale; so I don't know how much, but I went from a size 8 to a size 4-5. My friend thinks it amazing that I've made all these healthy changes in my life. I used to be a fast food and pizza girl. Eating only healthy foods is a huge change, but my skin and scalp are reaping the benefits of this new lifestyle. I do have more motivation during the day, and I feel more relaxed when in tense situations. I find I now have the strength and patience to analyze a situation before I react. This is a major improvement! I am so glad I read and followed your plan. I feel like a whole new person, and this is a good thing. Thank you."
—L.F., Illinois

◇ ◇ ◇

"I've been an entrepreneur and successful business owner for my entire life. I've always been highly motivated and extremely goal driven. I'm only 33 years old; however, the last 7 years of my life have been a fast downward spiral of fatigue and I've had to WILL myself to do almost anything. I've tried every single diet imaginable as I've fought to keep my weight between 235 pounds and 270 pounds for over 10 years. However, just 5 weeks ago I was referred to Doctor Jeffrey McCombs and the LifeForce Plan. I read his book and was educated about something called Candida and how it affects our bodies and our lives. Again, many thought it was another fad. However, after five weeks on the plan here is what has happened. My energy has skyrocketed to a level I haven't felt since I was a child. I have taken one nap in the 5 weeks since starting the plan and that was after only having slept 3 hours the night before. This may not sound impressive, but bear with me. I HAVE TAKEN TWO OR THREE NAPS A DAY FOR SO MANY YEARS I CAN'T REMEMBER. This has truly revolutionized my life. My employees, my fiancée, my adopted children, and everyone around me can't believe the changes. Now, for an added benefit! I've eaten 5-7 times a day. I eat more carbs than on any other DIET (I do not consider the LifeForce Plan a diet) I went from 256 pounds to 238 pounds and know that I'll be at my goal weight of 210 pounds very soon. Why am I writing this? Because I want anyone and everyone that has gone through the fatigue and mental anguish I went through for years to understand that there is hope. I know many doctors and your own family will have doubts and even tell you that Candida doesn't exist. Well...call it Candida or call it whatever you want. I know that this plan gets rid of whatever was causing me so much pain and suffering. I could literally fill 5 or 10 pages with my excitement. I'm doing this without knowing the doctor on a personal level at all and only speaking to him for about 15 minutes. So with all this I say THANK YOU Doctor for helping to radically change my life."

—L.N., New Jersey

◇ ◇ ◇

"I was afraid to spend money on yet another thing that would not help. Finally I got started 5 weeks ago. I have lost about 15 pounds. I was not trying to do that yet. I just wanted to get myself over the digestive problems and the Candida. My skin is so soft and beautiful I feel like I should be on an Ivory commercial. I can think and remember so much better. I can walk up and down the stairs without holding onto the rail and carry my 4-year-old granddaughter at the same time. I am so much stronger, maybe because of the energy I have and how much more I do now. I was walking the other day and realized NOTHING hurt. The only way I can describe my emotional state is the opposite of depressed. What would the proper word for that be? I want to thank you for doing what you do. I have to tell you, thank you is not a good enough word but there isn't one for this."

—B.S., California

◇ ◇ ◇

"I have been on the LifeForce Plan for only 3 weeks and 3 days now. I wanted to let you know that I have lost 21 pounds so far. This isn't the greatest thing since I started the diet. My blood sugar was at 317 and now and it is at 111. This is amazing. Thanks again and can't wait to continue and finish this wonderful program. Sincerely,"

—B.C., Canada

◇ ◇ ◇

"I have completed your LifeForce Plan, and I read from your book daily. The Plan is great, the book is like a health bible, and I have reaped immense benefits."

—A.L., North Carolina

◇ ◇ ◇

"Thank you for answering my questions and I also wanted to let you know that I purchased the LifeForce book this weekend. The book is so clear and concise and I really appreciate the two pages for easy reference, I am so impressed and pleased to have finally had all of the facts for easy reference.

I've lost 4 pounds in the first week. For the first time in 10 years I'm starting to feel more normal again. The struggles with going to the bathroom are starting to feel like a thing of the past. I'm so optimistic and plan to continue the program, I finally feel like there is hope in reversing my problems.

The last couple of years have been a learning curve for me and I've been slowly eliminating problems and many pills that I had been taking in the past.

Thanks for answering my questions and restoring my hope and faith in a better life. It's truly amazing to me that you take the time to answer the questions through email—it restores my faith that there are some who still want to help others."

—D.B., Arizona

◇ ◇ ◇

"I started the 'Life Force Plan' 8 weeks ago and it has changed my life dramatically. I follow everything recommended in the book (diet, sweating, drinking the required amount of water, etc.). I get colds very often and sneeze 24-7. But about 4 or 5 days after the program I stopped sneezing (I don't use a kleenex anymore at all). This is extremely unusual and surprising to me after 28 years of severe sinusitis, allergies, difficulties in breathing, chronic coughing and colds. To be honest, I was not expecting this kind of results."

—C.J., New Mexico

◇ ◇ ◇

"In 5 days I have lost 7 pounds. Unbelievable!! Thank you for your time,"

—C.H., South Dakota

◇ ◇ ◇

"First, I want to thank you so very much. I am start-ing my 9th week of the LifeForce Plan and I feel great. I have not experienced a migraine headache since I started the Plan."

—M.P., Iowa

◇ ◇ ◇

"My mother and I have been on the LifeForce Plan for 13 weeks now. Thank you for your help! We are both feeling SO MUCH BETTER than we have in years! Mom says she wishes everyone felt as great as she does! God bless you!"

—C.E., Florida

◇ ◇ ◇

"I have just completed your plan. Lost 50 lbs, went off blood pressure meds and allergy meds, feel great. Thanks."

—K.B., Texas

If you skipped over reading the above comments from people who have safely and effectively completed components in "the weight loss cure protocol," go back and read every single one. This is a very important part of "the weight loss cure protocol." Remember, we have to deprogram our mind from the mental triggers that have been implanted from the hypnotic and sublim-inal advertising messages that we have been bombarded with for decades. The other reason reading comments from people who have succeeded with this protocol is important, is that it begins to alter and change internal beliefs and automatic mental pro-grams that are partially responsible for our overweight condi-tion. Earl Nightingale, in his famous presentation *The Strangest Secret* discovered that we become what we think about. This is also called the "law of attraction." Whatever we picture in our mind, think about, put focus and attention on, and speak in words, becomes our future reality. When you focus and think about food, the fear of deprivation, the fear of hunger, or your overweight condition, you actually create more of the things you don't want! By consistently reading comments of people that have been successful at reducing weight, reducing hunger, increasing metabolism, and eliminating food cravings, you will begin to focus on these successful scenarios and cause them to be attracted into your life. What you think about becomes your reality.

These comments and testimonials from people that have actually done "the weight loss cure protocol" prove the claim that this protocol is 100% safe and effective. This kind of testimony is always the best and most compelling evidence that could be submitted in a court of law. However, as unbelievable as it may seem, the Food and Drug Administration, and the Federal Trade Commission say that the testimony of any person who has successfully benefited from "the weight loss cure protocol" can never be used, listened to, or relied on! These government agencies claim that what people have to say is irrelevant and doesn't matter! Even when over 100,000 people come forward giving their sworn testimony to the safety and effectiveness of "the weight loss cure protocol," the U.S. Government says none of their testimony can be used to determine the safety and effectiveness of this protocol! How absurd and outrageous. It is beyond rational comprehension, but this is how the glorious United States Government operates to allegedly protect its citizens.

Is this protocol safe and effective? Absolutely yes. Experts, Ph.D.s, biochemists, medical doctors, insiders at the FDA and National Institutes of Health, and patients who have used this protocol overwhelmingly attest to its safety and effectiveness. Hundreds of studies, peer reviewed articles, scientific documentation and substantiation, and the thirty-year test of time all support its safety and effectiveness. There is no legitimate evidence that can be produced anywhere in the world that would even suggest that this protocol is unsafe or ineffective.

Yes, it is true that government agencies will point to false and misleading studies or documents that suggest, but do not prove that the protocol is no more effective than diet and exercise alone. Every one of these alleged scientific studies were either funded by companies that have a financial interest in keeping this weight loss cure hidden, or were conducted in such a way as to guarantee failure.

Yes, "experts," "doctors," and government officials publicly state as fact that the Simeons "weight loss cure protocol" and the other suggestions in this book are dangerous and ineffective. However, none of these so-called experts have ever personally done the protocol exactly as described, treated patients with the protocol, interviewed doctors who are using the protocol successfully, talked to patients who have successfully done the protocol, or read the extensive amount of scientific documentation and substantiation. They speak as if they are omnipotent, all-knowing deities when, in fact, they are giving biased, unsubstantiated opinions. Most importantly, these naysayers are not independent, unbiased people. Upon close examination you find that they are all directly or indirectly on the payroll of companies that have a direct financial interest in keeping this truth hidden. They all financially benefit from suppressing and lying about this information.

Suppressing truthful information about anything that will have an adverse financial impact on the existing status quo is common and has been going on for years. It has been proven in court time and time again that this occurs.

When chiropractic treatment was threatening the profits of medical doctors and drug companies, the American Medical Association engaged in a false and misleading campaign to debunk and discredit chiropractors. They used fear, trying to convince people that chiropractors were quacks, their treatments were ineffective, and going to a chiropractor was dangerous and could cause permanent damage to the spine. The chiropractors fought back and sued the AMA for this blatantly false and misleading propaganda campaign. In court it was proven that chiropractic treatments were totally safe and, in fact, were much more effective in treating back pain than anything offered by members of the AMA, including drugs and surgery. The chiropractors won!

When Dr. Andrew Weil, a Harvard medical doctor, published his first book explaining that there were all-natural, inexpensive, effective and safe alternatives to drugs and surgery he was initially crucified in the press. His book could potentially have an adverse effect on the profits of the pharmaceutical industry.

John Gray, author of *Men Are From Mars, Women Are From Venus*, is a huge advocate of nutritional solutions to depression, anxiety, and stress. Even though his book has now sold over 30 million copies, he was initially attacked mercilessly when he suggested that the profitable anti-depressant drugs should be avoided and instead patients should consider inexpensive, safe nutritional remedies which are proven to be more effective.

Suzanne Somers' latest book on health is currently under fire.

The American Medical Association has put together a massive debunking campaign against the natural remedies outlined in Somers' book. Remember, the AMA is simply a union for companies and doctors in the pharmaceutical arena. They do not protect patients; they are an organization that is chartered to protect the financial interests and profits of its members. If people adopted Somers' suggestions, the profits of the pharmaceutical companies would be in great jeopardy.

Dr. Linus Pauling, the only doctor to win the Nobel Prize for science twice, discovered that the all-natural bioavailable form of Vitamin C, when given in high doses, killed every known virus. The drug companies immediately tried to get Vitamin C patented so it could be sold as the world's most powerful, effective, and safe antiviral agent. When it was determined that Vitamin C could not be patentable, therefore making its profit potential extremely low, the pharmaceutical cartel debunked Dr. Pauling's research and engaged in a massive campaign to discredit the use of Vitamin C in the treatment of viral infections. Even though it was proven that Vitamin C was the most powerful, most effective, and safest method of handling viral infections, any widespread use of Vitamin C would dramatically and negatively impact the profits being made on the dangerous and ineffective antibiotics sold by the pharmaceutical giants.

The truth about inexpensive, all-natural, safe, and effective cures is always suppressed because the drug companies need to continue to sell their expensive, profitable drugs, and surgical procedures.

Chinese doctors use a honey/herbal treatment to cure men for prostatitis with virtually 100% success. This was proven in a thirty-day clinical study. A year later 81% of them were still symptom free. This is without any dangerous drugs whatsoever. News of this is still suppressed.

For decades acupuncture was said to be a totally ineffective and very dangerous treatment causing severe negative side effects. Recently, a U.S. National Institutes of Health taskforce was forced to admit that problems caused by acupuncture were extremely rare. The NIH conducted studies which proved that acupuncture was just as effective and had much less side effects than western medicine's treatment used for stroke recovery, headache, menstrual cramps, tennis elbow, fibromyalgia, asthma, low back pain, and carpal tunnel syndrome. This information is also suppressed.

All-natural herbs combined with acupuncture lowered cholesterol levels dramatically in almost 80% of all patients in just twenty-seven days according to a recently published study. Of course, no side effects. These are better results than the incredibly profitable cholesterol reducing drugs that make the drug companies billions a year in profits. Your doctor will not tell you about these natural alternatives, and probably doesn't even know about them.

In my book *Natural Cures "They" Don't Want You To Know About* I go into great detail about how and why the drug companies, the AMA, the FDA, the FTC, and media routinely and systematically suppress the truth about inexpensive, safe, and effective non-drug and non-surgical ways to cure and prevent disease. The standard method of debunking is to use the word "quackery" and suggest that these treatment options are dangerous. Acupuncture, chiropractic, homeopathy, massage treatments, even believing that proper nutrition is important for your health, were all said to be forms of "quackery" and very dangerous to partake in. Imagine the U.S. Government stating that the belief that proper nutrition has anything to do with preventing disease was quackery seems ludicrous. The government has actually stated that taking nutritional supplements is dangerous!

According to insiders and whistle-blowers from the FDA, the FTC, the National Institutes of Health, and several pharmaceutical companies, the specific plan of attack that these organizations are following is to systematically try to convince people that all-natural inexpensive remedies, not sold by pharmaceutical companies, are "quackery" and very dangerous. Simultaneously they try to convince people that the drugs and surgical procedures drug companies sell are the only scientifically proven and safe methods of treating medical conditions. This is the great lie. This is the great deception. It is drugs and surgical procedures that are the most dangerous. In the last ten years it has been reported that using non-prescription over-the-counter drugs, and prescription drugs, exactly as the instructions stated, has resulted in the deaths of over one million people. This is a conservative estimate. Many advocacy and watchdog groups provide evidence that over ten million people worldwide are now dead because they took an over-the-counter non-prescription, or prescription medication. Aspirin is said to kill 2,000 people every year. It is the drugs that are dangerous. Remember that these are the same drugs that the FDA has stated emphatically are "totally safe and effective." Insiders and whistle-blowers who work, or have worked, within the FDA and American Medical Association have repeatedly stated that these organizations are not protecting the best interests of individuals. The FDA and AMA are actually protecting the profits of the companies that sell these dangerous drug and food products.

Is it really true that major publicly traded corporations work with government agencies in an unholy alliance to suppress the truth about information that ultimately would benefit people and society in general? Absolutely yes. Over the last seventy-five years, thousands of specific verifiable examples are available. These have been documented and reported on in major newspapers, magazines, books, and documentaries.

The most recent and fully documented exposé showing that this is true is the documentary *Who Killed The Electric Car?* This film is narrated by Martin Sheen and has onscreen contributions from Ed Begley, Jr., consumer advocate Ralph Nader, and Alexandra Paul. It shows how electric cars were produced that were so efficient, quiet, and powerful that the consumer demand overwhelmed the automakers. This is not what they expected. The automakers knew that if electric cars became mainstream, the need for gasoline and oil would be dramatically reduced. This would adversely affect the profits of the oil companies. Last year

Exxon posted profits in excess of $50 billion. Remember, these are profits posted after every accounting trick in the book was used. The real profits are estimated at over $250 billion. This movie is riveting and captivating. It shows how these beautiful, brand new, perfectly running automobiles were each collected and shredded by the car companies. It was as if they wanted to eliminate all evidence that an effective, popular alternative form of transportation was available. It shows in graphic detail how big companies and government lie and deceive the public, and will do anything and everything to protect their profits, even at the expense of people's health and wellbeing.

There is always an unholy alliance between big business and government causing the suppression of new technologies and information that could potentially have any adverse effect on corporate profits. There is a revolving door between government officials and big business. This is a global growing phenomenon. In America the U.S. Constitution starts with the words, "We the People..." In today's world, the reality is our government officials believe the Constitution reads, "We the Corporations..."

Did you know that over 85% of all of the commissioners of the FDA go to work directly, or indirectly, for the drug companies or food producers? This has been called by political insiders as nothing more than payoffs for the actions and decisions these commissioners made during their tenure to increase those corporations' profits. Did you know that the majority of government officials rotate between government jobs and working for lobbyists and corporations that their government positions are supposed to regulate? This creates an obvious conflict of interest and allows the government to simply do the bidding of these corporations, giving them competitive advantages.

Did you know that the majority of military personnel can be considered overweight, fat, or obese? This is because many food companies have gotten contracts to supply food to our military and have purposely designed menus that make our military fat. This way, the military requires more and more food each year to feed the troops. This means more profits for the food companies.

This interesting food company and government connection is prevalent in the U.S. school lunch program. I have inside sources and whistle-blowers that have told me directly that the suppliers of food for the school lunch programs specifically created menus and created food that would make school children fat very quickly. This is why the amount of food ordered each quarter continues to go up. Fat kids eat more food; the more food purchased means more profits for the food companies.

The profits we are talking about are astronomical. This is why there is such major suppression of the truth relating to the cause and cure of obesity.

Did you know the CEOs of various companies that get contracts with the U.S. Government have personally each earned as high as $40 million in a single year? The money being made in the government food company connection is staggering.

Every country that the U.S. Government creates strong diplomatic ties with has its food supply virtually taken over by U.S. food manufacturers. This is supposed to create exports from America to these respective countries, therefore benefiting the U.S. companies and the U.S. economy. When this occurs, fast food restaurants spring up throughout those countries. The influx of products, that for the first time contain such ingredients as high fructose corn syrup, trans fats, MSG, artificial sweeteners, growth hormones, and antibiotics, begins to permeate the diet of the local people. Almost instantly the local people of these countries begin to gain weight unexpectedly. I have visited dozens of countries around the world and have seen the meteoric rise of obesity occur in direct relation to the increase of fast food and these U.S. produced food products. Obesity in one particular country was up over 10,000% since fast food restaurants appeared!

Remember, the government, big business, and the media all have a financial self-interest in lying, and deceiving us about the truth of any product, technology, or discovery that could adversely affect profits of large corporations.

Some of the worst offenders are alleged consumer advocacy groups, watchdog groups, or associations that are supposed to be fighting the obesity epidemic. It has been proven in court that many alleged consumer advocacy groups and watchdog organizations are, in fact, fronts, set up and funded by food companies and drug companies. Therefore, they appear to be trying to stop and reverse the obesity epidemic; however, in reality, they work for the food industry and drug companies to actually increase obesity.

Associations such as the American Obesity Association, Overeaters Anonymous, North American Association for the Study of Obesity, National Eating Disorders Association, Eating Disorders Education Association, and others receive funding from the federal government and the food industry directly. The more obesity continues to increase means the more money they receive in the form of funding. They have no financial incentive to solve the obesity epidemic. Quite the opposite.

Publications such as the *International Journal of Obesity* are becoming more and more profitable as long as the worldwide obesity epidemic continues to grow. These financial conflicts of interest cannot be underestimated or overlooked. The world-wide overwhelming and consuming need for publicly traded cor-porations to increase profits at all costs is the driving, motivating force to make more people fatter every year and keep the real causes and effective cures hidden from the public.

In the Appendix of this book there is a list of medical refer-ences, scientific data, documentation, substantiation, and detailed technical scientific evidence supporting the safety and effective-ness of "the weight loss cure protocol."

The evidence and proof supporting the systematic debunking and suppression of "the weight loss cure protocol" can be found in news reports around the world, including the Associated Press and Reuters. It is highly recommended that you be educated about the growing worldwide debunking and suppression of new effective technologies and discoveries. Read the following books and watch the following DVDs that prove virtually everything that has been revealed in *this* book is true:

Books include:

- *Natural Cures "They" Don't Want You To Know About*, by Kevin Trudeau

- *More Natural "Cures" Revealed: Previously Censored Brand Name Products That Cure Disease*, by Kevin Trudeau

- *Sweet Deception: Why Splenda, NutraSweet, and the FDA May Be Hazardous to Your Health*, by Dr. Joseph Mercola and Dr. Kendra Degen Pearsall

- *Don't Eat This Book: Fast Food and the Supersizing of America*, by Morgan Spurlock

- *Fat Land: How Americans Became the Fattest People in the World*, by Greg Critser

- *The Hundred-Year Lie: How Food and Medicine Are Destroying Your Health*, by Randall Fitzgerald

- *Chew On This: Everything You Don't Want to Know About Fast Food*, by Eric Schlosser and Charles Wilson

- *The End of Food: How the Food Industry is Destroying Our Food Supply—And What We Can Do About It*, by Thomas F. Pawlick

DVDs include:

- *Supersize Me*
- *Who Killed The Electric Car?*
- *Iraq For Sale: The War Profiteers*
- *The Corporation*
- *The Constant Gardner*
- *Tucker*
- *Sister Kenny*
- *The Smartest Guys in The Room: The Story of Enron*

Additional recommended books and DVDs, which support and give indisputable evidence about all of the information reported on in this book, are listed in the Appendix. These books and DVDs are not only informative and eye opening, but are thoroughly entertaining as well.

An enormous amount of information has been covered in this book. All of the key points have volumes of backup information and substantiation. It is now time to put it all together in summary, and in an easy to follow going forward plan. Following "the weight loss cure protocol" exactly as described is the fastest, safest, and most powerful way to lose weight, reshape your body, permanently reduce hunger, reset your metabolism higher, eliminate food cravings, and most importantly, keep these benefits forever!

CHAPTER NINE

Putting It All Together: Summary and Conclusion

This book covers a large amount of material about the cause of obesity, the cures for obesity, and the reasons for the cover-up, denial, and suppression of these true facts. All of this information comes from, and is supported by, thousands of credentialed experts from around the world. Other experts, however, may disagree with these findings even though they are not merely opinion, but factually scientifically based. This is common in the medical field. There is virtually never a consensus among experts as to what is safe and effective or ineffective and dangerous; there is always constant debate. There are always opponents as well as proponents. There are always those that agree, and those that disagree.

So which experts do you believe? I would suggest, and historical facts back me up, that financial motivations almost always determine whether an expert is for or against a particular method of treatment. While not an "expert" in this field, you should know that I have no financial interests in anything recommended in this book. I have no financial motivations to report on these scientific discoveries. I am not compensated in any way, directly or indirectly, by any company or for any product mentioned in this book. Unlike virtually every other doctor who authors books, such as Dr. Weil, Deepak Chopra, Dr. Atkins, Dr. Pericone, Dr. Gary Null, and countless others, I do not sell supplements or products of any kind. I receive no royalties or endorsement fees for any products of any kind. I do not own or operate clinics as most doctors do and promote in their books. I do not own stock in any companies that I endorse. In this sense I am a true consumer advocate. I am probably one of the only completely unbiased sources of information relating to health and weight loss. I have no motivations other than to share what has worked for me and has worked for countless others.

This book, and all of the supporting substantiation, point to the facts that the ultimate cause of obesity is an abnormally operating hypothalamus. This causes intense and constant hunger, low metabolism, food cravings, and an abnormal excessive storing of fat in secure problem area fat deposits in the body.

The abnormal condition of the hypothalamus is caused by a combination of a large multitude of factors.

The exact Simeons "weight loss cure protocol" combining the very strict and specific diet with the exact amount of hCG, stimulates the hypothalamus to release abnormal fat deposits in the body, thus allowing the body to lose massive amounts of this secure fat extremely quickly. This results in a dramatic reshaping and re-sculpting of the body while retaining important structural fat and muscle mass. Little or no hunger occurs during the protocol.

The protocol also resets the abnormal hypothalamus condition, thus eliminating constant intense hunger, eliminating food cravings, increasing metabolism, and normalizing the hypothalamus so that the body does not abnormally store high amounts of fat in the secure problem area fat deposits in the future.

The protocol also cures and corrects the underlying cause of food cravings, binges, and uncontrollable urges to eat when a person is not hungry.

The protocol also gives the multitude of causes that created and exacerbate this condition. By eliminating the things that cause obesity, weight gain should never occur in the future.

This is why the Simeons "weight loss cure protocol" is being called a "cure" for obesity by medical doctors around the world. It corrects the condition and eliminates the causes so the condition does not return.

The protocol consists of four phases. Each phase consists of a series of things you must do, things you absolutely cannot do, things that are recommended and suggested you do, and things that are recommended and suggested you not do. Following these steps has been proven to be completely safe and totally effective at achieving the desired result of rapid and massive loss of abnormal fat, and a permanent correcting of the condition so that obesity does not return in the future.

As with any weight loss method, this protocol should be done under supervision of a medical doctor or licensed healthcare practitioner.

The following is a summary list of check sheets that contain the steps of each phase of the protocol. These check sheets may be reprinted or copied for your personal use to make following the protocol easier. Each of these items is defined in this book. The reasons they are recommended, and the benefits you receive from doing or not doing each item listed, is also explained in this book. Scientific substantiation and documentation as to the legitimacy and benefits of doing or not doing any of these items is listed in the Appendix or available at www.naturalcures.com.

Dr. Simeons, in his book *Pounds and Inches: A New Approach to Obesity* concluded the following, "The hCG plus diet method can bring relief to every case of obesity, but the method is not simple. It can be time consuming, and does require perfect cooperation between physician and patient. Each case should be handled individually. The physician must be available to answer questions, allay fears, and remove misunderstandings. The patient should be checked daily. Without a complete understanding of the protocol, it can be useless for a patient to be handed a diet sheet and simply take the shots. This method involves a highly complex bodily mechanism. Even though my theory may be wrong, the results speak for themselves. I must beg those trying the method for the first time to adhere very strictly to the techniques and instructions outlined. Do not embark on experiments on your own and refrain from introducing to this method innovations however thrilling they may seem. It has been proven that new method innovations or departures from the original technique has only led to failure and disappointment. The problems of obesity are perhaps not so dramatic as the problems of cancer. However, obesity often causes lifelong suffering. If this protocol in some way can be used to effectively address this fast becoming universal problem of modern civilized man, our world will be a happier place for countless fellow men and women."

I echo the words of Dr. Simeons.

You now have a choice. You can continue to live a life being a slave to the food companies. You can continue to leave your head in the sand, and remain unknowingly manipulated, lied to, deceived, and addicted to what is being called "food." You can continue to be nothing more than a "consumer" that the drug and food industry knowingly and unscrupulously extract money from on a regular basis. You can continue to be purposely made fat and obese against your will. Or...you can choose to be free!

You now know the causes of obesity. You now know the cure. Continued slavery or freedom...the choice is yours. Choose wisely!

Phase 1

Things you MUST do:

- Take ThreeLac as directed
- Drink one-half to one gallon of pure water with coral calcium daily
- Drink Wu Long tea as directed
- Walk one hour each day outside
- Do colonics as directed
- Eat two organic apples per day
- Eat organic grapefruits
- Eat breakfast
- Eat six times per day
- Finish dinner three and one-half hours before bed
- Do a colon cleanse
- Take organic extra virgin coconut oil
- Drink organic raw apple cider vinegar
- Take Eleotin as directed
- Use Callahan techniques as needed
- Eat a salad with lunch and dinner
- Take probiotics daily
- Take krill oil (Omega-3s) daily
- Take a whole food supplement daily
- Drink Yerba Mate tea daily
- Drink chamomile tea daily
- Take saunas as often as possible
- Take Acetyl-L Carnitine daily
- Take digestive enzymes with meals
- Look at and repeat the phrase "I weigh _____," using your ideal weight and look at pictures of you with your ideal body many times throughout the day

- Use stevia, organic agave nectar, organic raw honey, or organic raw sugarcane for sweeteners
- Get personalized individual care from a licensed healthcare practitioner who does not use drugs and surgery

Things STRONGLY SUGGESTED you do:

- Take a heavy metal cleanse product or get chelation
- Drink organic green tea daily
- Take Vitamin E daily
- Sleep eight hours, ideally between 10:00 p.m. and 6:00 a.m.
- Do deep breathing daily
- Listen to stress reducing CDs daily
- Eat 100% organic food
- Add hot peppers or hot salsa to food
- Use fresh cinnamon
- Do yoga
- Use a rebounder or mini trampoline daily
- Get twenty minutes of sun daily
- Get massages often
- Use AlphaCalm as needed
- Use a Q-Link, E-Pendant, or Biopro, or other such device
- Eat only 100% organic grass fed beef, veal, or lamb
- Eat only 100% organic poultry
- Eat organic raw (not pasteurized or homogenized) dairy products
- Take a homeopathic human growth hormone supplement as directed by your doctor
- Eat raw organic nuts and seeds in small quantities for snacks
- Use a shower filter
- Eat in a relaxed atmosphere at the table
- Chew thoroughly and eat slowly

- Play baroque classical music or other relaxing music at meal time
- Read books and watch DVDs for education and deprogramming from the suggested list in the Appendix
- Take flax
- Take a high fiber product
- Buy food each day
- Sing
- Go dancing
- Laugh
- Have a drink of wine, beer, or other alcohol to relax
- Play with pets or children often
- Give and get hugs often
- Play a musical instrument
- Try to include as many of the "tastes" in every meal or throughout each day
- Do resistance training
- Eat 100 grams of protein before bed
- Use Dianetics for psychosomatic and emotional ills

Things you MUST NOT do:

- No fast food, regional, or national chain restaurants
- Limit highly refined food, super highly refined food, such as white sugar and white flour
- No monosodium glutamate (MSG)
- No artificial sweeteners, such as NutraSweet and Splenda
- No trans fats, such as hydrogenated or partially hydrogenated oils
- No super highly refined sugars, such as high fructose corn syrup, corn syrup, sucrose, and dextrose
- No non-prescription, over-the-counter, or prescription medication (done only under the supervision of a physician)
- No nitrites

Things STRONGLY SUGGESTED you do NOT do:

- No meat, poultry, or dairy with growth hormone and antibiotics
- No restaurant food
- Don't go to restaurants that heavily advertise
- Don't buy products that are heavily advertised
- Limit homogenized or pasteurized dairy products
- No farm raised fish
- Limit wheat, choose rye instead
- Don't worry about calories, fat, carbohydrates, or sodium
- No microwaved food
- No diet food, low carb, low fat, "lite," or nonfat food
- No skin products with propylene glycol, sodium laureth sulfate, or mineral oil
- Don't watch, read, or listen to ads for food or restaurants
- No genetically modified food
- Limit ice cold drinks
- Limit exposure to air conditioning
- Limit exposure to florescent lights
- Limit carbonated drinks
- No juices that have been bottled, canned, or are in cartons

Phase 2

Things you MUST do:

- Be supervised and under the care of a licensed physician
- Weigh yourself daily
- Take before pictures
- Take daily injections of hCG as directed by your doctor
- Eat breakfast, snacks, lunch, and dinner as directed in the instructions
- Drink one-half to one gallon pure water with coral calcium daily
- Drink at least one cup organic chamomile tea daily
- Drink at least two cups Wu Long tea daily
- Drink at least one cup Yerba Mate tea daily
- Only 100% organic grass fed beef, lamb, and veal
- Only 100% organic poultry
- Use the Callahan techniques as needed
- Drink Eleotin tea
- Read "I weigh _____," out loud many times per day, and look at pictures with yourself with your ideal body throughout the day
- If your weight stays the same for four days in a row, use the "six apples protocol" as outlined in the instructions

Things STRONGLY RECOMMENDED you do:

- Drink organic green tea
- Do yoga
- Rebound or use mini trampoline
- Walk one hour per day
- Do resistance training
- Get twenty minutes of sun per day
- Use saunas as often as possible
- Get colonics as directed

- Eat only 100% organic food
- Eat in a relaxed atmosphere at the table
- Eat slowly and chew thoroughly
- Play baroque classical music or other relaxing music at mealtime
- Read books and watch DVDs for education and deprogramming from the suggested list in the Appendix
- Listen to stress reducing CDs daily
- Do deep breathing daily
- Wear a Q-Link, E-Pendant, or use Biopro or other such devices
- Get no more than one Thai massage per week
- Play with pets or children
- Play a musical instrument
- Sing
- Go dancing
- Laugh often
- Give and get hugs often
- Use a shower filter
- Sleep eight hours each night, ideally between the hours of 10:00 p.m. and 6:00 a.m.
- Use Dianetics for psychosomatic and emotional ills

Things you MUST NOT do:

- Put nothing on the skin
- No nitrites
- No monosodium glutamate (MSG)
- No artificial sweeteners, such as NutraSweet and Splenda
- No trans fats, such hydrogenated or partially hydrogenated oils
- No non-prescription, over-the-counter, or prescription drugs (must be done under the supervision of a licensed physician)

Things STRONGLY SUGGESTED you NOT do:

- No ice cold drinks
- Limit exposure to air conditioning
- Limit exposure to florescent lights
- No genetically modified food
- No restaurant food
- Don't watch, read, or listen to ads for food or restaurants
- Don't buy products heavily advertised
- Do not use a microwave
- No meat or poultry with growth hormone
- No farm raised fish

If you cannot or do not want to do the hCG and 500 calorie diet Simeons protocol, replace that protocol with the *Turbo Protein Diet* as explained in the book by Dieter Markert, available at www.almased.com. The Turbo Protein Diet will be your Phase 2.

Phase 3

Things you MUST do:

- Weigh yourself daily
- Take ThreeLac daily
- Drink one-half to one gallon pure water with coral calcium daily
- Drink at least one cup organic chamomile tea daily
- Drink at least two cups Wu Long tea daily
- Drink at least one cup Yerba Mate tea daily
- Use organic coconut oil daily
- Use organic raw apple cider vinegar daily
- Walk one hour per day outside
- Do a colon cleanse
- Do colonics as directed
- Eat breakfast
- Eat six times per day
- Finish dinner three and one-half hours before bed
- Eat 100% organic food
- Eat at least one organic apple daily
- Eat organic grapefruits often
- Take digestive enzymes with food
- Eat in a relaxed atmosphere, sitting at a table
- Eat slowly and chew thoroughly
- Take krill oil (Omega-3s) daily
- Take probiotics daily
- Use stevia, organic agave nectar, organic raw honey, or organic raw sugar cane as your only sweetener sources
- Eat only 100% organic grass fed beef, lamb, and veal
- Eat only 100% organic poultry
- Eat a salad with lunch and dinner

- Use Callahan techniques as needed
- Read out loud "I weigh _____," many times per day, and look at pictures with yourself with your ideal body throughout the day
- Take Eleotin tea as instructed
- Get personalized individual care from a licensed healthcare practitioner who does not use drugs and surgery
- If you gain two pounds use the skipping meals and steak method as described.

Things STRONGLY SUGGESTED you do:

- Take a whole food supplement daily
- Do yoga often
- Use a rebounder or mini trampoline often
- Do resistance training often
- Get twenty minutes of sun daily
- Use a sauna often
- Eat 100 grams of protein before bed on occasion
- Take a fiber drink often
- Add hot peppers or hot salsa to food
- Add cinnamon to your diet
- Play baroque classical music or other relaxing music at meal time
- Eat only 100% organic raw dairy products
- Take Acetyl-L Carnitine
- Take Vitamin E daily
- Use a Q-Link, E-Pendant, Biopro, or such devices
- Use AlphaCalm as needed
- Get massages often
- Sleep eight hours per night, ideally between 10:00 p.m. and 6:00 a.m.

- Do deep breathing daily
- Listen to stress reducing CDs daily
- Read books and watch DVDs for education and deprogramming from the list in the Appendix
- Take homeopathic human growth hormone (HGH) as directed by a licensed healthcare practitioner
- Eat raw organic nuts and seeds in small quantities as snacks
- Use a shower filter
- Take flax
- Buy food daily instead of stockpiling
- Sing
- Go dancing
- Laugh often
- Play with pets or children
- Play a musical instrument
- Give and get hugs often
- Use Dianetics for psychosomatic and emotional ills

Things you MUST NOT do:

- No sugar or starch
- No store bought bottled, canned, or carton juice
- No fast food, regional or national chain restaurant food
- No highly refined and super highly refined foods, including white sugar and white flour
- No meat, poultry, or dairy with growth hormone
- No monosodium glutamate (MSG)
- No artificial sweeteners, such as NutraSweet and Splenda
- No trans fats, such as hydrogenated or partially hydrogenated oil
- Don't worry about calories, fat, carbs, or sodium
- No non-prescription, over-the-counter, or prescription medications (done under the supervision of a licensed physician)

Things STRONGLY SUGGESTED you do NOT do:

- Limit ice cold drinks
- Limit exposure to air conditioning
- Limit exposure to florescent lights
- Limit carbonated drinks
- Limit restaurant food
- No skin products with propylene glycol, sodium laureth sulfate, and mineral oil
- Don't watch, read, or listen to ads for food or restaurants
- Don't buy heavily advertised products
- No diet, low carb, low fat, nonfat, or "lite" food
- Never use a microwave
- No food with nitrites
- Limit homogenized and/or pasteurized dairy products
- No farm raised fish
- Don't go to restaurants that heavily advertise

Phase 4

Things you MUST do:

- Weigh yourself daily
- Take ThreeLac as directed
- Do the LifeForce Candida cleanse
- Do a liver cleanse
- Do a parasite cleanse
- Take a heavy metal cleanse product, or get chelation
- Take a whole food supplement daily
- Drink one-half to one gallon pure water with coral calcium daily
- Walk one hour outside daily
- Do a colon cleanse
- Do colonics as necessary
- Eat breakfast
- Eat six times a day
- Finish dinner three and one-half hours before bed
- Eat organic apples daily
- Eat organic grapefruit often
- Take digestive enzymes with food
- Do a supervised fast within twelve months
- Do the Purification Program within twelve months
- Eat only 100% organic raw dairy products
- Take Acetyl-L Carnitine daily for three to six months
- Take Vitamin E daily
- Take krill oil (Omega-3s) daily
- Take probiotics daily
- Use stevia, organic agave nectar, raw organic honey, raw organic sugarcane as sweeteners
- Eat only 100% organic grass fed beef, lamb, and veal
- Eat only 100% organic poultry

- Always eat a salad with lunch and dinner
- Eat slowly and chew food thoroughly
- Be conscious of your hunger and stop eating when full
- Start meals with smaller portions
- Use Callahan techniques as needed
- Don't worry about calories, fat, carbohydrates, or sodium
- Eat raw organic nuts and seeds in small quantities as snacks
- Read out loud "I weigh _____," many times throughout the day, and look at pictures of yourself with your ideal body many times throughout the day
- Take Eleotin for at least six months
- Receive individual personalized care from a licensed health-care practitioner who does not use drugs and surgery
- Eat only 100% organic food

Things STRONGLY SUGGESTED you do:

- Drink organic chamomile tea
- Drink Wu Long tea
- Drink organic green tea
- Drink organic Yerba Mate tea
- Use organic coconut oil
- Use organic raw apple cider vinegar
- Do yoga
- Use a rebounder or mini trampoline often
- Do resistance training
- Get twenty minutes of sun daily
- Use saunas often
- Occasionally eat 100 grams of protein before bed
- Occasionally take a fiber drink
- Add hot peppers and hot salsa to food
- Add cinnamon to food

- Eat in a relaxing atmosphere sitting at a table
- Play baroque classical music, or other relaxing music while eating
- Read books and watch DVDs for education and deprogramming from the list in the Appendix
- Listen to stress reducing CDs
- Do deep breathing daily
- Get eight hours sleep per night, ideally between 10:00 p.m. and 6:00 a.m.
- Get various types of massages often
- Use AlphaCalm as needed
- Use a Q-Link, E-Pendant, and Biopro, or similar product
- Take homeopathic human growth hormone (HGH) as directed by a licensed healthcare practitioner
- Use a shower filter
- Sing
- Go dancing
- Laugh
- Have a drink of wine, beer, or alcohol to relax
- Play with pets or children
- Play a musical instrument
- Give and get hugs often
- Buy food each day for consumption, avoid stockpiling
- Take flax
- Try to include all "tastes" in all meals
- Use Dianetics for psychosomatic and emotional ills

Things you MUST NOT do:
- No fast food, regional or national chain restaurant food
- No diet, low carb, low fat, nonfat, or "lite" food
- No food with nitrites
- No monosodium glutamate (MSG)

- No artificial sweeteners, such as NutraSweet or Splenda
- No trans fats, such as hydrogenated or partially hydrogenated oil
- No super highly refined sugars, such as high fructose corn syrup, corn syrup, sucrose, and dextrose
- No non-prescription, over-the-counter, or prescription drugs (must be done under the supervision of a licensed physician)

Things STRONGLY SUGGESTED you do NOT do:

- Don't go to restaurants that heavily advertise
- Limit homogenized or pasteurized dairy products
- Limit wheat, use rye instead
- Limit ice cold drinks
- Limit air conditioning exposure
- Limit exposure to florescent lights
- Limit carbonated drinks
- No genetically modified food
- No store bought juice in bottles, cans, or cartons
- No food from any restaurant
- No skin products with propylene glycol, sodium laureth sulfate, or mineral oil
- Limit highly refined or super highly refined food, such as white sugar or white flour
- Don't watch, read, or listen to ads for food or restaurants
- Don't buy food products that are heavily advertised from publicly traded food corporations
- Never use your microwave

The Causes of Obesity

The following is a list of the main causes, sub-causes, and interrelating components that create the condition of obesity.

- Abnormal hypothalamus
- Genetics
- Intensely high and constant hunger
- Low metabolism
- Abnormally storing fat in abnormal secure problem area fat deposits
- Stressful incidents
- Eating high calorie, large meals, with highly refined food and little fiber after a long period of little or no eating
- Eating highly refined or super highly refined food with little fiber on a consistent basis
- Lack of walking
- Clogged liver
- Clogged colon
- Poor digestion
- Candida overgrowth
- Little or no enzymes in food
- Nutritional deficiencies, primarily calcium, zinc, Vitamin E, CLA
- Hypoactive thyroid
- Insulin resistance and abnormal pancreas
- Hormonal imbalances
- Uncontrollable urges to eat when you are not hungry
- Food cravings
- Artificial sweeteners
- High fructose corn syrup and other highly refined sugars
- Eating microwaved food
- Eating irradiated food
- Eating pasteurized food

- Monosodium glutamate (MSG)
- Pesticides, herbicides, and all chemical additives
- Non-prescription over-the-counter drugs
- Prescription drugs
- Antibiotics and growth hormone in meat, poultry, and dairy
- Mineral oil, propylene glycol, and sodium laureth sulfate in products put on the skin
- Lack of water consumption and dehydration of cells
- Drinking, showering, and bathing in chlorinated and fluoridated water
- Trans fats, including hydrogenated and partially hydrogenated oil
- Parasites
- Yo-yo dieting
- Skipping breakfast
- Not nibbling or eating six times per day
- Emotional and mental stress
- Lack of fiber in the diet
- Genetically modified food
- Homogenized and pasteurized dairy products
- Sluggish lymphatic system
- Lack of sun
- Heavy metal toxicity
- Poor circulation
- Lack of oxygen in the body
- Environmental and food allergies
- Poor breathing
- Not enough sleep
- Eating highly refined food late at night
- Exposure to electromagnetic frequencies from cell phones and other wireless devices

- Overexposure to air conditioning
- Overexposure to florescent lights
- Depression and anxiety
- Lack of muscle mass
- Ice cold drinks
- Carbonated beverages
- Not getting all "flavors" in food on a consistent basis
- Programming, mental triggers, and brainwashing from food and restaurant advertisers
- Constant dieting
- Lack of exercise
- Consuming too many calories
- Stockpiling food
- Lack of sweating
- Fast food restaurants
- Lack of raw fruits and vegetables
- Eating fast, standing up, in automobiles, or in front of the TV
- Toxins in the fatty tissue of the body
- Farm raised fish
- Overconsumption of wheat

Bibliography, References, Documentation, Substantiation

Recommended Books

- *Pounds and Inches: A New Approach to Obesity*, by A.T.W. Simeons

  (Available at www.naturalcures.com.)

- *Natural Cures "They" Don't Want You To Know About*, by Kevin Trudeau

- *More Natural Cures Revealed: Previously Censored Brand Name Products That Cure Disease*, by Kevin Trudeau

FDA, FTC, and Corporations

- *Sweet Deception: Why Splenda, NutraSweet and the FDA May be Hazardous to Your Health*, by Dr. Joseph Mercola and Dr. Kendra Degen Pearsall

  (In *Sweet Deception* you learn why artificial sweeteners are contributing to our skyrocketing rates of cancer, obesity, diabetes, and more. You'll see inside the motives of multinational corporations and the FDA as they promote these sweeteners as "safe" for consumption.)

- *Inside the FDA: The Business and Politics Behind the Drugs We Take and the Food We Eat*, by Fran Hawthorne

- *Politics in Healing*, by Daniel Haley

  (The suppression and manipulation in American healthcare. Former New York State Assemblyman Daniel Haley documents the suppression of new medical treatments. A well-researched investigation into the FDA and its policies of suppression.)

- *The Disease Conspiracy: "The FDA Suppression of Cures,"* by Robert Barefoot

  (Contains suppressed clinical studies documenting how vitamins and minerals cure cancer, heart disease, diabetes, MS, lupus, and dozens of other ailments.) www.cureamerica.net

- *Innocent Casualties: The FDA's War Against Humanity*, by Elaine Feuer

- *Stop the FDA: Save Your Health Freedom*, by Steven Fowkes (Editor)

  (Discover the FDA's hidden agenda; learn how to improve your health with supplements; discover the real reasons the FDA banned tryptophan; find out how the FDA suppresses medical breakthroughs; learn the true value of nutritional medicine; learn what you can do to save your health freedom.)

- *Hazardous to Our Health?*, by Robert Higgs

  (FDA Regulation of Health-care Products.)

- *Protecting America's Health: The FDA, Business and One Hundred Years of Regulation*, by Philip J. Hilts

Doctors, Medicine, and Drug Companies

- *Overdosed America: The Broken Promise of American Medicine*, John Abramson

- *Selling Sickness: How the World's Biggest Pharmaceutical Companies Are Turning Us All into Patients*, Ray Moynihan

- *On the Take: How Medicine's Complicity with Big Business Can Endanger Your Health*, by Jerome P. Kassirer

- *The $800 Million Pill: The Truth Behind the Cost of New Drugs*, by Merrill Goozner

- *Science in the Private Interest: Has the Lure of Profits Corrupted Biomedical Research?*, by Sheldon Krimsky

- *The Big Fix: How the Pharmaceutical Industry Rips Off American Consumers*, by Katharine Greider

- *The Truth About the Drug Companies: How They Deceive Us and What to Do About It*, by Marcia Angell, M.D.

- *The Great Bird Flu Hoax*, by Dr. Joseph Mercola

- *The Natural Bird Flu Cure "They" Don't Want You to Know About*, by David J. Kennedy

  (In this alarming investigation Nobel Prize-winning chemists and other top scientific minds share knowledge and facts about the inexpensive easily accessible cure that can stop this pandemic in its tracks.) Published by Wellness Research Publishing. Available at www.naturalcures.com

- *Over Dose: The Case Against the Drug Companies—Prescription Drugs, Side Effects, and Your Health*, by Jay S. Cohen, M.D.

  (Prescription drugs, side effects, and your health.)

- *Anatomy of an Illness as Perceived by the Patient*, by Norman Cousins

  (Reflections on Healing and Regeneration.)

- *The Great Betrayal: Fraud in Science*, by Horace Freeland Judson

- *Bitter Pills: Inside the Hazardous World of Legal Drugs*, by Stephen Fried

  (According to the *Journal of the American Medical Association* [JAMA], adverse drug reactions are the fourth-leading cause of death in America. Reactions to prescription and over-the-counter medications kill far more people annually than all illegal drug use combined. A work of investigative and personal journalism...the book is meant to help reform the system and inform your choices when using medications.)

- *The Drug Lords: America's Pharmaceutical Cartel*, by Tonda R. Bian

- *Disease-Mongers—How Doctors, Drug Companies, and Insurers Are Making You Feel Sick*, by Lynn Payer

- *Under the Influence of Modern Medicine*, by Terry A. Rondberg, D.C.

- *The Social Transformation of American Medicine: The Rise of a Sovereign Profession and the Making of a Vast Industry*, by Paul Starr

- *Confessions of a Medical Heretic*, by Robert S. Mendelsohn, M.D.

  (Approximately 2.4 million operations performed every year are unnecessary and cost about 12,000 lives. In six New York hospitals, 43 percent of performed hysterectomies reviewed were found to be unjustified. Historically, when doctors have gone on strike, the mortality rate has dropped.)

- *Medical Blunders*, by Robert M. Youngson and Ian Schott

  (Amazing True Stories of Mad, Bad, and Dangerous Doctors.)

- *Psychiatry: The Ultimate Betrayal*, by Bruce Wiseman

- *The Antidepressant Fact Book*, by Peter R. Breggin, M.D.

  (What Your Doctor Won't Tell You About Prozac, Zoloft, Paxil, Celexa, and Luvox.)

- *The Myth of Mental Illness*, by Thomas S. Szasz, M.D.

  (Foundations of a Theory of Personal Conduct.)

- *The Assault on Medical Freedom*, by P. Joseph Lisa

  (Why American Health Care Costs So Much!)

- *Racketeering in Medicine: The Suppression of Alternatives*, by James P. Carter M.D., Dr.P.H.

  (Can we assume that our health is always the prime concern of organized medicine? Or are Americans being deprived of effective, economical treatments because those treatments are not highly profitable for surgeons and pharmaceutical companies? Dr. Carter presents names, events and facts, which are of interest to all concerned Americans.)

- *The Truth About the Drug Companies: How They Deceive Us and What to Do About It*, by Marcia Angell, M.D.

- *The Fluoride Deception*, by Christopher Bryson

  (A chronicle of the abuse of power and the manufacture of state-sponsored medical propaganda that reveals how a secretive group of powerful industries...collaborated with officials from the National Institute of Dental Research to launder fluoride's public image.)

Food Industry

- *Fat Land: How Americans Became the Fattest People in the World*, by Greg Critser

- *Food Fight: The Inside Story of the Food Industry, America's Obesity Crisis, and What We Can Do About It*, by Kelly D. Brownell

- *The Hundred-Year Lie: How Food and Medicine Are Destroying Your Health*, Randall Fitzgerald

- *Don't Eat This Book: Fast Food and the Supersizing of America*, by Morgan Spurlock

- *The Fast Food Craze: Wreaking Havoc on Our Bodies and Our Animals*, by Tina Volpe

- *The End of Food: How the Food Industry is Destroying Our Food Supply—And What We Can Do About It*, by Thomas F. Pawlick

- *Aspartame (NutraSweet): Is it Safe?*, by H.J. Roberts, M.D.

- *Excitotoxins—The Taste that Kills*, by Russell L. Blaylock, M.D.

  (How monosodium glutamate, aspartame [NutraSweet] and similar substances can cause harm to the brain and nervous system, and their relationship to neurodegenerative diseases such as Alzheimer's, Lou Gehrig's disease [ALS], and others.)

- *In Bad Taste: The MSG Symptom Complex*, by George R. Schwartz, M.D.

- *Hard to Swallow: The Truth about Food Additives*, by Doris Sarjeant and Karen Evans

- *Fast food Nation—The Dark Side of the All-American Meal*, by Eric Schlosser

- *The Crazy Makers*, by Carol Simontacchi

  (How the Food Industry is Destroying Our Brains and Harming Our Children.)

- *Our Toxic World: A Wake Up Call*, by Doris Rapp

- *Chew On This: Everything You Don't Want to Know About Fast Food*, Eric Schlosser

- *Genetically Engineered Food—Changing the Nature of Nature*, by Martin Teitel, Ph.D. and Kimberly A. Wilson

  (What You Need to Know to Protect Yourself, Your Family, and Our Planet)

- *Food Politics*, by Marion Nestle

  (How the Food Industry Influences Nutrition and Health.)

- *Restaurant CONFIDENTIAL*, by Michael F. Jacobson, Ph.D.

  (Think a chicken Caesar salad is perfect for your diet? Think again. Choose a tuna sandwich over the roast beef sandwich? Wrong! The startling truth about our favorite foods from our favorite restaurants, with fat, calorie and salt content.)

- *Slaughterhouse*, by Gail A. Eisnitz

  (The Shocking Story of Greed, Neglect, and Inhumane Treatment Inside the U.S. Meat Industry.)

- *Mad Cow*, by Howard F. Lyman with Glen Merzer

  (Plain Truth from the Cattle Rancher Who Won't Eat Meat.)

- *Prisoned Chickens, Poisoned Eggs*, by Karen Davis, Ph.D.

  (An Inside Look at the Modern Poultry Business.)

- *The Chemical Feast*, by James S. Turner

  (Ralph Nader's Study Group Report on the Food and Drug Administration.)

- *A Chemical Feast*, by W. Harding Le Riche

  (A rational, commonsense discussion of chemicals in foods by a noted specialist in nutrition and epidemiology.)

- *Sowing the Wind*, by Harrison Wellford

  (A report from Ralph Nader's Center for Study of Responsive Law on Food Safety and the Chemical Harvest.)

- *The History of a Crime Against the Food Law*, by Harvey W. Wiley

  (The Amazing Story of the National Food and Drugs Law Intended to Protect the Health of the People—Perverted to Protect Adulteration of Foods And Drugs.)

- *Trans Fats: The Food Industry's Way of Giving You a Heart Attack*, by Judith Shaw

- *Rats in the Grain: The Dirty Tricks and Trials of Archer Daniels Midland, the Supermarket to the World*, by James B. Lieber

Water

- *The Drinking Water Book*, by Colin Ingram

  (A Complete Guide to Safe Drinking Water. There's nothing more important than the quality of the water that you drink.)

- *Water for Health, for Healing, for Life*, by F. Batmanghelidj, M.D.

  (You're not sick, you're thirsty! You always knew water was good for you. Now discover why it's nature's miracle.)

- *Water Wasteland*, by David Zwick with Marcy Benstock

  (Ralph Nader's Study Group Report on Water Pollution.)

- *Your Body's Many Cries For Water*, by F. Batmanghelidj, M.D.

(You are not sick, you are thirsty! Don't treat thirst with medications—A preventive and self-education manual for those who prefer to adhere to the logic of the natural and the simple in medicine.)

- *Fluoride, The Aging Factor*, by John Yiamouyannis, Ph.D.

  (How to Recognize and Avoid the Devastating Effects of Flouride. Find Out Who's Profiting from the Chronic Poisoning of Over 130 Million Americans!)

- *Don't Drink The Water*, by Lono Kahuna Kupua A'o

  (The Essential Guide to Our Contaminated Drinking Water and What You Can Do About It.)

- *Water—The Foundation of Youth, Health, and Beauty*, by William D. Holloway, Jr. and Herb Joiner-Bey, N.D.

- *The Water We Drink*, by Joshua L. Barzilay, M.D.; Winkler G. Weinberg, M.D.; and J. William Eley, M.D.

  (Water Quality And Its Effects On Health.)

- *Water Cures: Drugs Kill: How Water Cured Incurable Diseases*, by F. Batmanghelidj, M.D.

- *You Are Not Sick You Are Thirsty: How Water Cured Incurable Diseases—A Healer's Guide to Natural Health*, www.watercure.com

Milk

- *Homogenized Milk May Cause Your Heart Attack: The XO Factor*, by Kurt A. Oster, M.D.

  (And how it can destroy your arteries, your heart, your life!)

- *Don't Drink Your Milk!*, by Frank A. Oski, M.D.

  (New Frightening Medical Facts about the World's Most Overrated Nutrient.)

- *Milk—The Deadly Poison*, by Robert Cohen

Exercise

- *Rebounding to Better Health*, by Linda Brooks

  (A Practical Guide to the Ultimate Exercise.)

- *Urban Rebounding™...An Exercise for The New Millennium*, by J.B. Berns

  (The system known as Urban Rebounding brings together the science of the West and the philosophy and practicality of the East to form a holistic program of exercise in which people of all ages, sizes, shapes and states of physical condition can participate.)

Breathing

- *Super Power Breathing for Super Energy, High Health & Longevity*, by Paul C. Bragg, N.D. and Patricia Bragg, N.D., Ph.D.

  (Live Longer, Healthier, Stronger With Every Breath! Empower Yourself—stimulate your body's natural healing and brain power; Energize Yourself—39 simple exercises for a vibrant, energized body; Relax Yourself—35 calming effects of a healthier, fitter body.)

- *Flood Your Body with Oxygen*, by Ed McCabe "Mr. Oxygen"

  (Therapy for our polluted world.)

Mental Health

- *Dianetics*, by L. Ron Hubbard

  (The Modern Science of Mental Health.)

- *The Basic DIANETICS Picture Book*, by L. Ron Hubbard

  (A visual aid to a better understanding of man and the mind based on the works of L. Ron Hubbard.)

- *Scientology Picture Book*, by L. Ron Hubbard

  (Use it to understand yourself, life, and those you live with.)

- *Tapping the Healer Within*, by Roger J. Callahan, Ph.D. with Richard Trubo

  (Using Thought Field Therapy to Instantly Conquer Your Fears, Anxieties, and Emotional Distress.)

Cleansing and Detox

- *The Liver Cleansing Diet*, by Sandra Cabot, M.D.

  (Love Your Liver And Live Longer.)

- *The Amazing Liver Cleanse*, by Andreas Moritz

  (A Powerful Approach to Improve Your Health and Vitality.)

- *The Healthy Liver & Bowel Book*, by Sandra Cabot, M.D.

  (Detoxification Strategies for Your Liver and Bowel. Life Saving Strategies for those with many health problems, including liver disease, bowel problems and weight excess.)

- *Cleanse & Purify Thyself "And I Will Exalt Thee to the Throne of Power"*, by Richard Anderson, N.D., N.M.D.

  (Highly effective intestinal cleansing; removes pounds of Disease-Causing Toxins and Disease-Causing Negative Emotions.)

- *The Detox Diet: The How to and When to Guide for Cleansing the Body of Chemicals, Toxins, Sugar, Caffeine, Nicotine, Alcohol, and More*, by Elson M. Haas, M.D.

- *How to Cleanse and Detoxify Your Body Today!*, by Elson M. Haas, M.D.

  (Finally…You Can Look And Feel Better! A body freer of toxins, mucus, acids, dead cells and all irritants is STRONGER, HEALTHIER & more VITAL.)

- *Internal Cleansing*, by Linda Berry, D.C., C.C.N.

  (Rid your body of toxins to naturally and effectively fight: heart disease, chronic pain, fatigue, PMS and menopause symptoms, aging, frequent colds and flu, food allergies.)

- *Clear Body, Clear Mind*, by L. Ron Hubbard

  (The Effective Purification Program.)

- *Purification: An Illustrated Answer to Drugs*, by L. Ron Hubbard

  (Drugs cause the death of consciousness and awareness, and eventually of the body itself. If you value the ability to think clearly, emotional stability and a positive attitude about yourself, then *Purification: An Illustrated Answer to Drugs* is your answer.)

Additional Books

- *Kidnapped: How Irresponsible Marketers Are Stealing the Minds of Your Children*, by Daniel Acuff and Robert H. Reiher

- *Conspiracy of Fools: A True Story*, by Kurt Eichenwald

- *The Informant: A True Story*, by Kurt Eichenwald

- *Blood on the Street: The Sensational Inside Story of How Wall Street Analysts Duped a Generation of Investors*, by Charles Gasparino

- *Takedown: The Fall of the Last Mafia Empire*, by Rick Cowan and Douglas Century

- *LifeForce*, by Jeffrey S. McCombs, D.C.

    (A Dynamic Plan for Health, Vitality and Weight Loss.)

- *The Calcium Factor: The Scientific Secret of Health and Youth*, by Robert R. Barefoot and Carl J. Reich, M.D.

    (The relationship between nutrient deficiency and disease.)

- *Ancient Secret of The Fountain of Youth*, by Peter Kelder

    (Can five ancient Tibetan rites really make you look and feel years younger? The secret of youthful health and vitality.)

- *Four Arguments for the Elimination of Television*, by Jerry Mander

- *Serpent on the Rock*, by Kurt Eichenwald

- *Serpent on the Rock: Crime, Betrayal ad the Terrible Secrets of Prudential Bache*, by Kurt Eichenwald

- *Funny Money*, by Mark Singer

- *Holocaust American Style*, by Dr. James R. Walker, Director, Christian Health Research (www.ghchealth.com)

- *Townsend Letter: The Examiner of Alternative Medicine*

    (www.townsendletter.com)

- *Alternative Therapies in Health and Medicine: A Peer Reviewed Journal*

    (www.alternative-therapies.com)

Recommended DVDs and Films

- *Supersize Me*
- *The Corporation*
- *The Constant Gardener*
- *Who Killed the Electric Car?*
- *Tucker*
- *Sister Kenny*
- *The Smartest Guys in the Room*
- *Iraq For Sale: The War Profiteers*
- *Erin Brockavich*
- *Prescription for Disease* (www.garynull.com)
- *The Aviator*

Articles and Scientific Studies

- "Ten Pounds in Ten Days: A Sampler of Diet Scams and Abuse," by Laura Frazer—*Caremark*

- "Grapefruit May Help Obesity, Diabetes"—*UK Telegraph*

- "Want to Lose Weight? Get Enough Sunshine"—*Science Daily*

- "Green Tea May Aid Weight Loss"—*American Journal of Clinical Nutrition*

- "Mysterious Hormone's Role in Successful Weight Loss" —*Washington Post*

- "Bottoms Up! Peripheral Cues and Consumption Volume" —*foodpsychology.org*

- "Interactions Between Forms of Fat Consumption and Restaurant Bread Consumption"—*foodpsychology.org*

- "Does Stockpiling Accelerate Consumption? A Convenience-Salience Framework of Consumption"—*foodpsychology.org*

- "How Visibility and Convenience Influence Candy Consumption Volume"—*foodpsychology.org*

- "At the Movies: How External Cues and Perceived Taste Impact Consumption Volume"—*foodpsychology.org*

- "Can Package Size Accelerate Usage Volume?"
  —*foodpsychology.org*

- "Antecedents and Mediators of Eating Bouts"
  —*foodpsychology.org*

- "Out of Sight, Out of Mind: The Impact of Household
  Stockpiling on Usage Rates"—*foodpsychology.org*

- "Bad Popcorn In Big Buckets: Portion Size Can Influence
  Intake As Much As Taste"—*foodpsychology.org*

- "Why Visual Cues of Portion Size May Influence Intake"
  —*foodpsychology.org*

- "Food for Thought: An Inside Look At Food Psychology
  And The Unconscious Factors Causing People To Overeat"
  —*foodpsychology.org*

- "Chorionic Gonadotropin in Obesity: Further Clinical
  Observations," by Harry A. Gusman, M.D.—*The American
  Journal of Clinical Nutrition*

- "The Use of Chorionic Gonadotropin in the Treatment of
  Obesity," by James H. Hutton, M.D.—*The American Journal of Clinical Nutrition*

- "F as in Fat: How Obesity Policies are Failing in America"
  — *Trust for America's Health*

Literary References to the use of Chorionic Gonadotrophin In Obesity

THE LANCET

Nov. 6,	1954	Article	Simeons
Nov. 15,	1958	Letter to Editor	Simeons
July 29,	1961	Letter to Editor	Lebon
Dec. 9,	1961	Article	Carne
Dec. 9,	1961	Letter to Editor	Kalina
Jan. 6,	1962	Letter to Editor	Simeons
Nov. 26,	1966	Letter to Editor	Lebon

THE JOURNAL OF THE AMERICAN GERIATRIC SOCIETY

Jan.	1956	Article	Simeons
Oct.	1964	Article	Harris & Warsaw
Feb.	1966	Article	Lebon

THE AMERICAN JOURNAL OF CLINICAL NUTRITION

Sept.-Oct.	1959	Article	Sohar
March	1963	Article	Craig, et al.
Sept.	1963	Letter to Editor	Simeons
March	1964	Article	Frank
Sept.	1964	Letter to Editor	Simeons
Feb.	1965	Letter to Editor	Hutton
June	1969	Editorial	Albrink
June	1969	Special Article	Gusman

THE JOURNAL OF PLASTIC SURGERY (British)

April	1962	Article	Lebon

THE SOUTH AFRICAN MEDICAL JOURNAL

Feb.	1963	Article	Politzer, Berson & Flaks

References

1. Albrink MJ. *Chorionic gonadotropin and obesity?*. Am J Clin Nutr 1969 Jun;22(6):681-5

2. Ascheim S; Zondek B. Die Shwangerschafts Diagnose aus dem Harn durch nachweis der Hypophysovorderlappenhormone. Klin. Wochschr. 7:1401-1411. 1928

3. Asher WL. Harper HW. Effect of human chorionic gonadotrophin on weight loss. hunger. and feeling of well-being. Am J Clin Nutr 1973 Feb;26(2):211-8

4. Astrup A. VLCD compliance and lean body mass. Int J Obes 1989;13 Suppl 2:27-31

5. Atkinson JH. et al. Plasma measures of beta-endorphin/beta-lipotropin-like immunoreactivity in chronic pain syndrome and psychiatric subjects. Psychiatry Res. 1983 Aug;9(4):319-27

6. Bagshawe KD. et al. Pregnancy beta1 glycoprotein and chorionic gonadotrophin in the serum of patients with trophoblastic and non-trophoblastic tumors. Eur J Cancer. 1978 Dec;14(12):1331-5

7. Balducci R. et al. Effect of hCG or hCG+ treatments in young thalassemic patients with hypogonadotropic hypogonadism. J Endocrinol Invest. 1990 Jan;13(1):1-7

8. Ballin JC. White PL. Fallacy and hazard. Human chorionic gonadotropin-500-calorie diet and weight reduction. JAMA 1974 Nov 4;230(5):693-4

9. Bastow M.D. Anthropometrics revisited. Proc Nutr Soc 1982 Sep;41(3):381-8

10. Berry JN. Use of skinfold thickness for estimation of body fat. Indian J Med Res 1974 Feb;62(2):233-9

11. Birken S. et al. Isolation and amino acid sequence of COOH-terminal fragments from the beta subunit of human choriogonadotropin. J Biol Chem. 1977 Aug 10;252(15):5386-92

12. Birken S. Chemistry of human choriogonadotropin. Ann Endocrinol (Paris). 1984;45(4-5):297-305

13. Birmingham CL. et al. Human chorionic gonadotropin is of no value in the management of obesity. Can Med Assoc J. 1983 May 15;128(10):1156-7

14. Bonandrini L. et al. Chorionic gonadotropin (hCG) in the therapy of chronic peripheral obliterating arteriopathy (CPOA) of the lower extremities caused by arteriosclerosis. Minerva Chir. 1970 Mar 15;25(5):368-83

15. Borkan GA et al. Comparison of ultrasound and skinfold measurements in assessment of subcutaneous and total fatness. Am J Phys Anthropol 1982 Jul;58(3):307-13

16. Borkan GA, Hults DE, Gerzof SG, Burrows BA, Robbins AH.Relationships between computed tomography tissue areas, thicknesses and total body composition. Ann Hum Biol. 1983 Nov-Dec;10 (6):537-45.

17. Bosch B. et al. Human chorionic gonadotrophin and weight loss. A double-blind. placebo-controlled trial. S Afr Med J 1990 Feb 17;77 (4):185-9

18. Bousfield GR. et al. Structural features of mammalian gonadotropins. Mol Cell Endocrinol. 1996 Dec 20;125(1-2):3-19

19. Bozzola M. et al. Effect of human chorionic gonadotropin on growth velocity and biological growth parameters in adolescents with thalassemia major. Eur J Pediatr. 1989 Jan;148(4):300-3

20. Bradley P. Human chorionic gonadotrophin [letter]. Med J Aust Sep 25;2(13):510-1 1976

21. Brambilla F. et al. beta-Endorphin and beta-lipotropin plasma levels in chronic schizophrenia. primary affective disorders and secondary affective disorders. Psychoneuroendocrinology. 1981 Dec;6(4):321-30

22. Bujanow W. Hormones in the treatment of psychoses. Br Med J Nov 4;4(835):298 1972

23. Bujanow W.Letter: Is oxytocin an anti-schizophrenic hormone? Can Psychiatr Assoc J. 1974 Jun;19(3):323. No abstract available.

24. Cairella M. Drug therapy of obesity. Clin Ter. 1978 Mar 31;84 (6):571-92

25. Canfield RE. et al. Studies of human chorionic gonadotropin. Recent Prog Horm Res. 1971;27:121-64

26. Cole LA. Immunoassay of human chorionic gonadotropin. Its free subunit and metabolites. Clin Chem. 1997 Dec;43(12):2233-43

27. Emrich HM. Endorphins in psychiatry. Psychiatr Dev 1984 Summer; 2(2):97-114

28. Ferrari C. Use of a testosterone-gonadotropin combination in the treatment of pathological syndromes in adult males. Minerva Med. 1972 Jun 2;63(42):2399-408

29. Fiddes JC. et al. Structure. expression. and evolution of the genes for the human glycoprotein hormones. Recent Prog Horm Res. 1984;40:43-78

30. Fiddes JC. et al. The gene encoding the common alpha subunit of the four human glycoprotein hormones. J Mol Appl Genet. 1981;1(1):3-18

31. Fleigelman R. Metabolic effects of human chorionic gonadotropin (hCG) in rats. Proc Soc Exp Biol Med 1970 Nov;135(2):317-9

32. Gailani S. et al. Human chorionic gonadotrophins (hCG) in non-trophoblastic neoplasms. Assessment of abnormalities of hCG and CEA in bronchogenic and digestive neoplasms. Cancer. 1976 Oct;38(4):1684-6

33. Gallo RC. Bryant J. Antitumor effects of hCG in KS. Nat Biotechnol Mar;16(3):218 1998

34. Giudice LC. et al. Glycoprotein hormones: some aspects of studies of secondary and tertiary structure. Monograph. 1979 May 23

35. Greenway FL. et al. Human chorionic gonadotropin (hCG) in the treatment of obesity: a critical assessment of the Simeons method. West J Med 1977 Dec;127(6):461-3

36. Grzonkowski S. Analysis of the results of the measurements of adipose tissue in the human body based on the study of skinfold thickness. Przegl Epidemiol 1989;43(3):272-82

37. Gusman HA. Chorionic gonadotropin in obesity. Further clinical observations. Am J Clin Nutr 1969 Jun;22(6):686-95

38. Hashimoto TK. Chorionic gonadotropin preparation as an analgesic. Arch Intern Med 1981 Feb;141(2):269

39. Hayes PA. Sub-cutaneous fat thickness measured by magnetic resonance imaging, ultrasound, and calipers. Med Sci Sports Exerc 1988 Jun;20(3):303-9

40. Weiss LW, Clark FC.Three protocols for measuring subcutaneous fat thickness on the upper extremities.Eur J Appl Physiol. 1987; 56(2):217-21. PMID: 3552659; UI: 87190331

41. Heitmann BL et al. Evaluation of body fat estimated from body mass index, skinfolds and impedance. A comparative study. Eur J Clin Nutr 1990 Nov;44(11):831-7

42. Hermans P. Clumeck N. Picard O. et al. AIDS-related Kaposi's sarcoma patients with visceral manifestations. Response to human chorionic gonadotropin preparations. J Hum Virol Jan-Feb; 1(2): 82-9. 1998

43. LaPorte DJ. Predicting attrition and adherence to a very low calorie diet: a prospective investigation of the eating inventory. Int J Obes 1990 Mar;14(3):197-206

44. LaPorte DJ. Treatment response in obese binge eaters: preliminary results using a very low calorie diet (VLCD) and behavior therapy. Addict Behav 1992;17(3):247-57

45. Leshem Y. et al. Gonadotropin promotion of adventitious root production on cuttings of Begonia semperflorens and Vitis vinifera. Plant Physiol. 1968 Mar;43(3):313-7

46. Lustbader JW. et al. Structural and molecular studies of human chorionic gonadotropin and its receptor. Recent Prog Horm Res. 1998;53:395-424

47. Malkin A. The presence of glycosilated, biologically active chorionic gonadotropin in human liver. Clin Biochem 1985 Apr;18(2):75-7

48. Maruo T. et al. Production of Choriogonadotropin-like factor by a microorganism. Proc Natl Acad Sci U S A. 1979 Dec;76(12):6622-6

49. McGarvey ME. Tulpule A. et al. Emerging treatments for epidemic (AIDS-related) Kaposi's sarcoma. Curr Opin Oncol Sep;10 (5):413-21 1998

50. Miller R. et al. A clinical study of the use of human chorionic gonadotrophin in weight reduction. J Fam Pract. 1977 Mar; 4(3):445-8

51. Morgan FJ. et al. Chemistry of human chorionic gonadotropin. Monograph. 1976 May 25

52. Mueller WH. Relative reliability of circumferences and skinfolds as measures of body fat distribution. Am J Phys Anthropol 1987 Apr;72(4):437-9

53. Niebroj TK. et al. Effect of chorionic gonadotropins administration on water metabolism in glaucomatous women. Endokrynol Pol. 1971 May-Jun;22(3):251-5

54. Orphanidou C. Accuracy of subcutaneous fat measurement: comparison of skinfold calipers. ultrasound, and computed tomography. J Am Diet Assoc 1994 Aug;94(8):855-8

55. Orphanidou CI, McCargar LJ, Birmingham CL, Belzberg AS.Changes in body composition and fat distribution after short-term weight gain in patients with anorexia nervosa.Am J Clin Nutr. 1997 Apr ; 65 (4) :1034-41.

56. Perniola R. et al. Human chorionic gonadotrophin therapy in hypogonadal thalassaemic patients with osteopenia: increase in bone mineral density. J Pediatr Endocrinol Metab. 1998;11 Suppl 3:995-6

57. Pickar D et al. Clinical studies of the endogenous opioid system. Biol Psychiatry 1982 Nov;17(11):1243-76

58. Pierce JG. Eli Lilly lecture. The subunits of pituitary thyrotropin— their relationship to other glycoproteic hormones. Endocrinology. 1971 Dec;89(6):1331-44

59. Rabe T. et al. Risk-benefit analysis of a hCG-500 kcal reducing diet (cura romana) in females. Geburtshilfe Frauenheilkd. 1987 May; 47(5):297-307

60. Reiss M. Stunted growth and the mechanism of its stimulation in mentally disturbed adolescents. Int J Neuropsychiatry. 1965 Aug;1 (4):313-7

61. Rivlin RS. Therapy of obesity with hormones. N Engl J Med. 1975 Jan 2;292(1):26-9

62. Ross GT. Clinical relevance of research on the structure of human chorionic gonadotropin. Am J Obstet Gynecol. 1977 Dec 1;129 (7):795-808

63.Sanders S, Norman AP.Chorionic gonadotrophin in male growth-retarded adolescent asthmatic patients.Practitioner. 1973 May;210 (259):690-2.

64. Sarma JM. Houghten RA. Enzyme linked immunosorbent assay (ELISA) for beta-endorphin and its antibodies. Life Sci 1983;33 Suppl 1:129-32

65. Sarria A et al. Skinfold thickness measurements are better predictors of body fat percentage than body mass index in male Spanish children and adolescents. Eur J Clin Nutr 1998 Aug;52(8):573-6

66. Scaffidi A. Data on the pathogenesis and therapy of bronchial asthma in patients with secondary hypogonadism. Minerva Med Dec 1;65(86):4473-6 1974

67. Segal SJ (ed.). Chorionic Gonadotropin. Plenum Press: NY. 1980

68. Shetty KR. et al. Human chorionic gonadotropin (hCG) treatment of obesity. Arch Intern Med. 1977 Feb;137(2):151-5

69. Shomer-Ilan A. et al. Further evidence for the presence of an endogenous gonadotrophin-like plant factor: "phytotrophin" .Isolation and mechanism of action of the active principle. Aust J Biol Sci. 1973 Feb;26(1):105-12

70. Simeons ATW. The action of chorionic gonadotropin in the obese. Lancet II:1954: 946-947

71. Simeons ATW. Pounds and Inches: A New Approach to Obesity. Private Printing (1976)

72. Stein MR. et al. Ineffectiveness of human chorionic gonadotropin in weight reduction: a double-blind study. Am J Clin Nutr. 1976 Sep;29(9):940-8

73. Stern JS. Weight control programs. Curr Concepts Nutr. 1977; 5:137-55

74. Suginami H. et al. Immunohistochemical localization of a human chorionic gonadotropin-like substance in the human pituitary gland. J Clin Endocrinol Metab. 1982 Dec;55(6):1161-6

75. Tagliabue A et al. Application of bioelectric impedance measurement in the evaluation of body fat. Recenti Prog Med 1989 Feb;80 (2):59-62

76. Talbot LA et al. Assessing body composition: the skinfold method. AAOHN J 1995 Dec;43(12):605-13

77. Tavio M. Nasti G. Simonelli C. et al. Human chorionic gonadotropin in the treatment of HIV-related Kaposi's sarcoma. Eur J Cancer Sep;34(10):1634-7 1998

78. Torgerson JS et al. VLCD plus dietary and behavioral support versus support alone in the treatment of severe obesity. A randomised two-year clinical trial. Int J Obes Relat Metab Disord 1997 Nov;21(11):987-94

79. Vaitukaitis JL. Glycoprotein hormones and their subunits—immunological and biological characterization. Monograph. 1979 May 23

80. Veilleux H. et al. Gonadic and extragonadic effects in humans of 3.500 I.U. of hCG (human chorionic gonadotropin) in fractional doses. Vie Med Can Fr. 1972 Sep;1(9):862-71

80b.Vogt T, Belluscio D.Controversies in plastic surgery: suction-assisted lipectomy (SAL) and the hCG (human chorionic gonadotropin) protocol for obesity treatment. Aesthetic Plast Surg. 1987;11(3):131-56. Review.

81. Wattanapenpaiboon N. et al. Agreement of skinfold measurement and bioelectrical impedance analysis (BIA) methods with dual energy X-ray absorptiometry (DEXA) in estimating total body fat in Anglo-Celtic Australians. Int J Obes Relat Metab Disord. 1998 Sep;22(9):854-60

82. Weits T. et al. Comparison of ultrasound and skinfold caliper measurement of subcutaneous fat tissue. Int J Obes 1986;10(3):161-8

83. Yanagihara Y. Carbohydrate and lipid metabolism in pregnant albino rats during hunger after loading with gonad-stimulating hormones. Nippon Sanka Fujinka Gakkai Zasshi 1966 Nov;18 (11): 1293-301

84. Yanagihara Y. Carbohydrate and fatty acid metabolism in pregnant albino rats simultaneously loaded with fat emulsion and sex stimulating hormones during starvation. Nippon Sanka Fujinka Gakkai Zasshi 1967 Jan;19(1):8-14

85. Yanagihara Y. Carbohydrate and lipid metabolism in pregnant albino rats during starvation after loading with gonad-stimulating hormones. Nippon Sanka Fujinka Gakkai Zasshi 1966 Dec;18 (12): 1379-84

86. Yoshimoto Y. et al. Human chorionic gonadotropin—like material: presence in normal human tissues. Am J Obstet Gynecol. 1979 Aug 1;134(7):729-33

87. Yoshimoto Y. et al. Human chorionic gonadotropin-like substance in nonendocrine tissues of normal subjects. Science. 1977 Aug 5;197(4303):575-7

88. Young RL. et al. Chorionic gonadotropin in weight control. A double-blind crossover study. JAMA. 1976 Nov 29;236(22):2495-7

89. Zakut H. et al. hCG as tumor marker in non-trophoblastic neoplasms. Harefuah. 1985 Jan 15;108(2):82-5

90. Zondek B. Sulman F. The mechanism of action and metabolism of gonadotrophic hormones in the organism. Vit Horm 1945 3:297-336

Clinics That Use hCG and the Simeons "Weight Loss Cure Protocol"

Every doctor and clinic that I talked to that uses hCG and the Simeons protocol have requested that their names not be mentioned in this book. However, they are available at www.naturalcures.com.

- The one clinic and doctor that is public about his successful use of hCG in the treatment of obesity is Dr. Belluscio, M.D. His clinic can be found at www.hcgobesity.org.

Websites and Resources

General

    www.naturalcures.com
    www.thewhistleblower.com
    www.kevinfightsback.com

Nutrients, Vitamins, Etc.

    www.qnlabs.com
    www.eastwoodcompanics.com
    www.ericssonscoral.com
    www.trycorcal.com
    www.mercola.com
    www.advancedbionutritionals.com
    www.scienceformulas.com
    www.forevergreen.org (FrequenSEA)
    www.seasilver.com
    www.megafood.com
    www.tryseavegg.com
    www.sunchlorellausa.com
    www.alwaysyoung.com
    www.acgraceco.com

Food, Tea, Juices

    www.wulongforlife.com
    www.rapunzel.com (Raw evaporated cane juice)
    www.steviasmart.com (877) 836-9982
    www.freelife.com (Himalayan Goji Juice)
    www.xango.net (Mangosteen juice)
    www.monavie.com (Acai juice)

Cleansing

www.tryalmightycleanse.com
www.qnlabs.com
www.drnatura.com
www.dr-schulze.com
www.pbiv.com
www.123candida.com
www.rxvitamins.com
www.advancednaturals.com
www.lifeforceplan.com
www.liverdoctor.com
www.drstockwell.com
www.paradevices.com
www.purification.org
www.clearbodyclearmind.com

Water

www.ewater.com
www.wellnessfilter.com

Exercise

www.ultimate-rebound.com (888) 464-5867
www.urbanrebounding.com (262) 796-2009
www.cellercise.com (800) 856-4863
www.walkvest.com (877) 925-5837

Stress Reduction

www.alphacalm.com
www.u-cure.com
www.gentlewindproject.org
www.musictherapy.org
www.soundlistening.com
www.newagemusic.com
www.backroadmusic.com
www.innerpeacemusic.com
www.therelaxationcompany.com
www.emofree.com
www.tftrx.com

Emotional Issues

www.dianetics.com

www.emofree.com

www.tftrx.com

www.scientology.org

Breathing

www.breathe2000.com

www.oxycise.com

www.breathing.com

www.bestbreathingexercises.com

Electromagnetic Chaos

www.clarus.com

www.bioprotechnology.com

www.ewater.com

Dieting/Obesity

www.hcgobesity.org

www.tftrx.com (Callahan Technique)

www.tbfinc.com

www.almased.com

Find An Integrative M.D. or A Naturopathic Physician

www.mdheal.org (Foundation for Integrated Medicine)

www.citizens.org (Citizens for Health—(612) 879-7585)

www.healthfreedom.net

(American Association for Health Freedom—(800) 230-2762)

Exposing Fraud, Lies, Etc.

www.themeatrix.com

www.thetruthaboutsplenda.com

www.thewhistleblower.com

www.kevinfightsback.com

www.thecorporation.com

www.corpwatch.org

www.personsinc.org

www.prwatch.org

www.tvnewslies.org

www.foxbghsuit.com
www.disinfo.com
www.aldaily.com
www.fair.org
www.unknownnews.org
www.newstarget.com
www.bolenreport.net
www.cchr.org (Citizens Commission on Human Rights)
www.nancycartwright.com
www.alternet.org
www.indymedia.org
www.healthliesexposed.com
www.northamericanconsumersagainsthealthfraud.org
www.beyondpesticides.org
www.adbusters.org
www.worstpills.org (Public Citizen)

Miscellaneous

www.solarhealing.com
www.sungazing.com
www.drrathresearch.org
www.wolfeeyeclinic.com
www.therasauna.com (888) 729-7727
www.wecarespa.com (800) 888-2523
www.ota.com (Organic Trade Commission)
www.organicconsumers.org
www.bluesbuster.com (Full spectrum light bulbs—(888) 874-7373)
www.fullspectrumsolutions.com (Full spectrum lighting—
(888) 574-7014)
www.gordonresearch.com
www.aubrey-organics.com (Hair, skin, and body care)

About the Author

Kevin Trudeau shocked the publishing world with his first book *Natural Cures "They" Don't Want You To Know About*, selling over seven million copies in a little over a year, becoming the fastest selling, most read nonfiction book of all time. His second book *More Natural Cures Revealed: The Previously Censored Brand Products That Cure Disease* immediately became a *New York Times* best seller with millions of copies in print. As one of the world's leading consumer advocates and most fearless whistle-blower, Trudeau continues to expose corruption in both government and the corporate world. While continuing to receive threats and bribes in an attempt to keep him quiet, Trudeau continues to expose the dirty secrets that corporations and government officials around the world do not want you to know. As a member of the secret society "The Brotherhood" for almost twenty years, Trudeau secretly worked with the heads of state in over twenty countries, the most powerful royal families in the world, and the richest most influential corporations all over the globe. Trudeau knows firsthand how governments, royalty, and the rich and powerful deceive the public and take advantage of the masses all to increase their own personal profits and control. Trudeau is the first and only member of "The Brotherhood" to leave the secret society and still be alive to talk about it. Trudeau's mission is to empower the masses by educating them about suppressed secrets that can benefit a person's life in all areas. Trudeau has now given up his $2 billion global business empire to embark on this consumer advocacy and philanthropic mission.

For more information go to www.naturalcures.com, www.kevinfightsback.com, and www.thewhistleblower.com.

If you want to know more of what Kevin has to say, be sure to read *More Natural "Cures" Revealed: Previously Censored Brand Name Products That Cure Disease*

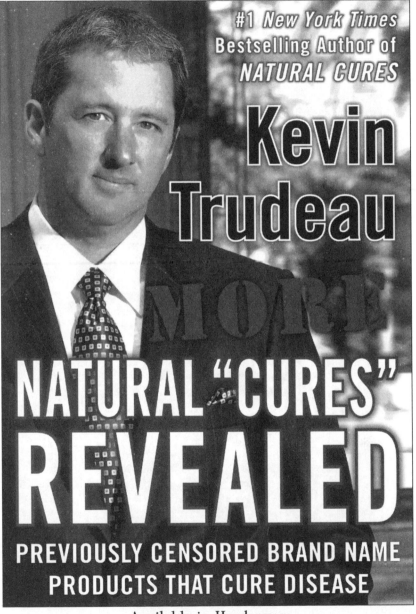

Available in Hardcover
ISBN-10: 0-9755995-4-2 ISBN-13: 978-09755995-4-9
Price: $24.95 US / $29.95 CAN

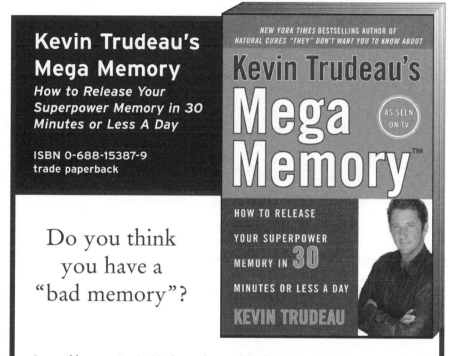